PASSING STRANGE

Passing Strange

SHAKESPEARE, RACE, AND
CONTEMPORARY AMERICA

Ayanna Thompson

OXFORD
UNIVERSITY PRESS

Oxford University Press is a department of the University of Oxford.
It furthers the University's objective of excellence in research, scholarship,
and education by publishing worldwide.

Oxford   New York
Auckland   Cape Town   Dar es Salaam   Hong Kong   Karachi
Kuala Lumpur   Madrid   Melbourne   Mexico City   Nairobi
New Delhi   Shanghai   Taipei   Toronto

With offices in
Argentina   Austria   Brazil   Chile   Czech Republic   France   Greece
Guatemala   Hungary   Italy   Japan   Poland   Portugal   Singapore
South Korea   Switzerland   Thailand   Turkey   Ukraine   Vietnam

Oxford is a registered trade mark of Oxford University Press
in the UK and certain other countries.

Published in the United States of America by
Oxford University Press
198 Madison Avenue, New York, NY 10016

Library of Congress Cataloging-in-Publication Data
Thompson, Ayanna, 1972–
Passing strange : Shakespeare, race, and contemporary America / Ayanna Thompson.
   p.   cm.
Includes bibliographical references and index.
ISBN 978-0-19-538585-4 (cloth : alk. paper); 978-0-19-998796-2 (paperback)
1. Shakespeare, William, 1564–1616—Dramatic production.
2. Shakespeare, William, 1564–1616—Stage history.
3. Shakespeare, William, 1564–1616—Film adaptations.
4. Shakespeare, William, 1564–1616—Appreciation—United States.
5. Race in literature.
6. Theater—Casting. I. Title.
PR3091.T53   2011
792.9'5—dc22   2010033675

9 8 7 6 5 4 3 2 1

Printed in the United States of America
on acid-free paper

*This book is dedicated to
all the race men and women
who keep the conversation going*

Contents

Acknowledgments

THIS BOOK HAS benefited from the generous feedback of many colleagues. Its redeeming qualities are probably due to their thoughtful engagements, but the faults are definitely all of my own. Although these lists are always incomplete (even when long), I want to thank several organizations and individuals for supporting the progress of this project.

I presented early versions of chapter 5 at the Harvard Renaissance Colloquium, the University of New Hampshire Speakers Series, and in a seminar led by Jeremy Lopez at the Shakespeare Association of America conference. An earlier and slightly shorter version of this chapter originally appeared in *Shakespeare Bulletin* ("The Blackfaced Bard: Returning to Shakespeare or Leaving Him?" *Shakespeare Bulletin* 27, no.3 (2009): 437–456), and I am grateful to the editors and publishers of the journal for granting permission to print a revised version here. I also presented early versions of chapter 7 at the Arizona State University Renaissance Colloquium and at the Shakespeare Association of America conference on a panel organized by Alfredo Michel Modenessi. A shorter version of this chapter was originally published in *Shakespeare Quarterly* ("Unmooring the Moor: Researching and Teaching on YouTube," *Shakespeare Quarterly* 61, no.3 (2010): 337–356), and I am grateful to the editors and publishers of the journal for granting permission to print a revised version here. Finally, The Public Theater and the LAByrinth Theater Company in New York invited me to participate in their "Sunday Speaker Series," in which I presented an early version of chapter 8. The discussions and debates that I had in these various venues helped to sharpen my thinking and writing, and I am deeply appreciative for the generous invitations to attend these events.

Shamelessly and selfishly I have asked colleagues along the way both to read and discuss certain portions of this book. For their thoughts, suggestions, and encouragement I would like to thank Jonathan Burton, Valerie Fazel, Cora Fox, Daniel Gilfillan, Maureen Goggin, Stephen Guy-Bray, Andrew Hartley, Jonathan Gil Harris, David Hawkes, Madhavi Menon, Ian Moulton, Alyssa Robillard, Katherine Rowe, Bradley Ryner, Beth Tobin, Henry Turner, and Will West. The colleagues to whom I am the most indebted, however, are Peter Erickson, Scott Newstok, and Francesca Royster. All three scholars have served as judicious interlocutors throughout the development of this project, and I cannot thank them enough for their generosity and thoughtfulness.

For their generous willingness to offer their time for interviews (sometimes on multiple occasions), I would like to thank Ken Adelman of Movers and Shakespeares, Rafe Esquith of Hobart Elementary School, Harvard University's Professor Henry Louis Gates, Jr., Dana Gioia of the Aspen Institute (and formerly of the National Endowment for the Arts), and Kimiko Shimoda of the Oregon Shakespeare Festival. I benefited immensely from the interactions I had with these very busy individuals.

A special note of thanks is reserved for my graduate research assistants. I could not have found the wealth of material included in this book without their super sleuthing. Geoffrey Way was particularly helpful finding the Internet materials cited, and Heather Ackerman is a researcher *par excellence*. She is a top notch thinker, and this book has benefited from the sustained conversations we have had about the materials she found.

Everyone at Oxford University Press has been amazing. I particularly want to thank Shannon McLachlan and Brendan O'Neill for encouraging this project from its inception. I would also like to thank the anonymous reviewers whose suggestions truly helped to shape the content and form of the final book.

Last, but never least, I would like to thank my family for their love, encouragement, and unflagging support (even in the face of long days away writing). Derek and Dashiell have made this journey with me (Dashiell calls it "black work"), and I love them so much for it. Dashiell is a great hockey player; he wanted to make sure that appeared in print!

All citations from Shakespeare in this book are taken from the Norton anthology. *The Norton Shakespeare: Based on the Oxford Edition*, ed. Stephen Greenblatt et al. (New York: W. W. Norton & Company, 1997).

PASSING STRANGE

FIGURE 1.1 Stephen Paul Johnson (Touchstone) and Paul Bates (Audrey) in The Hudson Valley Shakespeare Festival's 2007 production of *As You Like It* (directed by John Christian Plummer). Photo by Walter Garschagen.

And the only way to do something more substantial onstage—then and now—is to discuss one of the defining features of the American experience: race. I don't know how anyone, black or white, in America can stand up in front of an audience with a microphone and never mention it. It's as if there's an elephant in the room, and it's spraying out elephant diarrhea all over everyone, and no one's mentioning it. It's surreal. My impulse is always to call people's attention to the situation. *Uh, the elephant? Shitting on you?*
—PAUL MOONEY[1]

Shakespeare can serve as an important signifier for the "native" and minority cultures in a variety of locations as well as in conditions of contingency and flux. Of course, there are no overall guarantees of a progressive outcome.
—JYOTSNA SINGH[2]

It's like Shakespeare, with a nigga twist.
—AKALA[3]

1

Introduction

THE PASSING STRANGENESS OF SHAKESPEARE IN AMERICA

LIKE THE BLACK American comedian Paul Mooney, I find it impossible to ignore the shitting elephant in the room. Notions, constructions, and performances of race continue to define the contemporary American experience, including our conceptions, performances, and employments of Shakespeare. When I teach Shakespeare in my university classes, when I see a contemporary Shakespearean production on film, the stage (see Figure 1.1), or the Internet, when I hear and see allusions to Shakespeare in commercials, television shows, and the popular media, I see race: whiteness, blackness, Hispanic-ness, Asian-ness, the normatively raced, and the deviantly raced. It is always there; it is always present; it always impacts the way Shakespeare is being employed. And, like Mooney, I am always surprised when others don't mention it—the good, the bad, and the ugly—because race is the giant elephant in the room. Thus, *Passing Strange* is my attempt "to call people's attention to the situation." It is my attempt to bring contemporary race studies and contemporary Shakespeare studies into an honest and sustained dialogue.

It is probably worthwhile at this early moment to define what I mean by "Shakespeare" and "race." Both terms are loaded in unique ways in popular American parlance, and I want to be sure that their multivalent meanings are understood from the beginning of this book. While William Shakespeare was a sixteenth- and seventeenth-century British playwright, his name is not consistently employed in common discourse to refer to this historical figure alone. Rather, Shakespeare is often used to mean his now-canonical body of work: a synecdoche of sorts in which the name Shakespeare stands in for his entire creative output. But the name is also employed to signify a mythical fantasy about the author as a symbol for artistic genius, or as a symbol for the difficulty of the work created by that genius. While some scholars employ quotation marks to denote the difference between the historical figure, Shakespeare, and the symbols his name may evoke, "Shakespeare," I am not convinced these differences can be easily, or neatly, disentangled in contemporary American parlance. Therefore, I do not employ the quotation marks, even when I am clearly evoking Shakespeare-as-symbol.[4] I think it is important to keep all of the meanings, references, and ambiguities in play just as many of the modern employments of his name capitalize on these multiplicities. It is all Shakespeare.

Race likewise has multiple, and at times contradictory, uses in contemporary American discourse. While, in the most basic sense, race is the categorization of humans into groups based on heritable traits, many Americans have a limited notion of heritable traits as only referring to skin color (black, white, brown, etc.), facial features (lips, noses, eye shape/size, etc.), and hair type (straight, curly, kinky, etc.). Based on these traits, many would identify the races as white/Caucasian, black/African, and Asian. At times Hispanic/Latino/Chicano and Native American/American Indian are identified as races, and at other times they are identified as ethnicities. When Americans use the word race, it is often difficult to discern what they include in the term and what they exclude. If this is not muddled enough, there are times when race is also used to signify a set of cultural practices, such as specific ways of speaking, cooking, eating, and socializing and the historical narratives created that relate to these cultural practices. And there are also times when race is used to denote only nonwhite people, as if white Americans have no race.[5] While I do not agree with all of these uses, I want to keep the multivalent meanings for race in play, as with my use of Shakespeare, within *Passing Strange*. Part of the tension that arises when one discusses Shakespeare and race together is that one must interrogate which definitions are being employed, and which are being elided, at any particular moment.

So when does the pairing of Shakespeare and race occur? And when it occurs, is it worthy of a book-length examination? Is the pairing not just a sign of the social progress being made in contemporary America? It is generally assumed that contemporary Shakespeare studies and Shakespearean performance have benefited from an attention to, and the incorporation of, race studies. Our increased knowledge about the complexity of the Renaissance world (through increased international trade) and our incorporation, or explicit rejection, of that knowledge in modern performances seems to have enhanced our understanding of Shakespeare. Although there are still skeptics who argue that it is anachronistic to analyze depictions and constructions of race in Renaissance texts, many others have integrated aspects of race studies into their research and performances.

It has yet to be debated, however, whether race studies and racial activism benefit from Shakespeare. *Passing Strange* analyzes how well and how comfortably Shakespeare and race fit together in the American imagination through an examination of specific moments in contemporary film, novels, theatre, prison programs, programs for at-risk youth, Internet postings, and scholarship. Far from offering one set of answers to these questions, *Passing Strange* demonstrates both how and why instability is the nature of the relationship between Shakespeare and race in American popular culture. In fact, *Passing Strange* might just be a manifesto advocating for the maintenance of that instability, but more on that later.

Two anecdotes exemplify the push and pull between Shakespeare and race in the American imagination. Anecdote One: At a recent Shakespeare conference, a scholar delivered a paper about the need for Shakespeareans to get out into "the community" to deliver Shakespeare to "the people." She told a story about an illiterate, black, recovering drug addict who was learning to read by studying Shakespeare's plays. Her message was that this black man was being *freed by* Shakespeare; he was being freed from the shackles of his illiteracy and drug dependence through the richness of Shakespeare's language and stories. In her story Shakespeare was constructed as an essential tool in both this black man's recovery and advancement.

Anecdote Two: At the same conference I asked a colleague about another black Shakespearean whom I had not seen, and my colleague said, "It's great, isn't it? She has been *freed from* Shakespeare to focus on race." My colleague's message was that our friend was finally free to pursue a project that was devoted to issues of racial justice; she was freed from the shackles of Shakespeare to investigate topics of real and immediate social relevance. In this comment Shakespeare was constructed as an essential obstacle in the pursuit of racial justice.

These anecdotes neatly encapsulate the linguistic and theoretical extremes of the debate this book seeks to address. The notion of being *freed by* Shakespeare encourages espousing and promoting an uncomplicated view of Shakespeare's cultural capital: Shakespeare can uplift the people because his works are aesthetic masterpieces that speak to all humans, in all times, in all cultures. The notion of being *freed from* Shakespeare constructs Shakespeare studies as an obstacle that must be overcome to conduct research on contemporary race issues: Shakespeare can oppress the people because the promotion of his universality makes white, Western culture the norm from which everything else is a lesser deviation. Or to frame the extremes in another way, while it is often assumed that Shakespeare's plays are not only universal and timeless but also humanizing and civilizing, it is also assumed that Shakespeare may actually disable the advancement of racial equality. As Jyotsna Singh (cited as the second epigraph for this chapter) saliently warns, when it comes to Shakespeare and Shakespearean appropriations, "there are no overall guarantees of a progressive outcome."

Of course, these are the extremes of the debate. *Passing Strange* examines the greyer areas between American constructions of Shakespeare and American constructions of race by asking: How is Shakespeare's universalism constructed within explicit discussions and debates about racial identity? Is there a value to claims to an essentialized racial identity for Shakespeare (e.g., Shakespeare was black, a woman, a Jew, etc.)? How should Shakespeare's Moors be performed on the contemporary stage, and how does, or should, our understanding of the original staging practice of blackface impact these ideas and practices? Of what benefit is the promotion of Shakespeare and Shakespearean programs to incarcerated and/ or at-risk persons of color? Are the benefits merely tied to the aesthetic value of Shakespeare, or is there some other value that providing access to Shakespeare's works affords these populations relative to their life experiences and circumstances? Do Shakespeare's plays need to be edited, appropriated, revised, updated, or re-written to affirm racial equality and relevance? Do the answers to these questions impact our understanding of authorship, authority, and authenticity? How do performances involving actors of color affect contemporary notions of Shakespeare's racial politics, and does the medium employed (film, television, stage, Internet, etc.) alter these receptions? What does the history of Shakespearean scholarship and performance tell us about the possibilities for employing Shakespeare as a theoretical and practical tool for negotiating *contemporary* race relations?

I include one line from the chorus to the song "Shakespeare" from Akala, a young, black hip-hop artist, as the third epigraph for this chapter because the lyrics clearly articulate the distance between the popular image of Shakespeare and the popular image of black culture. "It's like Shakespeare, with a nigga twist" implies that Shakespeare does not already have a "nigga twist" within it. Whatever the "nigga twist" is imagined to be, it must be added to Shakespeare. This book explores the way the distances and proximities between popular constructions of Shakespeare and popular constructions of racial identity are forged. It asks who and what benefit from thinking about adding a "nigga twist" to Shakespeare.

Akala's song, however, is also important within this project because the dissemination of his material and the popularity of his work grew out of a twenty-first century technology and medium: a video on YouTube. Because in *Passing Strange* I am deeply invested in gauging and engaging in American popular culture, I employ disparate, nontraditional sources: not just film (which can rightly be considered a traditional form now) but also nontraditional performance spaces (like prisons and the Internet). Shakespeare's American cultural value and legacy cannot be weighed through performances in traditional venues only. One must look beyond the theatre (and the movie theatre) to see a more complete picture of the popular American construction of Shakespeare. When one colorizes this picture—that is, when one adds the dimension of race to the portrait—it is imperative to examine less traditional venues like a black hip-hop artist's video on YouTube. *Passing Strange*, then, expands the material focus of Shakespeare studies to include lesser-studied areas of cultural creation *and* distribution.

ON THE MEANING OF "PASSING STRANGE"

When Brabanzio complains to the Duke of Venice that his beautiful, Venetian daughter, has been tricked into marrying the "extravagant and wheeling stranger" (1.1.137), Othello the Moor, the Duke demands that Othello explain how this relationship came to be. Othello promises to deliver "a round unvarnished tale" (1.3.90), relating how he "won" Brabanzio's daughter (1.3.94). Then he reveals that it was "the story of [his] life" (1.3.128) to which Desdemona was attracted: "She'd come again, and with a greedy ear / Devour up my discourse" (1.3.148–149). Othello explains that after the course of several months:

My story being done,
She gave me for my pains a world of kisses.
She swore in faith 'twas strange, 'twas passing strange,
'Twas pitiful, 'twas wondrous pitiful.
She wished she had not heard it, yet she wished
That heaven had made her such a man.
(1.3.157–162)

Based on this encouragement from Desdemona, Othello says, he dared to woo her more openly. He, thus, makes it clear that it was the story of his adventures from his "boyish days" (1.3.131) to being sold into "slavery" (1.3.137) to his encounters with "the cannibals that each other eat" (1.3.142) that wooed Desdemona: "This only is the witchcraft I have used" (1.3.168). And the Venetian Duke approvingly responds, "I think this tale would win my daughter, too" (1.3.170).

From this famous passage in Shakespeare's *Othello* (c. 1603) we get the oft-cited phrase, "passing strange." Here I begin with a discussion of the Renaissance understanding of the phrase, but I also explore and exploit the phrase's expanded and stretched use over the centuries. In the Renaissance, the adverbial use of "passing" (modifying the adjective "strange") meant surpassingly, preeminently, or exceedingly. According to the Oxford English Dictionary, this meaning is now extremely rare and is only used poetically.[6] In *Othello*, however, Desdemona uses the phrase to indicate that Othello's story is exceptionally unusual. Interestingly, Shakespeare plays on the multiple meanings of "pass," both the adverbial and verbal uses, just a few lines later when Othello says, "She loved me for the dangers I had passed, /And I loved her that she did pity them" (1.3.166–167). The verb form of "pass" here signifies a survival (to outlive), but we can also hear the echoes of the meaning of loss and death (to pass beyond). The Renaissance audience may have heard ambiguities written into Othello's narrative of his winning of Desdemona: exceptionality is tied to both survival and loss.

The richness of the phrase "passing strange" has made it a frequently cited Shakespearean passage, even when the text and plot of *Othello* are not included in the allusion. Of course, there are far too many to cite here, but I briefly mention three from the nineteenth century to exemplify the phrase's appropriation to express moments of exceptionality. In her 1849 novel *Shirley*, Charlotte Brontë has one of her characters comment on the nervousness exhibited by a young woman. Miss Helstone remarks, "[P]assing strange! What does this unwonted excitement about such an everyday occurrence as a return from market portend? She has not lost her senses, has she? Surely the burnt treacle has not crazed her."[7] According to Miss Helstone, the madness brought on by eating burnt treacle is the only thing that could warrant such outlandish behavior; everyday occurrences, on the other hand, should not produce such "passing strange" behavior.

Similarly in Robert Louis Stevenson's 1888 novel *The Black Arrow*, Dick notes that it is "passing strange" that his stakeout is being observed by others.[8] Again, the appropriation of the phrase signifies the exceptional nature of the event: it signifies an occurrence that no one could predict. And in Thomas Hardy's 1891 novel *Tess of the D'Urbervilles*, the narrator describes the meeting of Alec D'Urberville and Tess Durbeyfield as an accident of timing: "In the ill-judged execution of the well-judged plan of things the call seldom produces the comer, the man to love rarely coincides with the hour for loving. . . . Out of which maladroit delay sprang anxieties, disappointments, shocks, catastrophes, and passing-strange destinies."[9] In Hardy's appropriation, one's fate can be rendered exceptionally unique precisely because of the "ill-judged execution" of life's significant events. For Hardy, "passing strange" signifies the very nature of life.

While these types of nonreferential allusions help to keep the meaning of the phrase "passing strange" as "exceptionally unusual" in wide circulation, allusions that keep race at the heart of the allusion have tapped into the more modern sense of "passing." In Joseph Conrad's *Heart of Darkness* (1899), for instance, Marlow explains to his auditors aboard *The Nellie*, who are drifting on the river Thames, that even when he discovers the horrible atrocities that Kurtz committed in Africa (e.g., Kurtz's "pamphlet" that advises to "Exterminate the brutes"), he still cannot forsake him and relegate his memory to the "dustbin of progress."[10] Marlow explains,

> But then, you see, I can't choose. He won't be forgotten. Whatever he was he was not common. . . . No, I can't forget him, though I am not prepared to affirm the fellow was exactly worth the life we lost in getting him. I missed my late helmsman awfully—I missed him even while his body was still lying in the pilot-house. Perhaps you will think it passing strange this regret for a savage who was no more account than a grain of sand in a black Sahara. Well, don't you see, he had done something, he had steered; for months I had him at my back—a help—an instrument. It was kind of a partnership.[11]

Marlow begins by explaining that he cannot forget Kurtz because he was an extraordinary man of action, but he ends by explaining that he cannot forget his African pilot because "he had done something." Thus, he unites these seemingly disparate figures in his mind, and he is able to bridge his memories of them through the Shakespearean allusion from *Othello*. In this way, Marlow becomes the feminized Desdemona figure who struggles to relate his love for what should be (and in these cases are) unattainable figures (both sexually and racially). For Marlow, then, the appropriation of Shakespeare's "passing strange" signifies both the attraction and repulsion one feels when one acknowledges one's desire both to be Other and to be with the Other.

Although it is clear that Conrad is referencing Shakespeare, the American reader might hear echoes of a more modern usage. The modern usage of "passing," of course, is a uniquely American one that stems from the racial segregation of the Jim Crow era in which racial mingling was prohibited and clear racial identification was required. In this sense, to "pass" means to identify oneself as another race (usually black identifying as white for social and economic privileges). As Linda Schlossberg explains, "Because of [the] seemingly intimate relationship between the visual and the known, passing becomes a highly charged site for anxieties regarding visibility, invisibility, classification, and social demarcation. It disrupts the logics and conceits around which identity categories are established and maintained—even as it may seem to result in the disappearance or denial of a range of 'minoritized' or queer identities."[12]

It is this racialized appropriation of passing that attracted Mark Stewart (aka Stew) to the phrase "passing strange" in *Othello*. As one of the creative forces behind the Broadway hit musical, *Passing Strange*, Stew heard important resonances in the Shakespearean phrase for his own narrative of self-discovery in Europe.[13] A middle-class black American who fled to Europe to escape "the limitations of being an American black artist only to tangle with the European fascination with 'the American Negro,'" Stew experimented with "passing for ghetto" in his European performances.[14] It was only when he began to work on the semi-autobiographical musical, however, that he discovered how appropriate the phrase "passing strange" was for his own life.

> I opened the comic book version of *Othello* that Maria Goyanes at The Public Theater handed me, and I opened it to the passage where Othello talks about how he wooed Desdemona. It moved me as close to tears as anything I'd ever read in my life. In that scene, Othello reminded me of a guy in a rock band who got the girl by spinning his rock-and-roll war stories. I thought "that's what the Youth in *Passing Strange* would do when he meets all these European girls." He'd tell them a stack of tales from a land they'd never been to, and—like all storytellers—he'd, uh, embellish just a bit. Obviously, the term "passing" has deep historical meaning for any African American my age [45] or older. My grandmother was light enough to pass. But the kid in this play discovers there's more to passing than just black folks passing for white. The term "passing" also has to do with time passing, of course.[15]

In Stew's musical, then, it is important to maintain the multiple resonances of the phrase "passing strange." He leads his audience back to Shakespeare's original usage which signifies the exceptionality, and perhaps fictionality, of Othello's narrative, but he folds into it the modern American anxiety about the performative and nonessential nature of racial identity. Throughout the musical the Youth struggles to find "the real," and ultimately experiments with "Black folks passing for black folks."[16] In addition, the musical is performed by an all-black cast, many of whom must perform/pass for the white characters in the scenes in Amsterdam and Berlin.

Harkening back to Marlow's feelings of desire for the unattainable Other expressed in Conrad's *Heart of Darkness*, Stew also highlights the strange attraction-repulsion that comes through the notion of "passing." The desire to be other can be both attractive and repulsive because it requires both a creation and an

erasure. Theorizing the multiple manifestations of passing, Linda Schlossberg perfectly anticipates the emotional cross sections that Stew's musical explores:
"Passing is not simply about erasure or denial, as it is often castigated but, rather,
about the creation and establishment of an alternative set of narratives. It becomes
a way of creating new stories out of unusable ones, or from personal narratives
seemingly in conflict with other aspects of self-presentation. . . . The risk and pleasure of narrative thus seems intimately connected to the risk and pleasure of
passing."[17]

I have provided this rather lengthy deliberation on "passing strange" and
"passing" because the examination this book affords the modern constructions of
racial identity through Shakespearean reference/performance and the modern
constructions of Shakespearean identity through racial reference/performance
necessitates the activation of these multiple meanings. Like the multivalent meanings of Shakespeare and race, I want to keep active the various meanings of
"passing" and "strange" because they are rich and entangled in significant ways in
our modern parlance. Of course, on the most basic level I am interested in exploring
notions of authenticity when it comes to the pairings of Shakespeare and race. Is
a highly racialized performance of a Shakespearean play (say, for example, by Will
Power to Youth in Los Angeles, California) read as a type of passing? Are the young
Hispanic actors hired by WPY passing for Shakespeare's white characters? Or do
Shakespeare's characters pass for other races when they are performed by actors of
color? What is deemed as authentic, and who is afforded the authority to determine authenticity: the original text, the director, the performers, the critics, the
general audience, the theatre historians?

The central metaphor for passing, however, is not only apt for questions of
authenticity. Rather the phrase "passing strange," with the imbedded notion that
passing entails "creating new stories out of unusable ones" (to borrow Schlossberg's words), allows one to think about what makes a story (un)usable, whether
the narrative is constructed as universal, timeless, adaptable, updatable, or just
plain out of date. In fact, the feelings of "risk and pleasure" that are inherent to the
act of passing *and* narrative construction are exhibited in many of the texts I
examine. The risk and pleasure of making Shakespeare a dog (as in the film *Bringing
Down the House*), of claiming that Shakespeare was essentially Other (as in the
young adult novel *Black Swan*), or of constructing a dialogue between Renaissance
imperialism and Chinese independence (as in the YouTube *Othello* video) are
central to this book. The desire to rewrite a story from a different point of view,
like the desire to pass, offers both the hopes and limits of authorship.

And finally, like Stew, I am interested in the implications for time and space in
the notion of passing. This book examines what happens when Shakespeare

moves—passes—between historical, cultural, national, and racial borders. While my analysis in *Passing Strange* is tightly focused on contemporary American culture, implied in the examinations in all of the chapters is the distance from Shakespeare's originary moment. That moment is not fully recoverable, just as anything from the distant past is not, but the ways people figure the distances between disparate historical and cultural moments reveal a great deal about their own spaces, places, and times. Thus, the tools used to measure the distance—the historical, cultural, national, and racial passes—are as important as the distance itself.[18]

For these various reasons and more that will become apparent as the book continues, I have embraced the risk and pleasure of naming this book—a passing in and of itself—with a Shakespearean phrase. The title is far from unique, the appropriation is far from unusual, and the attempt to rewrite its meaning is far from *passing strange*, but it is nevertheless the right title for the stories I want to tell about the pairings of Shakespeare and race in our contemporary popular-American culture.[19]

INFLUENCES, METHODOLOGIES, AND TARGETED READERS

Although this is the first book to offer a sustained examination of a type of contemporary-Shakespearean-cultural-race studies, it is indebted to a wealth of research that has come before it. First and foremost this book is indebted to the scholars who first brought Shakespeare studies and race studies together by analyzing how race was defined, constructed, and performed in Renaissance England. The early publications of Eldred Jones, Anthony Barthelemy, Ania Loomba, and Kim Hall alerted scholars and later practitioners to the fact that race is present in Shakespeare's works: in his constructions of whiteness, blackness, Jewish-ness, Arab-ness, etc.[20] Because they were performing a type of historical recovery—highlighting the references many scholars and practitioners had taken for granted and/or ignored for centuries—their work was deeply tied to the historical moment of the Renaissance. In other words, their research and writing did not extend into an examination of Shakespeare in the present moment. Nevertheless, their historical recoveries have been extremely important for my thinking and writing.

This book is also indebted to the scholars who perform cultural-studies analyses of the roles Shakespeare has played in the United States. Some of these scholars perform historical research, revealing the specific work Shakespeare performs at specific historical moments, like for instance the nineteenth-century Astor Place Riots in New York.[21] And some of these scholars address American Shakespeares—that is, the multiple ways Shakespeare is configured in the American imagination—in broader and more theoretically informed ways.[22] At times both the historical and the theoretical works address issues of race, but race is never central to their analyses. Instead it remains on the periphery as part of the analysis but not the lens through which the analysis is conducted. *Passing Strange* could not have been produced, however, without this ground-breaking historical and cultural research.

More recently there has been a wave of books that place contemporary constructions of Shakespeare and race in dialogue through an examination of Shakespeare's position in formerly colonized regions like the Caribbean, Africa, and Asia. Of course these works are heavily influenced by postcolonial approaches, and they bring issues of race, identity, and the social and cultural capital of Shakespeare to the forefront of their analyses.[23] Nevertheless, the United States rarely figures into their analyses. While Tom Cartelli's watershed book, *Repositioning Shakespeare*, placed American Shakespeares within a postcolonial frame, reading them alongside African and Caribbean ones, his analyses of American Shakespeares did not extend beyond the early twentieth century (1916 to be exact).[24] Cartelli's analyses, of course, opened the door for a similar approach to later American texts and performances.

The two scholars whose work has influenced me the most are Peter Erickson and Francesca Royster because their research forces readers to acknowledge that Shakespeare and race are inextricably linked in the contemporary American imagination. Erickson's *Citing Shakespeare* demonstrates in a clear and comprehensive fashion how often black artists (primarily novelists, poets, and sculptors) engage in dialogues with Shakespeare's works.[25] For Erickson, these artists' reinterpretations of Shakespeare offer the hope for the progressive creation of new narratives about race. Likewise, Royster's *Becoming Cleopatra* provides an analysis of African-American counter narratives about Cleopatra's race and place in history.[26] This book was particularly influential for my own thinking and research because the counter narratives Royster privileges all stem from pop culture sources (especially film).

Thus, *Passing Strange* is influenced by these earlier works and moves beyond them in specific ways. First, because I am interested in contemporary constructions of Shakespeare and race in the broadest sense, I am not limiting my attention to black and white America. Instead, I examine white (chapter 2), black (chapters 2, 3, and 5), Hispanic (chapter 6), and Asian (chapter 7) Americans and Americas. And chapter 4 treats the broader area of multiculturalism as it relates to classical theatre companies. Furthermore, there are moments in the book when my research extends beyond the borders of the United States. For example, chapter 3 is centered on a novel by a British author of Indian descent, Farrukh Dhondy. Nevertheless, this non-American novel offers the perfect lens for the American approach to strategic essentialism.

Second, because I adopt a cultural studies approach, the texts and productions I examine in *Passing Strange* are intentionally disparate in format, style, and tone. There is no way to gauge the American cultural engagement, assessment, and employment of Shakespeare and race without looking beyond traditional sources. Thus, I examine two films (chapter 2); a young adult novel (chapter 3); modes of casting in classical theatre companies (chapter 4); three legal cases involving the use of blackface (chapter 5); prison arts programs, NEA programs for at-risk youth, and inner-city arts programs (chapter 6); and Asian-American amateur Shakespeare performances that are uploaded to YouTube (chapter 7). There are moments in the book that seem to stray very far from Shakespearean texts. In fact, I imagine that many of the texts discussed will be unfamiliar, even to the most ardent of Shakespeare scholars and fans. I have provided as much information about these texts as possible (including plot summaries and overviews when applicable), and my hope is that this book will inspire some readers to seek out these sources for themselves. There are such rich and diverse materials available that I hope they inspire further discussions and analyses of Shakespeare and race.

Obviously, the diversity of these materials requires different methodological approaches. No one approach works equally well for films, novels, legal cases, and Internet videos, to name just a few. Thus, each chapter tailors a methodological approach to the material analyzed, but there is more continuity than this might suggest. In fact, the chapters progressively move from the theoretical to the practical, at first offering ways of seeing and interpreting the pairings of Shakespeare and race in the contemporary United States and then providing ways to introduce and advance conversations about Shakespeare and race in the contemporary United States. I am not ashamed to admit that there are polemical moments in the book because this is a project that requires action and not just passive reflection. I would not be content creating a book that merely analyzes moments of tension and debate. Instead, it is important to me to offer ways to create new dialogues, but I will address this more fully in the final section of this chapter.

Despite the disparate materials examined, there are unifying throughlines within *Passing Strange*. Although I would not have predicted this when I started this project, the culture wars of the 1980s and 1990s provide an important point of reference for the early chapters (especially chapters 3 and 4). For those who do not know, the culture wars in the late twentieth century focused on what should be required and taught in college and university English departments (primarily). In the aftermath of the civil rights era, many literary scholars began to specialize in noncanonical authors and fields such as African-American, Chicano, Native American, and Asian-American literature.[27] In addition, with the rise of postcolonial studies, non-Western literatures were frequently introduced into the curriculum, and, in tandem, the traditional Western literary canon was often questioned because of its ties to colonialism and imperialism.[28] Thus, on college and university campuses, and in the popular media as well, debates raged about what should be the required readings and courses for educated persons.[29] While the debates have largely subsided about literary studies in general, there are still intense flare-ups over Shakespeare's place in the canon. And it is within these flare-ups that notions of race (or, frequently, the call for an end to notions of race) rise to the surface most perceptibly. As a result, in the early portions of *Passing Strange* I situate these debates within the larger historical context of the culture wars of the late twentieth century.

Another throughline that unifies the seemingly disparate points of analysis in *Passing Strange* is the tension between assumptions that Shakespeare's texts and appropriations of his texts are either progressive or conservative. Like the continuing debates about Shakespeare's place in the canon, the debates about the exact nature of Shakespearean production, reproduction, appropriation, and revision are fraught and frequently tense. And, once again, race often comes to the surface in these debates. Like the difficulty of controlling the exact meaning and significance of contemporary blackface performances (about which I write in chapter 5), Shakespeare may exist in the collective American imagination as a symbol that cannot fully be directed and managed in predictable and knowable ways. While some employ Shakespeare to serve as the ultimate tool to reform and unify a population into a cohesive identity (nationally, culturally, socially, *and* racially), others employ Shakespeare to reveal and unscript the desire for cohesion, hoping instead that Shakespeare will create a space for individuality and autonomy (again, nationally, culturally, socially, *and* racially). Both beliefs and employments of Shakespeare exist, and this book seeks to untangle the moments when these narratives are constructed to see how race figures into them. As the epigraph from Jyotsna Singh at the beginning of this chapter attests, however, the outcomes of appropriation are never guaranteed. And this reveals another throughline: the tension between intention and reception. While many authors, directors, activists, etc. appropriate Shakespeare for a specific socio-political purpose (whether progressive or conservative), the reception of that appropriation is impossible to control. *Passing Strange* analyses the tensions between intention and reception, alternating its focus between the two to reveal the nature of the instabilities.

Because of the broad focus of this book, my hope is that I am addressing a wider audience than the traditional work of Shakespeare criticism. In other words, I am not writing solely to and for the Shakespeare scholar. Although I proudly count myself as a member of this scholarly community, and although I value and utilize works written solely for this community, the dialogues that I intend this book to inspire must occur beyond the borders of the academy. Therefore, I hope I am addressing those both inside and outside of academia: scholars, practitioners, and activists alike. There are moments in the book when I directly address secondary school teachers (chapter 7), the artistic directors of classical theatre companies and the actors of color employed by them (chapter 4), the artistic directors of arts education programs and the funding organizations that support them (chapter 6), racial activists (chapter 3), and Shakespeare scholars and performance theorists in general (chapters 2 and 5). Because of this, there will be moments when segments of this diverse readership will feel alienated and uncomfortable (for example, specialists may find certain sections reductive, while others may find the theoretical sections challenging).

Despite the fact that I have intentionally written this book to be reader friendly by avoiding the specialist's jargon whenever possible, my discourse and rhetoric may not be familiar to all readers at all times. While this creates certain difficulties, it does offer the opportunity to create a more comprehensive dialogue and debate. If a diverse readership works through *Passing Strange*, then the comprehensiveness, complexity, and productivity of our future dialogues and debates about the roles Shakespeare and race have played, continue to play, and should play in the future of our contemporary American society will be the ultimate pay off. If we are to advance the conversation, then we can no longer talk in segregated and siloed environments and discourses. So I challenge my readers to be patient and to read with open hearts and minds.

PASSING BEYOND STRANGENESS

As Carla Kaplan argues in her introduction to the Norton critical edition of Nella Larsen's 1929 novel *Passing*, "Contemporary scholarship on passing, much of which has at least touched on this novel, generally remains divided."[30] There are those who believe that passing is a radical act, one "that demonstrates the instability and fictionality of race and destabilizes . . . identity categories."[31] And on the other side of the scholarly divide, "there are those who believe that passing reinforces identity categories by suggesting that there are meaningfully racialized states of being to pass *between*."[32] One side privileges the individual's ability to rewrite his/her racial identity, and the other side privileges the staying power of the original racial categories.

The poles of the scholarly debate about passing seem apt to appropriate to a discussion of Shakespeare, race, and the contemporary American imagination. There are those who believe that acts of appropriating Shakespeare empower the appropriator, and there are those who believe that acts of appropriation reveal the power of Shakespeare's original script. While *Passing Strange* will not resolve or unite the extremes of this debate, it will demonstrate and explain which side is popularly espoused in various situations. In other words, popular American culture does not simply embrace and promote one side of this debate. Rather, both extremes are exhibited at various moments.

Although it is helpful to articulate and analyze these extremes, this book hopes to accomplish more. As I indicated earlier, I would not be content merely exposing when, how, and why authorship, authority, and authenticity are conveyed to either Shakespeare or race in the contemporary imagination. Instead, I want to offer ways to move the debates beyond the passing strangeness of contemporary American constructions of Shakespeare and race, and I propose that this will occur through popular acknowledgements and celebrations of Shakespeare's instability. As recent textual scholarship has engaged with performance scholarship, there has been a scholarly recognition that the notion of a stable, fixed, and perfect Shakespeare text is a myth.[33] And it is not just a myth in the textual realm; it is also a myth in the practical performance realm. The earliest performers of Shakespeare's plays certainly did not have stable and full texts to perform from, and the earliest adaptors of his plays certainly did not treat them as whole and complete.[34] Likewise, when contemporary performers approach Shakespeare's plays, they freely cut, move, and clarify lines to suit their performance situation with regard to timing, audience, and space.

Shakespeare (again I stress the multivalent meanings of this name), then, *was* never and, therefore, *is* never coherent, stable, fixed, and defined. Instead, he was/ is always defined through the recreation of his identity, image, texts, and performances. If the question remains whether race studies and racial activism benefit from attention to or the inclusion of Shakespeare, then we must advocate for an unstable Shakespeare to get to the answer. Some gains can be made from the pairing of Shakespeare and race when Shakespeare's instability is explored and exploited. This does not mean denigrating Shakespeare—the man or the plays— through claims of cultural, historical, or racial irrelevance; those arguments are based on notions of Shakespeare's stability. Rather, Shakespeare needs to be rendered as contingent—as in process and as passing—as the creative moment in which his name, image, text, and performance are invoked.

Although this does not frequently occur in the texts, performances, and situations that I explore in *Passing Strange*, there are several examples of the benefits of instability. For example, in chapter 6 I analyze the way the Will Power to Youth program in Los Angeles, California implicitly destabilizes Shakespeare through the program's emphasis on collaboration. The program directors, who hire at-risk Hispanic youth to work through and perform a Shakespearean play during their school breaks, never articulate a belief in the stability of Shakespeare—the man, the texts, or the cultural icon. Instead, their focus is always on the needs and unique dynamics that their groups explore, create, and then perform. Shakespeare is central to their project, but his importance is only revealed through the group's collaborative creations.

Likewise, in chapter 7 I explore what I am calling the unmooring of *Othello* that occurs in Asian-American YouTube performances. In the videos discussed, Othello is unmoored historically, linguistically, and narratively. But the clips are disturbingly moored in a familiar performance strategy: they update Othello's narrative by framing it in a fantasy of contemporary, black-American culture. While these videos provide a conflicted sense of what it means to be outside popular American culture, they offer another avenue to destabilize Shakespeare. The interactivity of the Internet may present the best pedagogical vehicle to deconstruct regressive racial politics of Shakespearean performance history. The expansive dialogues that occur across national, cultural, racial, religious, and temporal borders on interactive Web sites like YouTube enable one to challenge "unusable" narratives and to create new ones in their stead. In other words, the medium plays a vital role in its ability to destabilize.

And finally in chapter 3 I explore the frequent examples of strategic essentialism that attempt to claim Shakespeare as Other (black, a woman, an Arab, etc.). While I provide an in-depth analysis of the theories and practices of strategic essentialism, I want to highlight here the potential for what I would like to coin "strategic confusion": that is, moments when Shakespeare is strategically confused for an artist of color. It is fashionable to claim that "Shakespeare was black," as Maya Angelou famously did, but Shakespeare is not destabilized in that claim. On the other hand, the claim that "It never occurred to us that a white man could write that good" destabilizes whiteness and Shakespearean authorship in surprising and productive ways.[35]

In other words, to pass beyond the strangeness of American constructions of Shakespeare and race, we will have to destabilize both race *and* Shakespeare. To destabilize does not mean to destroy, vilify, or denigrate; rather, it means to shift the foundation so that new angles, vantages, and perspectives are created. My hope is that *Passing Strange* will reveal that it is not only our modern conceptions of race that need to be challenged, but also our modern conceptions of Shakespeare.

I have dedicated this book to "race men and women" because I see *Passing Strange* as a work of scholarly intervention and activism. Although the term race man is somewhat anachronistic (a phrase first defined in 1945 by St. Clair Drake and Horace Cayton), I want to appropriate it to this moment and this work.[36] As

Mark Anthony Neal explains, "'Race man' is a term from the beginning of the 20th century that describes black men of stature and integrity who represented the best that African Americans had to offer in the face of Jim Crow segregation. It has lost some of its resonance in a post-civil rights world, but it remains an unspoken measure of commitment to uplifting the race. Race men inspire pride; their work, their actions and their speech represent excellence instead of evoking shame and embarrassment."[37] While Neal focuses on the historic importance of the race man to uplift the race through positive representation, Henry Louis Gates, Jr. employs the phrase to describe experts in black culture: "In the black tradition it's like being a Talmudic scholar, a person of letters who writes about African-American culture."[38] For Gates, a race man is a scholar who passes on racial history and knowledge. Yet Hazel Carby reminds us that the initial race men, like W. E. B. Du Bois and Booker T. Washington, specifically focused on the gender of those doing the uplifting, representing, and cultural transmitting: women were not thought appropriate as race men.[39]

By including women in my dedication, I hope I have made it clear that I think both sexes can do this important work, which I do not see as limited to representation. Instead, I appropriate the phrase to signify those who are willing to recognize, identify, and question the significance of the elephant in the room (to return to the epigraph from Paul Mooney): the men and women who work to uplift the race by encouraging scholarly and practical debates. *Passing Strange*, then, is designed to begin the conversation, and my hope is it will continue well after the covers of the book are shut.

FIGURE 2.1 Kidnapping the Bard. Film still from *Bringing Down the House*.

The meaning of a classic can rarely be recovered or revived; it must nearly always be re-created. The supposedly universal ideas commonly ascribed to classics originally clarified a certain range of human experience under a particular aspect of eternity that can never again have exactly the same significance.
—LEE SIMONSON[1]

2

Universalism

TWO FILMS THAT BRUSH WITH THE BARD, *SUTURE*

AND *BRINGING DOWN THE HOUSE*

IT IS COMMON to hear Shakespeare's plays referred to as universal, as depicting universal themes, plots, emotions, and characterizations. Simply perform an Internet search for the terms "Shakespeare" and "universal" and you will find a plethora of essays for sale about the "universal themes" in Shakespeare plays, such as "Universal Themes: Othello Essays" and "Universal Themes of Politics and Violence in Shakespeare's Works."[2] As Michael Bristol argues, the institutionalization of Shakespeare in contemporary American academic settings makes Shakespeare a part of the American consciousness "whether or not [we] have read any of the plays."[3] My college students, for example, often begin the semester by making statements about the value, importance, and enduring relevance of Shakespeare's plays in the twenty-first century because of their universality. These statements affirm Bristol's point that an "expression of interest in Shakespeare . . . is interpreted as an unambiguous sign of cultural advancement" because "the tyranny of Shakespeare's goodness, is an indication of just how powerfully situated this material is within the ensemble of social and cultural relations in contemporary society."[4] Or, as Gerald Nachman argues, "Shakespeare becomes theatrical spinach" in America's schools because "He's good for you."[5]

Of course, theatre reviewers often assess productions based on their ability to communicate Shakespeare's universal themes. Writing about The Bridge Project, the transatlantic collaboration between the Old Vic and the Brooklyn Academy of Music, Tim Auld praised Sam Mendes's 2009 production of *The Winter's Tale* because it expresses the "universal theme of longing" that left Auld with a "heavy lump in [his] throat."[6] In other words, productions are often judged on their ability to inspire emotional responses, which are assumed to occur through the plays' universal appeal. Thus, directors, producers, and actors often refer to Shakespeare's universality when pitching their new and often radically updated productions of his plays. When discussing his 2009 television series "10 Things I Hate About You," which is based on the 1999 film with the same name, which is in turn based on *Taming of the Shrew*, Carter Covington described the "staying power" of *Taming of the Shrew* as one that is dependent on the "universal archetypes" of the characters and their relationships.[7] Despite the fact that Covington is creating a television series from a movie that contains none of the language from Shakespeare's original play, he still feels the need to espouse the universal appeal of the original even as he espouses the need to update it.

Similarly, the Aboriginal activist Noel Pearson discusses his desire to translate all of *Richard III* into his native Guugu Yimithirr language because he wants his audience to "understand that these things are universal, that Richard III is like politics in Hope Vale."[8] Although Pearson is actually discussing the political landscape of contemporary Australia—"the play also resonates deeply with the politics and kin-conflicts of my own hometown (I have several cousins who could play the part of Richard to perfection)"—he employs the rhetoric of Shakespeare's universality to advance his cause (his "affiliation with English literature").[9]

Film treatments of Shakespeare's plays also tap into the rhetoric of Shakespeare's universality because the promotion of his perpetual relevancy provides a way to invite diverse audiences to the box office. To gain a larger share of the movie-going population, especially the coveted younger, frequent movie-visiting audience, film treatments of Shakespeare's plays are pitched as broadly as possible. Thus, films as disparate in style, tone, language, and historical setting as Kenneth Branagh's *Henry V* (1989)[10]—a film set in the play's historical moment with Renaissance costumes and Shakespeare's original language—and Billy Morrissette's *Scotland, PA* (2001)[11]—an adaptation of *Macbeth* set in the 1970s with none of Shakespeare's original language—end up marketing themselves as Shakespeare for the people, *all* people. In these films Shakespeare is sold as the universal story teller because the universal can be marketed to all.

So what exactly does the universal mean? In these disparate references to the universal one can detect schisms in the very meaning of the term. While it is clear they work off the common notion that the universal is applicable to all subjects, conditions, and/or situations, embedded within them are challenges to this universal applicability. In one, universality is emotional veracity; in another, it is longevity; in another, it is translatability; and, in many, it is simply marketability. In fact, it seems difficult to reconcile a formal dictionary definition of universal with more popular uses of the term. These definitions are not—I have to say it— universal. While it seems difficult for film versions of Shakespeare's plays to sell themselves as anything other than universal, the conflicted views of Shakespeare's universality come across in films that treat Shakespeare only tangentially. That is, films whose plots, themes, characters, and settings are not directly tied to Shakespeare's plays seem to address the questions of the particular, historical, and traditional in more explicit and complex fashions than straight-forward film versions, adaptations, or even spin-offs do.

For example, Andrew Fleming's irreverent 2008 comedy *Hamlet 2* provides an extremely complex portrait of Shakespeare's position within the contemporary multicultural world by mocking simplistic universalist statements (made primarily by the lead character played by Steve Coogan), juxtaposing them with racist statements that clearly belie an espousal of the universal, and ultimately creating a heart-felt performance that does reify the universal.[12] This, to me, represents a more complex portrait of the push-pull between differing notions of the universal than anything represented in more straightforward film versions of Shakespeare's plays.

Therefore, in this chapter I examine two films that are specifically *not* film versions or film adaptations of Shakespeare texts. Instead, I have chosen *Suture* (1993) and *Bringing Down the House* (2003) because they reveal important clues about the racial and cultural work Shakespeare performs in our twenty-first century American world without being tied to recreations of the plots or themes. These films come from opposite ends of the American-film spectrum: *Suture* is a small-budget independent film that receives a lot of scholarly attention; *Bringing Down the House* is a big-budget Hollywood blockbuster that receives very little scholarly attention. Yet both films address how perceived racial and cultural differences affect contemporary American life; both have a great deal to say about Shakespeare's role in the effects on that life; and both grapple with the notion of universality in informative ways. What emerges from these films are two contradictory notions of the universal in relation to racial difference. While in common parlance it is typical to define the universal as that which pertains to the universe in general and all things within it without division, these films traffic in slightly more nuanced common notions of the universal. In one, the universal is meant to elide racial differences, to create a unified whole that is colorblind. In the other, the universal is meant to exclude anything that is not white and Western, to create a unified whole that does not permit or contain racial divisions.

THE UNIVERSAL AS THE COLORBLIND: *SUTURE*

A type of modern film noir set in the glaring bright light of Phoenix, Arizona, *Suture*, an independent film written and directed by Scott McGehee and David Siegel, examines the connections between personal identity and notions of the universal and the colorblind.[13] Although Shakespeare plays an extremely minor role in the film, the references to him and his works are central to the film's critique of universalism in the guise of colorblindness. Two brothers, who have never met, unexpectedly discover each other at their father's funeral. One brother, Vincent Towers, has lived a life of opulence and luxury in Phoenix, while the other brother, Clay Arlington, has lived a life of poverty and manual labor in Needles, California. Yet they immediately discover their secret kinship because their "physical similarity is disarming."

In what appears to be an effort to develop a relationship, Vincent invites Clay to Phoenix for a weekend visit after the funeral. After dressing Clay in his own clothes and furtively swapping their driver's licenses, however, Vincent attempts to fake his own death by blowing Clay up in his car. We later learn that Vincent has been the chief murder suspect in his father's death and seeks to evade the law by substituting his brother's body for his own. In spite of Vincent's efforts, Clay survives the blast but loses his memory. Everyone assumes that Clay is Vincent because of his clothes, car, and photo identification, and they attempt to help reconstruct Vincent's identity and memory for him. Prominently featured within the film are two doctors—a psychiatrist who hopes to cure "Vincent's" memory loss and a plastic surgeon who hopes to heal "Vincent's" facial scars. In the end, Vincent returns to kill Clay, but is instead killed by him. Despite the fact that this violent episode helps to restore all of Clay's true memories, he decides to live his life as the wealthy and privileged Vincent Towers, forever forsaking his identity as Clay Arlington. He ends by declaring, "I am Vincent Towers."

A film that is obviously interested in identity formation, *Suture* depicts the plastic surgeon and the psychiatrist as scientists whose work is informed by their beliefs in, and adherences to, universal principles. For example, the plastic surgeon Dr. Renee Descartes (played by Mel Harris) comes "from a long line of plastic surgeons." Her grandfather was a plastic surgeon, and Dr. Descartes explains that her father was an art historian who wrote a book about a fifteenth-century plastic surgeon: "He was pursuing a theory about Renaissance ideals of beauty and he came across Gaspare Tagliacozzi, the father of rhinoplasty . . . the father of modern plastic surgery." Coming from this stock, Dr. Descartes presents herself as someone who believes not only in the art of her science—at one point we see her sculpting a clay model of "Vincent's" head—but also in the science of artistic ideals. For instance, when "Vincent" expresses doubts about his innocence even though he cannot remember committing a crime, she assures him that he could not have committed murder because he has "too elegant a nose to have shot someone." While at first this seems like a joke, she explains that she actually "collect[s] books on characterology and physiognomy. It used to be a complete science." For Dr. Descartes, identity is both tied to and revealed by universal aesthetic principles: beautiful people do not commit murder, only ugly ones do. Thus, Dr. Descartes reads and interprets "Vincent's" face in terms of these universal aesthetic principles just as she tries to heal and recreate him according to them.

Likewise, the psychiatrist Dr. Max Shinoda (played by Sab Shimono) attempts to heal "Vincent" through what he assumes are the universal principles of Freudian psychoanalysis. His cavernous white office, for example, is framed by two floor-to-ceiling Rorschach blots, and he is constantly attempting to analyze "Vincent's" dreams in Freudian terms. Exhorting "Vincent" to remember the specific details of his dreams, Dr. Shinoda provides a deliberately simplistic example about cars in dreams: "We all know names like Chevrolet, Chrysler, Buick, Dodge, Ford, or Oldsmobile to be names of car companies, but think about, say, Oldsmobile: Olds Mobile, Old Mobile, an old person's car, an antique car.... Dodge, dodging, moving quickly, getting away." Then he underscores his point by referencing Sigmund Freud: "As Freud said, 'Dreams appear like a coded puzzle.'" Assuming their universal applicability, Dr. Shinoda employs cultural markers to help spark "Vincent's" memory. Weaving a type of guide to the great quotes from the great books into his discussions with "Vincent," Dr. Shinoda implicitly trusts that these works have something valuable to say to and about "Vincent's" condition. He quotes Freud again to stress that details are always readable: "As Freud said, 'Nothing is insignificant.'" He quotes W. H. Auden when he wants "Vincent" to interpret his dreams: "The poet Auden said, 'Learn from your dreams what you lack.'"

Not surprisingly, then, Dr. Shinoda also cites William Shakespeare to support his claims that there are universal ways to analyze the mind. In a line that is often misquoted from *Hamlet*, Dr. Shinoda says, "To sleep is to dream." Of course, the line in *Hamlet* is, "To sleep, perchance to dream" (3.1.67). And, likewise, Dr. Shinoda attributes a line to Shakespeare that might loosely stem from *Hamlet* as well: "Just try and regard everything here as 'fodder for remembrance,' as Shakespeare said." Although Shakespeare never pairs "fodder" with "remembrance," Ophelia offers flowers to her loved ones and says, "that's for remembrance. Pray, love, remember" (4.5.173–174). While it is interesting that Dr. Shinoda misquotes and/or misattributes lines to Shakespeare, the force of his point works even if the citations are incorrect because their universal applicability stems from the cultural capital of the author to whom he attributes them. He believes that there are certain authors, texts, and lines that speak to the human condition universally—that these references are meaningful precisely because they are universally applicable.

Privileging both Freud and Shakespeare, and in particular *The Interpretation of Dreams* and *Hamlet*, Dr. Shinoda references passages that have the most cultural significance for him.[14] And it is no accident that these texts do; Freud, as the father of psychoanalysis, privileged Shakespeare above all others. Analyzing the modern fascination with identifying or debunking Shakespeare's identity as the genius dramatist of the Renaissance, Marjorie Garber argues that Freud was thinking about *Hamlet*, a play about remembrance, when he penned *The Interpretation of Dreams*. "While Freud thus confers upon Oedipus a primacy he denies to Hamlet," Garber writes, "Hamlet remains a half-hidden center of preoccupation throughout Freud's work. . . . [The] writings of Freud himself seem uncannily to circle back upon the subject—the subjects—of *Hamlet*."[15] Similarly, Stephen Greenblatt examines *Hamlet* as a play that specifically addresses the problems of cultural memory. It is no accident, Greenblatt argues, that Western civilization is obsessed with *Hamlet* because it both addresses and creates "our" cultural memory.[16] *The Interpretation of Dreams* and *Hamlet*, however, do not spark any memories for Clay as "Vincent."

Thus, the two doctors in *Suture*—one who works on the external aspects of the body and one who works on the internal aspects of the mind—operate according to what they assume are the universal principles of their disciplines. Nonetheless, the film reveals their adherence to these principles to be shortsighted and limited because they cannot actually restore Vincent Tower's body and mind when it is Clay Arlington they are treating. The film puts a great deal of pressure on the blind spots of universal principles because neither plastic surgery nor psychoanalysis can fully remake Vincent Towers from Clay Arlington. Moreover, while on paper the film's plot reads like a standard type of mistaken identity double plot, *Suture* muddies matters by employing a salt and pepper cast: Vincent is white (played by Michael Harris), Clay is black (played by Dennis Haysbert), and they look nothing alike. The attempts by the doctors to recreate their vision of "Vincent Towers" through plastic surgery and psychoanalysis, then, are rendered even more bizarre because they are literally—not just figuratively—blind to the reality of the differences between the brothers. The film depicts the doctors as ignoring or being blind to the specific and the particular because of their belief in the universal.

Because no one within the film notices, or at least comments on, the color discrepancy between Vincent Towers and Clay Arlington, the audience is left in the awkward position of experiencing something entirely different from the characters within the film. Upon first seeing the film, I kept expecting each new character that encountered Clay as "Vincent" to notice the racial difference and then reveal

FIGURE 2.2 The identical twin brothers Vincent Towers (played by Michael Harris) and Clay Arlington (played by Dennis Haysbert). Film still from *Suture*.

it to the others. When no character did, I slowly realized the film was offering a commentary on the desire for colorblindness in contemporary American life. As Michael Omi and Howard Winant remind us, the late 1980s and early 1990s when *Suture* was produced were the decades in which neoconservatives pronounced their desired social end as the end of all race consciousness.

> In such a vision recent history is seen as a period of enlightened progress— an unfolding drama of the social, political, and economic incorporation of minorities which will not be thwarted or reversed. The "color-blind" society, it is argued, will be the end result of this progress. Yet viewed more deeply, recent history—particularly the period from the 1960s to the 1980s—reveals a more complex and contradictory trajectory in which the pattern of race relations seems far less certain, and much less tranquil.[17]

As Omi and Winant go on to argue, rather than promoting "an egalitarian society," the neoconservatives' appropriation of the term "color-blind" actually promotes a type of historical amnesia that eradicates the need to address and work through past injustices, inequalities, and difficulties.[18] According to Omi and Winant, the neoconservatives are all too willing to embrace colorblindness because it is part and parcel of a larger historical erasure. The past becomes irrelevant at best and unreadable at worst in this neoconservative version of colorblindness.

Likewise, Omi and Winant critique the "neoliberal racial project" for supporting a "racial universalism" which is founded upon the notion that there should be "a 'single society,' rather than a 'we and they' orientation to race."[19] "The universalist view of race does not recognize the instability inherent in racial politics and identity. It treats race as something we can 'get beyond.'"[20] In other words, they critique neoliberals for ignoring the practical challenges to living as if contemporary American society is unified racially and culturally. Thus, in *Racial Formation in the United States* it is not merely the political right that is accused of whiting out race consciousness in the latter decades of the twentieth century; rather, the political left is also depicted as sacrificing the important work that noticing race accomplishes. Aligned with Omi and Winant's prescient arguments, *Suture* asks its audience to interrogate simplistic presentations of universalism and colorblindness.

Suture also seems tapped into the debates about colorblind casting that were circulating in the late 1980s and early 1990s. As the theatrical trailer for the film announces, "*Suture* [is a] thriller where nothing is black and white," and the back of the DVD declares that "*Suture* takes a non-traditional approach to casting." Of course, August Wilson, the black American playwright who won two Pulitzer Prizes for plays in his Pittsburgh Cycle of plays about African-American history and culture, created a firestorm by publically and vociferously opposing colorblind casting, the practice of casting actors of color in roles traditionally conceived as and written for white actors:

> Colorblind casting is an aberrant idea that has never had any validity other than as a tool of the Cultural Imperialists who view their American culture, rooted in the icons of European culture, as beyond reproach in its perfection. It is inconceivable to them that life could be lived and even enriched without knowing Shakespeare or Mozart. . . . To mount an all black production of *Death of a Salesman* or any other play conceived for white actors as an investigation of the human condition through the specifics of white culture is to deny us our humanity, our own history, and the need to make our own investigations from the cultural ground on which we stand as black Americans.[21]

According to Wilson, "Cultural Imperialists" claim that their cultural and artistic traditions are universal, and, thus, they advocate for productions with nontraditional casting in the form of colorblind casting. Like Omi and Winant, Wilson famously argued that there is a desire in white America to ignore and even eradicate the differences between races and cultures because then past and current injustices based on race can be ignored: "America often expects blacks to be carbon copies of whites and white culture."[22]

McGehee and Siegel's film effectively exposes what Wilson labels as the imperialists' desire to white out blackness, to make black white. In *Suture* Clay is actively made into a "carbon copy" of his white brother by Drs. Descartes and Shinoda. For example, Dr. Descartes' pursuit of universal aesthetic facial beauty renders her all too blind to Clay's differences from Vincent. In one of the more disturbing scenes in *Suture*, Dr. Descartes comments on "Vincent's" "elegant" features while removing the sutures from his scarred face:

> You have what they call a Greco-Roman or American nose, sleek with a small prominence at the bridge and point. Physiognomists were sure that people with Greco-Roman noses were inclined towards music and literature and the arts. Definitely not deviant behavior like killing people. . . . And your fine, straight hair [is] almost always a sign of good mental temperament, not to mention digestion. And your mouth—thin, smooth lips, slightly open. Lips that are a sign of an affectionate, kind-hearted, and generous person.

Dr. Descartes pulls the sutures from Clay's black face and strokes his curly hair, all the while creating him anew in her own image—white, slender nosed, thin lipped, and straight haired. Far from promoting the philosophy her namesake declared three hundred fifty years earlier—"I think, therefore, I am"—Dr. Descartes echoes something closer to Genesis's notion, "I declare, therefore, you are." As one critic notes, "Renee sutures over the difference between her desired vision of Clay and what we, the audience, can see."[23] This scene clearly exposes the white society's attempt to ignore racial differences (and thus to see society narcissistically).

Although not operating in the physical realm, Dr. Shinoda also works to make Clay malleable, to make him into the man he both assumes he is and wants him to be. His reliance on the assumed universal greatness and applicability of Western artists and philosophers is presented as equally blind as Dr. Descartes' methods in *Suture*. Shakespeare's position within Dr. Shinoda's list of the greats should not be surprising considering Shakespeare's position within the debates about colorblind casting. As I have argued elsewhere, "the practice of colorblind casting is inextricably enmeshed in the contemporary history of Shakespearean production," and

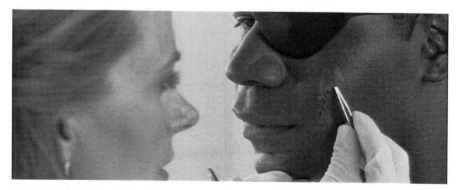

FIGURE 2.3 Dr. Renee Descartes (played by Mel Harris) sutures Clay Arlington (played by Dennis Haysbert) into Vincent Towers. Film still from *Suture*.

"the immense and enduring weight of Shakespeare's cultural legacy has helped to create the perceived need for colorblind casting."[24] The debates about nontraditional casting between Robert Brustein, the white artistic director of the American Repertory Theatre, and August Wilson frequently circled around Shakespeare, just as Dr. Shinoda circles back to Shakespeare in his attempt to recreate "Vincent."[25] Thus, *Suture* links colorblindness with historical amnesia, cultural imperialism, and social, political, and cultural alienation.

McGehee and Siegel, however, interrogate and apply the most pressure to the notion of the universal through their use of suture theory. The audience is never sure whether or not it is supposed to see Clay's blackness. Seeing the film, one constantly asks: Has *Suture* employed colorblind casting? Is there something wrong because I can see, *do* see, Clay's/Dennis Haysbert's blackness? Or, is there something wrong with the characters in the film because they refuse to see color? Because of these uncertainties, the film disrupts the audience's ability to suture into the film.[26] Although suture theory is often deemed Lacanian, Jacques-Alain Miller introduced the concept into the field of psychoanalysis.[27] Suture theory describes the difficulty of having to fit oneself into society's discourse. In order to participate in society one must acquire language, but language limits one's ability to exist (think) freely (without governed constructions). A doubleness exists in which the subject realizes that there is a gap between his/her unique individual (and yet inexpressible) view of him/herself and his/her (expressible and yet alienating) pronoun/name. Jean-Pierre Oudart helped appropriate suture theory for film studies, by arguing:

> Every filmic field is echoed by an absent field, the place of a character who is put there by the viewer's imaginary, and which we shall call the Absent One. At a certain moment of the reading all the objects of the filmic field combine together to form the signifier of its absence. At this key-moment the image enters the order of the signifier, and the undefined strip of film the realm of the discontinuous, the "discrete." It is essential to understand this, since up to now film-makers believed that, by resorting to cinematic units as discrete as possible, they would find their way back to the rules of linguistic discourse, whereas it is cinema itself, when designating itself as cinematography, which tends to constitute its own *énoncé* in "discrete" units.[28]

According to Oudart, the camera's frame is read by the viewer as his/her absence from the scene. Film's connection with Lacan's focus on the relationship between the individual and language, for Oudart, stems from the viewer's absence from the filmic frame. Obviously, viewers cannot understand a film if they are constantly questioning their absence from what is depicted. Film works, then, because viewers suture themselves into the world they see. Kaja Silverman, a critic who helped solidify suture theory in film studies, goes on to explain that certain film/ shot rules are derived "from the imperative that the camera deny its own existence as much as possible, fostering the illusion that what is shown has an autonomous existence, independent of any technological interference, or any coercive gaze."[29] Thus, suture theory identifies the necessary loss (absence) of a private and personal identity in order to function within a communicable society. In film, the camera must help audiences suture over their own absence from the events depicted in order to communicate the plot effectively.

The most obvious connection with suture theory in McGehee and Siegel's film *Suture* is the audience's inability to suture seamlessly into the filmic world. We are constantly aware that we are seeing and experiencing something differently from the characters within the film—that the camera's eye divides us from the characters within the film—and this ruptured suturing enables the audience to recognize the racial blind spots within simplistic notions of universality. Commenting on the title of their film, McGehee and Siegel discuss their interest in suture theory:

> The name came early on, as a joke. You don't want to make a film that's about theory from that end: it would be very dull. This film's very loosely about suture theory; it's more about identity and identification. . . . We might have come up with some elaborately structured system where point-of-view shots were reserved for certain situations about suture, but we didn't do anything like that. It's really on a metaphorical level that you can talk about suture in film.[30]

Although McGehee and Siegel claim that they are not strictly following point-of-view shots that challenge the viewer's ability to suture into the filmic world, their use of nontraditional casting accomplishes as much as these specific shots would. In interviews McGehee and Siegel declare that their use of a racially-mixed cast is not a "casting issue" because it is "integral to the film and the story [they] were trying to tell."[31] The alienation the audience is expected to feel—the recognition that the camera's point-of-view represents the "Absent One" and not one's own view—makes the audience painfully aware that colorblindness is neither achievable *nor* desirable.

In interviews McGehee and Siegel explain that *Suture* is not meant to offer a meditation on black American culture: "We didn't set out to make a film about black experience in America. How we've attempted to control those social metaphors in the film is pretty broad—we've attempted to keep the film more in the parameters of sociology than race, the way the homogeneity of society affects the

construction of personal identity."[32] McGehee even declares that the film deliberately does not employ references to black history and black culture, stating that
"the soundtrack features Johnny Cash, not James Brown."[33] Thus, *Suture* disavows
employing explicit markers of black culture, and Clay's/Dennis Haysbert's blackness floats freely. As Roy Grundmann notes, the film depicts "a black man, not an
African-American."[34]

While *Suture* does not engage in the cultural aspects that make up black
American life—Clay's memories of his life in Needles, California, for example, are
more about the town's poverty than his race—it places the construction of white
American culture from European classics under a close microscope. The musical
landscape of the film, for instance, provides the aural equivalent to the citations
of Freud and Shakespeare—musical "classics" that are assumed to be universal:
Richard Wagner's *Tannhauser* and *Siegried*, Johannes Brahms's "Alto Rhapsody"
and "German Requiem," Giacomo Puccini's *Turandot*, and Joseph Haydn's "String
Quartet No. 82 Op. 77." Vincent Towers and his friends and family adore classical
music. Vincent listens to Wagner in his car, Dr. Descartes is dressed to go to the
opera in one scene, and Vincent's friends arrange for an opera singer to serenade
him in the hospital.

But Clay does not seem to relish the supposed universal appeal of classical
music. In fact, when he drives Vincent's Bentley—the car that is rigged with the
bomb—he switches the music from Wagner's *Tannhauser* to Johnny Cash's "Ring
of Fire," and remarks, "Right" and smiles. As one critic points out, the film explodes
"the Hollywood cinematic tradition of presenting whiteness as an 'invisible'. . . .
[It] presents a critical reading of whiteness as a dominant social and cultural
construction."[35] Only the colorblind, the film suggests, are incapable of seeing the
visibility of whiteness and markers of white culture. In other words, the colorblind
are the ones who trumpet white cultural constructions, like Freud, Shakespeare,
and Wagner, as universal.

In the end, Clay's memory slowly returns, but his desire to return to an existence as Clay Arlington does not. Clay's memory is fully restored after he shoots
Vincent in the face, ensuring that his brother cannot be identified as the true Vincent Towers. He explains to Dr. Shinoda in a calm and emotionless voice that he
will not return to living as the poor, working class Clay Arlington because the
world still sees him as "Vincent."

I am Vincent Towers. . . . When I look in the mirror, I see Vincent Towers.
When I go to the club, people call me Vincent Towers. Renee's in love with
Vincent Towers. . . . There's a dead body that cannot be identified, and in a
most real way it is not the body of Vincent Towers. I am Vincent Towers.

The world's treatment of Clay as "Vincent" becomes more important to him than the memories that have been restored. Society's projection of Vincent's identity onto Clay has been fully internalized by "Vincent." Despite the fact that Dr. Shinoda repeatedly calls him Clay, "Vincent" can only respond, "I am Vincent Towers." Clay's adoption of "Vincent's" identity perfectly enacts W. E. B. Du Bois's theory of the "double-consciousness": he has "no true self consciousness" and only sees himself "through the eyes of others."[36] Or, to return to August Wilson's rhetoric, Clay accepts his place as a "carbon copy" of "white America."[37]

Of course, the fascinating twist in *Suture* is the fact that society's projection of "Vincent" onto Clay seems to afford him wealth, power, acceptance, and love, the exact opposite of the "contempt and pity" that Du Bois identified as white America's projection onto blacks.[38] *Suture* ends with "Vincent" marrying Dr. Descartes, and a photo essay of their travels together is projected on the screen with their smiling faces featured in each image. And yet, in becoming "Vincent," Clay accepts what Omi and Winant identify as "the incorporation of our ['more radical'] demands (equality, justice, inclusion) in the warped and denatured form of 'color blindness'" which simply reinforces "the underlying racist system we set out to destroy."[39] Clay becomes the colorblind mold of a neoconservative's creation, a creation that is provided its finishing touches by a neoliberal's espousal of universalism.

Although parodied in the film for his blind adherence to psychoanalysis, Dr. Shinoda offers an amazing statement of insight and metadrama early in *Suture*. In explaining what amnesia is, Dr. Shinoda renders the universal signs of amnesia as culturally constructed: "Research suggests that your own understanding of how and what an amnesiac forgets . . . [Dr. Shinoda pauses and starts over] What is seen in movies or TV has created a pattern by which you yourself have forgotten. If you thought you could forget how to talk, for example, we would not be having this conversation right now." *Suture* as a whole attempts to wrest the audience from accepting these filmic and televisual patterns as natural and/or universal. Rather they are revealed to be artistic creations that are both informed by *and* inform the social, cultural, political, and historical world in which they were conceived. Of course, this means these patterns can be changed.

Reflecting on the impact of *Racial Formation in the United States*, Omi and Winant conclude: "We ended the second edition of *Racial Formation* with an injunction to 'notice' race. The contradiction between that necessity and the uncertain denial involved in color blindness identifies the racial battlefield of the twenty-first century."[40] As Omi and Winant make clear, a critique of colorblindness and an espousal of the universal will be central to racial and social justice issues in the twenty-first century. While some scholars, activists, teachers, and students are uncomfortable by their call to "notice race," even fewer will be comfortable with a claim that an espousal of Shakespeare's universality might just imply a neoconservative view of colorblindness.[41] *Suture*, however, shows in glaring black and white how pathological it is to go blind to race and how chauvinistic it is to assume that texts are universal—even those by William Shakespeare.

THE UNIVERSAL AS EXCLUSIVE: *BRINGING DOWN THE HOUSE*

If Scott McGehee and David Siegel's *Suture* is a small-budget, high-concept film that engages film theory, then Adam Shankman's *Bringing Down the House* can only be described in oppositional terms, as a big-budget, low-concept film. Where *Suture* is intellectual, *Bringing Down the House* is physical. Where *Suture* is theoretical, *Bringing Down the House* is slapstick. Where *Suture* is alienating, *Bringing Down the House* is inclusive. Despite these obvious differences from *Suture*, *Bringing Down the House* nevertheless raises similar questions about the meaning of Shakespeare's universality. It does so, however, by engaging a popular assumption about Shakespeare's universalism: that claims of universality are really codes for racial exclusivity. Where *Suture* investigates the neoconservative hijacking of color blindness, *Bringing Down the House* investigates the popular belief that universalists are racists.

Bringing Down the House follows the relationship between Peter Sanderson (played by Steve Martin), a divorced tax attorney, and Charlene Morton (played by Queen Latifah), a convict who seeks to clear her name. Peter, whose career always seems to interfere with his personal life, makes a date with a woman in an online legal chat room. When Charlene arrives for their first date, Peter is surprised to find her a street-talking black woman who is not a lawyer at all, but an ex-con who wants help with her legal troubles. As their date quickly sours, Charlene blackmails Peter into letting her stay with him. The film posits that the prospect of Charlene publicizing their online interracial relationship terrifies Peter enough to let this black stranger move into his house. The racist social pressures in the world around him are so great (almost every white character in the film exhibits immense bouts of xenophobia) that Peter agrees to help Charlene as long as she does not publicize their cyber-relations.

The film ends up commenting a great deal on popular assumptions about Shakespeare because one of the film's most explicitly racist characters has a dog named "William Shakespeare." Virginia Arness (played by Joan Plowright), a wealthy coffee heiress, is said to "bring new meaning to the term conservative." She is an "arch conservative."[42] Peter, of course, is attempting to win the big account with this "arch conservative." When first we see Mrs. Arness waiting to have tea with

Peter in an exclusive country club, she is seated next to a French bulldog wearing a starched Elizabethan collar. "This is William Shakespeare," she intones haughtily to Peter.

Jason Filardi and Adam Shankman, the writer and director respectively of *Bringing Down the House*, provide the audio commentary on the DVD, and they discuss how the Bard came to be in their film.

> SHANKMAN: And there's William Shakespeare. We had a lot of debate over [the dog's name] . . . What did the dog's name used to be?
> FILARDI: God, we went through so many. Oh, Margaret Thatcher.
> SHANKMAN: Joan [Plowright] didn't like it to be Margaret for some weird reason. She didn't want the dog to be a girl. Oh, because you could see the dog's penis. We thought that was funny, but she said, "No, it should be William Shakespeare."

Shankman goes on to discuss how he decided to play up the dog's new name by changing his outfit for every scene in which he appears: the dog wears an Elizabethan ruff, an ascot, a golf visor, and an Elizabethan soft collar. So although the dog was not initially envisioned as Shakespeare, the writer and director decide to play up the humorous possibilities of this new identity, even nicknaming the dog "The Bard" in the DVD's montage of film stills that appear under the DVD's options page. In other words, Plowright's revision to the dog's name was fully embraced by the writer and director as a change to the dog's "character."

It is worth asking, however, why it is supposed to be humorous for a racist to name her dog after the most famous English playwright in history. It is worth

FIGURE 2.4 The canine-ization of the Bard. DVD menu still from *Bringing Down the House*.

questioning why this alteration fits so seamlessly into *Bringing Down the House*'s filmic world. Is the joke based on the idea that a racist would never name her dog "Shakespeare"? Is the joke based on the idea that cultured people who read Shakespeare could not possibly be so socially "conservative"? Is the name meant to be read as ironic because Shakespeare's purported universality stands in opposition to Mrs. Arness's racism and classism? Unfortunately, it is more likely the exact opposite. The joke seems to be based on the idea that it is only natural for a racist to come up with the name "Shakespeare," and that an interest in the classics goes hand-in-hand with conservative social values.

While most Shakespeareans—that is, teachers, scholars, actors, directors, and fans—would agree that this assumption is an utter fallacy, the film is trafficking in contemporary popular stereotypes about cultural capital, the classics, and contemporary issues of race and power. Despite the fact that *one* popular notion is that Shakespeare is timeless and universal, there is *another* popular notion that the universal does not really include everyone. One need only think about the number of theatre companies that bill themselves as doing something different with Shakespeare by bringing his plays to "the people" to realize that there is a popular notion that Shakespeare is not already for, by, and with the people (for more on this topic see chapter 4). In fact, the canine "Shakespeare's" role in the film promotes this popular assumption in very clear ways.

Emphasizing the stereotype that a love of Shakespeare means "arch" conservatism, *Bringing Down the House* does not merely allow "William Shakespeare" to be a passive lapdog. On the contrary, he plays an active and central role in sniffing out the true identity of Charlene. When Charlene pretends to be Peter's nanny/cook to impress Mrs. Arness, Mrs. Arness reminisces:

That smells like our Ivy's jambalaya. She was so wonderful. We paid her nothing, of course, you know. But then people had standards of service in those days. . . . Our Ivy was with us for so long we really thought of her as one of the family. After every meal our mother would scrape all of the food we had not eaten and put it on one big plate and give it to Ivy. . . . You know, there's a lovely, sad Negro spiritual that Ivy's brother used to sing when he came in from the tobacco fields:

Mama, is massa' goin' sell us tomorrow?
Yes, yes, yes.
Mama, is massa' goin' sell us tomorrow?
Yes, yes, yes.
Mama, is massa' goin' sell me tomorrow?

Yes, yes, yes.

So watch and pray.

Now, there's a second verse if you'd like to join in the chorus.

During this scene, Plowright emphasizes the horror of the "Negro spiritual" by singing it with great bathos, and as she sings one of the characters chokes on her food out of sheer shock. Completely insensitive to the inappropriate linking of the poor black servants of her childhood with Charlene, Mrs. Arness seems to expect that all blacks will be in positions of happy and grateful servitude.

The direct relationship between Mrs. Arness's racism and her choice to connect her dog's identity with William Shakespeare becomes explicit immediately following her reminiscences. Just after Mrs. Arness finishes her serenade, "William Shakespeare" hops away from the table, where he too has been served by Charlene, and runs to the television. Although he never barks, whimpers, wines, or makes any other noises in the course of the entire film, at this crucial moment "William Shakespeare" barks and coughs loudly, drawing everyone's attention to the TV show, "Criminals at Large." On the show Charlene is revealed to be an *escaped* convict and not a recently released one as she led them to believe. In other words, "William Shakespeare" rats out Charlene (if I may mix my animal metaphors), thus obfuscating the need to confront Mrs. Arness's racism. Not only does "William Shakespeare" literally protect Mrs. Arness from this potentially dangerous prisoner, but also from the potential threat of a confrontation over her outrageously insensitive behavior. Charlene actively and aggressively prepared to defend herself against the overt racism exhibited by Mrs. Arness by coming out of the kitchen wielding a large knife, but she is interrupted by "William Shakespeare's" revelation of her true identity. Thus in *Bringing Down the House*, "William Shakespeare" serves as a protector of the white, racist, exclusive establishment, as represented by Virginia Arness.

As a film that explicitly interrogates contemporary race relations, *Bringing Down the House* reveals what I think has become the unspoken back-story to Bardolatry: Shakespeare represents the epitome of Western culture because he represents the exclusivity of white culture. The levels of conflation in this back-story are complex. On the one hand, Shakespeare is taken to mean the man, the plays, and the modern literary bedrock of Western civilization. But on the other hand, Shakespeare is taken to mean two contradictory, but not mutually exclusive, ideas: the exclusivity of Western civilization *and* the fantasy of the racial homogeneity of that civilization. In other words, Shakespeare's cultural capital comes precisely from the contradictory ideas that his works exclude everything that is not Western (which, of course, is also popularly a synecdochical conflation/substitution for "white"), and conversely, that "our" civilization, culture, and society, which Shakespeare helped to create, have nothing to do with issues of race. This assumption only functions, however, when it is imagined that whiteness is the norm from which everything else is a lesser deviation. In these terms, then, whiteness has nothing to do with race. This contradictory construction, that Shakespeare is universal and exclusive, is vital, but has been under analyzed in popular culture.

Bringing Down the House does a brilliant job of revealing the contradictions in the popular construction and perception of Bardolatry. Worshipping the Bard is often assumed to mean that one must prostrate oneself before an all-knowing white God, but the notions of universality and exclusivity can come into conflict in this construction. In the film, this is revealed by the fact that Plowright's character Mrs. Arness cannot be without her beloved dog, "William Shakespeare." It is almost as if the film is arguing that her position in society is as much a function of her wealth as it is a function of her proximity to the Bard. In addition, the dog/God/Bard conflation is demonstrated most clearly when "William Shakespeare" reveals Queen Latifah's character's true identity: "Shakespeare" knows all, even the true identity of felons. Knowing all and being invested in all are two separate matters when it comes to Bardolatry, however. In *Bringing Down the House*, "Shakespeare" is not allowed to have any connections with nonwhite subjects and subject matters. In fact, to the contrary, "Shakespeare" seems to stand in the way of being able to enter into nonwhite culture. Mrs. Arness's only access to black culture when "Shakespeare" is around is her distant memory of black servants who ate her leftovers and sang spirituals about the horrors of a modern-day, quasi-slavery.

While this may seem like an extreme position, one that is exaggerated in *Bringing Down the House* simply for comic effect, these notions are popular and that is precisely what enables the comic effect in the film. Harold Bloom's 1998 book *Shakespeare: The Invention of the Human*, for example, continues to be an amazingly popular and well-selling book because Bloom's brand of Bardolatry is popular, and its rhetoric is not that far off from what is satirized in *Bringing Down the House*. Bloom writes about Shakespeare's "universalism" in terms of Shakespeare's "invention" of both "personality" and "humanity."[43] For Bloom, however, this omniscience does not mean that Shakespeare interested himself in issues of race. In fact, Bloom declares that Shakespeare's "politics, like his religion, evades [him], because [he] think[s] he was too wary to have any."[44] Critics who explore these issues in Shakespeare are "knowers and resenters," "erotomaniacs and bespoilers," and simply "destructive," according to Bloom.[45] Again, the unspoken assumption behind Bardolatry is that Shakespeare was (and still is) an all-knowing white God who was not (and, it is argued implicitly, that he cannot be, and should not be made to be) interested in anything outside a fantastically constructed homogenous Western civilization. Bloom constructs a contradictory image of what Shakespeare's legacy is: it is the creation of "our" civilization, or as Bloom puts it, "our humanity," which imagines a homogenous society and culture. And it is the creation of what our society should be: a society that does not *have* to address issues of race, class, sexuality, and gender.

Bringing Down the House, however, presents an increasingly conflicted view of Bardolatry and sets up a binary that takes Bloom's rhetoric to its logical end: equality and justice can only be achieved when Bardolatry, claims to universalism, and the Bard himself are kidnapped. An interest in contemporary issues of race and power, the film suggests, are at odds with a love of the Bard. When Charlene attempts to mend things between Peter and Mrs. Arness, Mrs. Arness threatens to call the police. Defensively reacting to the threat that would land her back in jail, Charlene and Howie (played by Eugene Levy) kidnap "William Shakespeare." Howie enters the room with "William Shakespeare," complete with stiff Elizabethan ruff, bound in a leather leash and gagged with a bone. Howie and Charlene believe that the most effective way to pressure Mrs. Arness is through her beloved canine companion (see Figure 2.1). But what also becomes clear through their actions is the fact that Howie and Charlene implicitly believe that the most effective way to change Mrs. Arness's opinions (including the racist ones) is to kidnap "Shakespeare." It seems no accident that the two characters most closely associated with black culture and the possibilities of interracial relationships are the ones to steal "Shakespeare," the symbol for what the film euphemistically deems as "conservative" English values. The two characters who code switch between standard English and a black urban vernacular steal the canine stand-in for the father of modern standard English.

As illogical as this scheme may seem, it actually seems to work on Mrs. Arness. With "Shakespeare" out of the picture she begins to loosen up; she becomes more accepting; and she begins to engage others in a more liberal way. She goes to an all-black hip-hop bar, befriends two black men, and all three get drunk and stoned together. Later Mrs. Arness can be heard code switching by talking a black urban vernacular with her newfound black friends. When they say that they will see her around, Mrs. Arness responds, "Fa-sheezy, homies" (*for sure, friends*). At this point, Mrs. Arness is decidedly less interested in her beloved dog. She declares that "William Shakespeare" is ugly and heavy, and she actually hands him back to Peter. In other words, "William Shakespeare" seems to have been part of what was impeding the opening of Mrs. Arness's mind. When she was tied to "Shakespeare," Mrs. Arness's only access to black culture was her distant memory of her black servants. Having the Bard kidnapped, Mrs. Arness accepts, enjoys, and even promotes what the film posits are the wonders of black culture (language play, generosity, and affability). Again, this rejection of "Shakespeare" seems to signal a rejection of Shakespeare's universalism as exclusion.

The audio commentary on the DVD by Adam Shankman and Jason Filardi reasserts this conflation of Bardolatry with "arch" conservatism. They admit that many of their jokes are based on the audience's awareness of Joan Plowright's personal and professional background. It would not be overstating it to argue that they thought the audience would easily conflate Plowright's Shakespearean theatre history with the "arch conservative" tone she adopts for Mrs. Arness; and it is definitely not going too far to argue that they wanted the audience to think about Plowright's biography. Describing the scene in which Plowright's character gets stoned, Adam Shankman comments, "Joan Plowright is, like, Franco Zefferelli's muse, and I am getting her stoned and making her say 'Pussies!'" It is interesting to note how easily Shankman collapses Plowright's identity with that of her character's. He does not describe the scene as depicting Mrs. Arness getting stoned; instead, he says that it is "Franco Zefferelli's muse" to whom he does this. Because the director verbalizes this conflation of identities so clearly, it seems obvious that he imagines the audience will participate in this conflation as well.

In addition, in Shankman's filmic world, the conflation of Joan Plowright's identity with that of her character's can never be separated from her biography as a famous Shakespearean actress and the wife of the most famous Shakespearean actor of the twentieth century, Sir Laurence Olivier. Again, discussing the scene in which Plowright's character gets stoned with two black men, Shankman states:

These three, this was the best, these three ended up becoming, like, buddies while we were shooting. Joan was hanging out. I was, like, there's Laurence Olivier's children's mother sitting with these two guys at the bar, like, hanging out with these guys. Like, when we were not shooting, she was hanging out with them. It was great.

Shakespeare, Shakespearean production, and Shakespearean cultural legacy loom large in Shankman's imagination. And once again it is assumed that Bard-hood does not have anything to do with black people: any woman whose life has been so marked by her proximity to the Bard (through her professional and personal lives) should not want to befriend two black men (even though they share the same profession!).

Instead, Plowright should be tied to a dog named "Shakespeare" and speak only Shakespeare's English. Thus, films like *Bringing Down the House* traffic in the contradictory functions Shakespeare plays in popular culture; Shakespeare is revered perhaps in part because he represents a racial exclusivity that is often unspoken. A large part of the humor of these films comes from the irreverence of culturally kidnapping a venerated subject (which is thus made into an object). The pleasures of cultural heterogeneity—like Mrs. Arness's enjoyment of black culture—can only be achieved when Bardolatry is fully rejected and exposed.

Through an engagement with the film's canine-ization of Shakespeare, one hears the questions that are often suppressed through claims to his universality. If race studies and racial activism have opened up new venues for Shakespearean research and performance, do Shakespearean research and performance open up new fields for race studies and racial activism? More fundamentally, do Shakespeare studies and Shakespearean performance work against the primary tenets of racial activism—promoting equity and exposing ideological/structural systems of power based on race—by implicitly supporting the perpetuation of a white, paternalistic literary canon? Do Shakespeare studies and Shakespearean performance inherently work at cross purposes from race studies and racial activism?

CONCLUSION: BEYOND THE UNIVERSAL?

Book titles often promote the way Shakespeare anticipates, supports, and even endorses other artistic, cultural, historical, and political endeavors. A search for book titles that begin *Shakespeare and . . .* yields such disparate finds as *Shakespeare and . . .* America, Brecht in Nigeria, Cognition, Decorum, Eastern Europe, Feminist Criticism, Gender, Hawaii, Intertextuality, Jungian Typology, Keats, Love, Medicine, National Culture, Our World, Public Execution, the Question of Theory, Revision, Science, Temperance, the Uses of Ideology, Violence, World Peace, and Youth Culture.[46] The popular belief in and espousal of Shakespeare's universality fuels these varied projects and enables them to continue to be produced without apparent contradiction: Shakespeare is universal and, thus, is essentially congruent and harmonious. There have only been two books that titularly place Shakespeare in opposition to something else—two nineteenth-century texts with the same title, *Shakespeare or Bacon?*—but these books do not really question the universal compatibility of Shakespeare.[47] Instead, they engage in the centuries' old debate about the authorship of the plays: these books ask "Was it Shakespeare?" over "Is this oppositional to Shakespeare?" And yet it is clear from an analysis of *Suture* and *Bringing Down the House* that there are conflicting notions of Shakespeare's universality.

I am not arguing that when someone declares that Shakespeare is universal that the listener is (or should be) immediately throne into paroxysms of doubt as to the meaning of the word. As my students do on the first day of class, most people will assume that an avowal of Shakespeare's universality is universally applicable, encompassing, timeless, and, well, good. The tensions arise, however, when race enters into Shakespeare's universe. In my classes, for example, my students feel comfortable making statements about Shakespeare's universality until they read plays like *Titus Andronicus* or *The Merchant of Venice*, or when they read (without skimming over lightly) pejorative lines about an "Ethiope" in *Much Ado about Nothing* or a "Jew" in *Henry IV*, to list only a few examples. When confronted with Shakespeare's presentations of racial difference, my students often abandon their espousals of universality for those of historical specificity: that these portraits are products of Shakespeare's age. Thus, my students give voice to the pendulum swing between declamations of Shakespeare's universality and declarations of his particularity. Interestingly, Ben Jonson seems to be one of the first to give voice to this swing in his elegy in the first folio of Shakespeare's plays. After all, in that poem Jonson proclaims that Shakespeare is both "for all time" and the "Soul of the Age"—that is, both the timeless and the timely.[48]

Of course, debates about the veracity of the universal and the particular are common and do not necessarily involve discussions about race, as the Jonson poem proves. Nonetheless, in twenty-first-century popular American culture the debate is more heated precisely because we have not been able to go blind to race, to become colorblind, or even to blend seamlessly. And this is precisely why McGehee and Siegel's *Suture* and Shankman's *Bringing Down the House* are important cultural texts with which to begin this analysis. If Shakespeare's universality is commonly understood to represent the timelessness of his plays, then these films expose the other, less openly discussed notions of universality. In *Suture* it is clear that another popular understanding of Shakespeare's universality is actually a narcissistic colorblindness, a colorblindness that is not only blind to the important cultural differences between races, but also blind to the cultural specificity and cannibalistic tendencies of white, Western cultural production, with Shakespeare's plays featured as one example. *Bringing Down the House*, on the other hand, reveals another popular understanding of the universal as an exclusive and excluding white culture, one that promotes unity solely through the elimination of other cultural productions. In this model Shakespeare, in the form of a dog (from canonization to canine-ization), must be kidnapped for the lure of racial, cultural, and class exclusion to be broken.

It is important to stress once again that these films stem from radically different filmic traditions—the art house versus the big studio, the theoretical versus the comic, the film-school inspired versus the music-video inspired[49]—because they stem from and represent different versions of popular American culture. And yet both films operate through an interrogation of the universal. While they reach radically different ends through radically different means, *Suture* and *Bringing Down the House* place the popular assumption of Shakespeare's universality under a tight and color-filtered microscope. The results are a clear rejection of the rhetoric of colorblindness and exclusion. The focus on race's role in twenty-first century American culture in both films renders the notion of Shakespeare's universality as not only suspect but also dangerous.

If we take from *Suture* and *Bringing Down the House* that an espousal of the universal is something to be avoided when pairing discussions of Shakespeare and race, then are we only left with discussions of the particular? Clearly, this is articulated in the epigraph for this chapter by Lee Simonson. He is able to caution against the "supposedly universal" only by acknowledging the "particular aspect" of a classic's creation.[50] Does this not simply lead us back to the new historicists' claims that everything is particular, that everything is historical, that everything is timely (but not necessarily timeless)? Yes and no. Many early-modern race scholars have turned to historicizing race precisely because the new historicists failed to do so. Think, for example, about the numerous excellent books that historicize race in the early modern period: Eldred Jones's *Othello's Countrymen*, Anthony Barthelemy's *Black Face, Maligned Race*, Ania Loomba's *Gender, Race, Renaissance Drama*, Kim Hall's *Things of Darkness*, and Joyce Green MacDonald's *Women and Race in Early Modern Texts* are only a few.[51] As excellent, informative, and necessary as these works are, they do not encourage one to engage in the cultural work Renaissance texts perform in the twenty-first century. While they combat simplistic espousals of Shakespeare's universality by investigating the particulars of Renaissance culture, they do not engage in contemporary notions of the universal. So there is a way in which a turn towards an investigation of Shakespeare and race in the twenty-first century is a version of new historicism, a version that takes on the current moment instead of a past one.

And yet, my readings of *Suture* and *Bringing Down the House* seem to indicate that it is not simply enough to become a new historicist of the present moment. Rather, to engage contemporary notions of Shakespeare, race, and universalism, one must be attuned to a wider variety of sources: one must be willing to engage in cultural studies in the broadest sense. Doing so, one realizes that one does not have to forgo either the historical or the particular because, like Jonson's elegy, they continue to operate forever in tandem and tension. The rhetoric of the universal will not be abandoned simply because the particular is always more particular, more specific, and yet a fuller understanding of the undercurrents of meaning within the term allows one to reexamine the ways Shakespeare and race operate in discord in the contemporary world. Some have attempted to exploit the friction through dramatic effect (*Suture*) and humorous effect (*Bringing Down the House*), and some have attempted to appropriate and redirect the tension through claims to racial essentialism, the focus of the next chapter.

FIGURE 3.1 If, as Paul Mooney says, "Jesus is black, and so was Cleopatra," then is Shakespeare black too? DVD menu still from *Know Your History: Jesus Was Black . . . So Was Cleopatra*.

Our lives were saturated with Paul Laurence Dunbar. I mean, if we didn't know ten Dunbar poems we were considered blithering idiots. . . . We did Shakespeare, but we thought Shakespeare was black because of the language. It never occurred to us that a white man could write that good. He certainly didn't sound white. All the great people we knew who did Shakespeare, whether it was [Paul] Robeson or anybody else at Howard [University], the drama students, it sounded like a black way of speaking.

—JOHN H. BRACEY, JR.[1]

3

Essentialism

MEDITATIONS INSPIRED BY FARRUKH DHONDY'S NOVEL

BLACK SWAN

IN HIS INFAMOUS manifesto against liberal multiculturalism, *The End of Racism*, the conservative critic Dinesh D'Souza includes chapters with the titles "Is Eurocentrism a Racist Concept? The Search for an African Shakespeare" and "Uncle Tom's Dilemma: Pathologies of Black Culture."[2] Although the chapters are numbers nine and twelve respectively, juxtaposing the titles in one sentence highlights the differences D'Souza imagines exist between Shakespearean, African, and African-American cultural productions. According to D'Souza, ancient Africans did not produce a Shakespeare because their civilizations were not as advanced as their European counterparts, and black Americans are currently incapable of producing a Shakespeare because our culture values pathology, which according to D'Souza is

characterized by extremely high rates of criminal activity, by the normalization of illegitimacy, by the predominance of single-parent families, by high levels of addiction to alcohol and drugs, by a parasitic reliance on government provision, by a hostility to academic achievement, and by a scarcity of independent enterprises.[3]

D'Souza does not spend a great deal of time analyzing what made Shakespeare a great writer (how about his "parasitic reliance" on rich patrons and the royal court?), or alternatively what factors make his works so culturally important in contemporary American society because "Shakespeare" is really just a cultural marker for him, a type of shorthand referent for greatness, high culture, and universal value. On the other hand, black, African, and African American become markers for "pathology," which are obviously set against Shakespeare-as-panacea. In other words, D'Souza constructs Shakespeare and blackness in oppositional terms, and the twain shall not meet (at least not in D'Souza's construction of the foreseeable future).

Although an extremely different impetus, aesthetic, and ideology fueled the production of the BBC Radio 4's 2006 show "Lenny and Will," one critic located a similar stereotype in the marketing materials: that black and Shakespeare are necessarily at odds. "Lenny and Will" documented the black, working-class comedian Lenny Henry's "quest to find out if Shakespeare is for everybody or just an elite."[4] Henry described himself as being "slightly allergic to Shakespeare" because "it always seemed to be for people who talked posh."[5] Henry even declared in an interview that "Shakespeare is not part of my life."[6] Thus, BBC Radio 4 sends Henry "in search of the magic of Shakespeare in performance," which the show posits will transform his opinion of "Will."[7] One critic objected, however, that

> The trailers promised that comedian Lenny Henry would discover here that the plays of William Shakespeare were not just unintelligible messages from the past about posh people but could, and I quote, "rock." Perhaps I am alone in finding this quite amazingly patronising, or in being equally offended at the implication that Henry, being black and of working-class origins, cannot understand Hamlet. The programme revealed that he can, he does. But surely to assume otherwise from the start, or be encouraged in such a delusion, is outrageously prejudiced?[8]

The fact that Radio 4 advertised "Lenny and Will" as Henry's surprising discovery of a "late-flowering passion for the plays" implicitly traffics in a rhetoric that is similar to D'Souza's—a rhetoric that implies that such a discovery for a black person of working-class origins is *inherently* a *surprise*.[9] The twain are not supposed to meet but sometimes they do, the radio show implied.

With the implication that Shakespeare and blackness are at odds as a backdrop (think back to the excluding notions of universalism explored in chapter 2), it is clear why several artists and scholars of color have claimed Shakespeare as one of their own racially. In 1983, for example, the Nobel Prize winning Nigerian writer, Wole Soyinka, claimed in a tongue-and-cheek manner that Shakespeare was "a gifted Arab" writer.[10] Shakespeare's portrait of Othello's "jealousy complicated by racial insecurity" could only have been written by "a man from beneath the skin—an

Arab at the very least," Soyinka bemused.[11] Soyinka's essay, originally published in the academic journal *Shakespeare Survey*, puts into dialogue Shakespeare's genius at conjuring the foreign (Soyinka specifically focuses on *Antony and Cleopatra*) with ancient Arab tales (he highlights the ancient Arabic legend of Majnun Layla, which resembles the plot of *Romeo and Juliet*). In Soyinka's essay there is no divide or distance between these literatures; instead, they are afforded the same intellectual and cultural weight.

Similarly, when editing the first edition of the *Norton Anthology of African American Literature*, Henry Louis Gates, Jr. used to joke that he wished he could prove that Shakespeare "had a black ancestor" so that he could be included in the anthology.[12] Gates's gag, of course, rested on capital grounds—both financial and cultural. He could sell more books if Shakespeare were included in the anthology not only because Shakespeare's books sell in multiple lucrative markets (grade school curricula; college curricula; and public, private, and personal libraries), but also because Shakespeare's cultural capital could make an anthology of African-American writers even more culturally viable and valuable. Gates literally wanted to put black American writers on the same page as Shakespeare; he wanted to force the twain to meet.

The most famous statement of racial essentialism, however, was made in 1985 when Maya Angelou claimed: "I know that William Shakespeare was a black woman."[13] In an address delivered at the National Assembly of Local Arts Agencies in Cedar Rapids, Iowa, Angelou discussed how her grandmother urged her *not* to recite one of Portia's speeches from *The Merchant of Venice* at their C. M. E. Church in Stamps, Arkansas. Instead, Angelou's grandmother wanted her to recite something by a black artist, something by "Mister Langston Hughes, Mister Countee Cullen, Mister James Weldon Johnson, or Mister Paul Laurence Dunbar."[14] Looking back years later, Angelou claimed that certain lines by Shakespeare still spoke to her in uniquely personal *and* racial ways:

> I found myself and still find myself, whenever I like, stepping back into Shakespeare. Whenever I like, I *pull* him to me. . . . Of course he wrote it for me: that is a condition of a black woman. Of course, he was a black woman. I understand that. Nobody else understands it, but I know that William Shakespeare was a black woman. That is the role of art in life.[15]

Angelou makes Shakespeare one of her literary ancestors in terms of both race and gender (Shakespeare was a *black woman*). In this fashion she can both step backwards in time to read about her past *and* pull Shakespeare to her to make him/her fit the current moment. An act of appropriation, Angelou's statement renders the assumed divide between Shakespeare and black cultural production at odds with "the role of art in life," which works to create connections, reveal legacies, and demonstrate heritages.

As many other scholars have noted, Angelou's statement of affiliation with Shakespeare was employed by the conservative leader of the National Endowment for the Humanities at the time, Lynne Cheney, as proof that Shakespeare is universal, and that there are "truths that, transcending accidents of class, race, and gender, speak to us all."[16] While Cheney is all too willing to promote Angelou's love of Shakespeare as the "eloquent voice" that proves that "the humanities are about more than politics, about more than social power," she does not take seriously Angelou's claim that Shakespeare was black.[17] As Marjorie Garber argues, "What makes Angelou's appropriation of Shakespeare as a black woman acceptable—and a fitting climax to Cheney's indictment of ideologues in the academy—is . . . the fact that this is only a figure, an allegory, a 'transcendent' 'truth.'"[18] If Cheney did take Angelou's claim seriously, however, she would have to revise her final recommendation that "Colleges and universities should work toward intellectually coherent curricula . . . [in which students] study texts of Western civilization. . . ."[19] Implied in Cheney's rhetoric, which resembles those employed by D'Souza and the promotional materials for the BBC Radio 4 show "Lenny and Will," is the notion that black literature and culture are neither "Western" nor universal—that an "intellectually coherent curricula" is also a racially coherent white one.

STRATEGIC ESSENTIALISM

It seems worthwhile at this point to return to the idea that an appropriation of Shakespeare as a person of color is an act of strategic essentialism. As a glance at several online white supremacist blogs and Web sites makes clear, the claim that Shakespeare was black rankles white supremacists as much as the fact that the United States currently has a black president.[20] Likewise, this claim seems to bother white conservatives who position themselves against "self-hating white liberals." "Laban," a self-described "white" blogger from Dorset, for example, derided the "perfect cross-section of received liberal opinion" on Simon Mayo's BBC 5's radio show for "discussing Shakespeare and his relevance to young people. In passing they touched on theories that Shakespeare was black or an aristocrat."[21] "Laban" cannot contain his disdain for this conversation, and his blog inspires numerous comments by others who are equally outraged. There must be something strategic about the claim that Shakespeare was black if it instigates so much anxiety by certain culturally conservative whites (see Figure 3.1). Despite the fact that the debates about the meaning, value, and utility of strategic essentialism are widely viewed as passé in the academy—as something that came and went with the culture wars of the 1980s and 1990s—Shakespeare's presence in this formulation keeps the debate current. When notions of strategic essentialism have predominantly been overthrown and even re-written (see, for example, Paul Gilroy's notion of "strategic universalism"[22]), there continue to be statements that "Shakespeare was black," "Shakespeare was a Jew," "Shakespeare was a woman," and so forth. Essentialist notions and claims still thrive and multiply when it comes to the Bard.

Essentialism has many different meanings in different fields (education, philosophy, philosophy of art, biology, etc.). Although in common parlance it is frequently used as a synonym for the universal—as something that transcends cultural/historical specificity—that is not the definition I am employing. Rather I am employing the definition for strategic essentialism that is commonly used in literary criticism. In its most basic and reductive sense, strategic essentialism is the practice of promoting racial differences as inherent, fundamentally different, and therefore fixed in order to create affiliation, cohesion, and unity within a racialized group. Of course, Gayatri Chakravorty Spivak famously defined, refined, and redefined the idea of strategic essentialism. Discussing her collaboration with the Subaltern Studies collective of historians who were attempting to "re-write the history of colonial India from below, from the point of view of peasant insurgency,"[23] Spivak critiqued the group's focus on "making a theory of consciousness or culture rather than specifically a theory of change."[24] She then posited a method of "transactual reading" that deconstructs traditional methods of historiography and presents "an active transaction between past and future."[25] By imagining an essential relationship—based on race and ethnicity—between the historians in the Subaltern Studies collective and their subjects, Spivak argued that it must be a *strategic* alignment: "the discourse of the unified consciousness of the subaltern *must* inhabit the strategy of these historians" through the constructed "complicity between subject and object of investigation."[26]

Does the notion of strategic essentialism, then, apply to the claim that Shakespeare was a person of color? While it does seem to promote a type of transactual reading in which there is an active transaction between past and future, neither Shakespeare nor the artist/scholar of color aligns neatly, and in an uncomplicated fashion, with the "the massive historiographic metalepsis" of the subaltern peasant.[27] In fact, Spivak refined her definition of strategic essentialism to emphasize the importance of the contextual element of the *strategy*. Spivak warned:

A strategy suits a situation; a strategy is not a theory. . . . The strategic use of essentialism can turn into an alibi for proselytizing academic essentialisms.

The emphasis then inevitably falls on being able to speak from one's own ground, rather than matching the trick to the situation, that the word strategy implies.[28]

The strategic part of strategic essentialism, Spivak intones, is precisely in "matching the trick to the situation," or in being "situation-specific."[29] Thus, Spivak is highly critical of "gesture politics," the phrase she uses to describe moments of "affirming one's own identity very strongly as black, Mexican," or any other marginalized race or ethnicity within an academic institution and by "a very militant opposition to the Western canon."[30] This stance, she states, "is precisely not a strategic use" because it will not change the system from within.[31]

Of course, Spivak was writing during the height of the culture wars when there were wide-sweeping debates about what texts and methods should be included in college curricula primarily in the humanities. Close to twenty years later, the debates have died down and Spivak's calls for strategic essentialism are largely disregarded as not only passé but also as unstrategic.[32] Yet Spivak ended her redefinition of strategic essentialism on a surprising, and critically neglected, note about the important role humor can play in gesture politics.

> Within gesture politics, there is a wonderful critical moment that one can use without learning all of this jargon that we are talking, which is humor, humor. That political use of humor, which we know in the general African American struggle in the United States, I have looked at with incredible admiration.[33]

In thinking about statements like "Shakespeare was black" and "I know Shakespeare was a black woman," I hear precisely the humor about which Spivak writes—a humor that Glenda Carpio cites as a strategy black Americans have used to address the horrors of American slavery.[34] Of course, Spivak argued that the *strategy* behind strategic essentialism carries the most theoretical *and* practical weight, and here she links humor with an ability to "change the system from within." If Spivak's original definition of strategic essentialism—the one about transactual readings that seek to correct historiographic metalepses—does not map neatly over the relationship between the artist/scholar of color and Shakespeare, does that preclude statements that actively revise Shakespeare's race and/or gender from being strategic acts of humor *and* essentialism?

Let us turn for a moment to the epigraph for this chapter by John H. Bracey, Jr. and his declaration that as a child he thought "Shakespeare was black." A professor at the University of Massachusetts, and the son of a professor at Howard University, Bracey was neither uneducated nor misinformed as a child. Instead, through humor he disrupts the artificial divide between the assumed high culture (often racialized as white) of Shakespeare and the assumed folk culture (often racialized as black) of Paul Laurence Dunbar. Implied in Bracey's comment is the strength and certainty of his racial pride. He associates great cultural production with the black community in which he was raised, and, thus, the greatness of Shakespeare's text is necessarily filtered through this lens. Bracey's logic can be rephrased as a clear syllogism: if great cultural productions are produced by black artists, and if Shakespeare's plays are great cultural productions, then Shakespeare must be black. This is humorous, of course, because it turns traditional assumptions about the race of great artists upside down. A similar strategy is employed in Soyinka's claim that Shakespeare is Arab and in Angelou's claim that he is a black woman. The humor in these statements comes from the fact that these artists/scholars know that white Americans *do not* associate great cultural production with people of color.

Of course, the Dinesh D'Souzas and Lynne Cheneys, who are often the loudest in proclaiming the universal and timeless appeal of Shakespeare's works, and who are often the harshest in denying the value of situating his works historically and culturally, welcome these types of statements. Cheney focused on Angelou's claim that "Shakespeare was a black woman" precisely because it sounds as if it affirms Shakespeare's universality. But the D'Souzas and Cheneys can only appropriate these statements by ignoring the larger implication: that Shakespeare's blackness, Arab-ness, or otherness would destabilize a racialized cultural hierarchy. This realignment of the margin and center, then, is precisely what Spivak imagined as the potential outcome for strategic essentialism, and it is also the ground Farrukh Dhondy explores in his little-known 1992 novel *Black Swan*.

FARRUKH DHONDY'S *BLACK SWAN*

An ambitious and complicated young adult novel, *Black Swan* tells the tale of young Rose Hassan, a biracial British girl, who must become the personal aid to the mysterious Mr. B when her mother falls suddenly ill. It is slowly revealed that Mr. B, who is also referred to as Mr. Bernier, Mr. Claude, and Mr. Johnson, although we are certain by the end of the novel that none of these names is actually his own, is a West Indian dissident who faked his own death to abscond with millions of dollars in foreign aid money from his tiny Caribbean homeland. Despite the fact that Rose is hired to cook and clean for Mr. B, when he discovers that she is bright and well-read—she is a scholarship recipient at a prestigious secondary school and plans to attend university for an acting degree—he asks her to transcribe the

diaries of Simon Forman, a Renaissance "scientist and a magician and necroman-
cer and all sorts of other things," from a manuscript that was copied in the nineteenth century from the original (the original was destroyed in a fire).[35] The diary,
according to Mr. B, is extremely valuable and controversial because "the stuff in it
is quite incredible."[36] He makes it clear that he is in hiding because the diaries are
so valuable that he is constantly followed and pursued for them.

Forman's diaries, which form a narrative within the larger narrative of *Black
Swan*, relate Forman's relationships with Christopher Marlowe, William Shakespeare, and an escaped African slave from Hispaniola (who is named Lazarus by
the Spanish priest who helps to free him and Henry Walsh by the English captain
who educates him). Shakespeare is characterized as a "drunkard from Warwick-
shire," who is therefore incapable of penning great verse but who is all too willing
to accept "any credit that may come to him" from pretending to do so.[37] Lazarus/
Henry and Marlowe, then, write several of the plays together and separately, and
these plays become expressions of their feelings for each other, which evolve from
love and passion to jealousy and disdain.[38] Rose assumes the secrecy of the diaries—the reason she must transcribe them instead of merely photocopying
them—arises from the fact that they reveal that "Shakespeare" is merely a front
for an interracial and homosexual union between Lazarus/Henry and Marlowe:
that the "spear [is actually] held in this black hand."[39]

The novel becomes more complicated as Mr. B's relationship with Shakespeare
and the politics of his native Caribbean island are implicated in the narratives told
in Forman's diaries. It seems by the end of the novel that the diaries were really
Mr. B's "stories," with all of the multivalent meanings for this word in play. For
example, Lazarus/Henry and Marlowe both fake their own deaths in the diaries,
as does Mr. B. Likewise, in the end Forman notes that the sonnets were actually
written by Marlowe and dedicated to Lazarus/Henry, whose adopted last name is
Walsh (hence "Mr. W. H."). Forman writes, "My particular favorites are XX, CXXVII
and CXLVII as these hold the secret I have laid bare."[40] These numbers, however,
are actually the numbers for the Swiss bank account in which Mr. B has hidden the
stolen millions. And when Mr. B relates to Rose how he escaped death at the hands
of the militant revolutionaries on his island, he explains that it was because he
"was known in the whole country for the finest style of teaching Shakespeare ever.
Better than all the Englishmen they had had right down the years in the school."[41]
His countrymen even referred to him as "old Shakey—from Shakespeare, you
know."[42] In other words, Mr. B constructs an identity that is in competition with,
and even betters, not only "Englishmen," but also Shakespeare. Mr. B is as willing
to stand in for Shakespeare as he is willing to appropriate works of high art as his
own. He tells Rose they should run away to America together because

A black man and a lady of your color, no matter what age they were, could lose themselves. I could be the poet and you could be my granddaughter and I would shamble from hotel to hotel on your arm and recite the most exciting poetry. John Donne, Yeats, Eliot, and I could pretend some of it was my own. These Americans wouldn't know the difference. . . . I shall call myself Longfellow from today on.[43]

From "old Shakey" to "Longfellow," the unnamed Mr. B understands the value of literary cultural capital, and he repeatedly attempts to seize it for himself, to put the spear in his own black hand.

But ultimately what Mr. B understands is the power of stories. At the beginning of the novel he mocks Rose for wanting to be an actress because actors "want to be someone else for the significant part of their lives. They want to be directed. The story is written by someone else. The emotions are supplied. The rest of us, we write our own stories, we fight for our own emotions."[44] Mr. B's life, then, is dedicated to making sure that he has the power to script his own story. At the end of the novel when Rose asks "What does the story matter," he declares, "stories always matter. Because it's my story. I don't mean that I invented it, I mean, it's my own story."[45] Mr. B, like all authors, wants the ability to construct the narrative, emotional, and moral arc of his own story—even if it is cloaked under the name of Forman, Shakespeare, Lazarus, or Longfellow—so that he can combat the ways others attempt to script and limit the meanings of his life. In the voice of Lazarus/Henry, Mr. B expresses the horror that we may be limited by the expectations of others: "Maybe we only see what we expect to see."[46] *Black Swan* makes it clear that this is especially true when race is part of the story being told.

Despite the fact that Dhondy is an acclaimed author whose other books have garnered awards (including a nomination for the Whitbread Literary Award), *Black Swan* landed rather quietly with only a handful of reviews in venues geared primarily towards secondary teachers. These short reviews (mostly around 250 words) devote most of their limited word count to summaries of the complicated plot, and very few mention the important role race plays in the narrative. For example, one positive review notes that "Dhondy's pulse-quickening novel makes crystal-clear the revolutionary power of the written and spoken word," but it never mentions that Rose, Mr. B, and Lazarus are black characters who all comment extensively on the significance of their races on their stories.[47] One negative review, which critiques the novel for being "a wobbly mystery with a very muddy solution," even whited-out the Lazarus/Henry narrative by claiming that: "Teenaged Rose learns, through her employer, of a secret that will supposedly 'shock the world of letters': Christopher Marlowe was the actual author of Shakespeare's works."[48] In this review, gone are the parallel narrative structures that link Rose, Mr. B, Lazarus, and Shakespeare, and gone is the notion that "Shakespeare was black." In other words, the reviews seem to re-center the great literary production in whiteness, while the novel seeks to de-center an unexamined assumption of that connection. Only one review highlights the fact that Dhondy's novel makes the "bard's plays as the creation of a cruelly tormented black man," and that this might "stretch young minds" in positive, informative, and educational ways.[49]

Likewise, there has been a deafening silence within early modern race/appropriation studies about *Black Swan*. As *Black Swan* was released in the United Kingdom in 1992 and the United States in 1993, during the height of the culture wars, it is surprising that no one on either side of the wars sought to capitalize on the claims put forward in the novel. While this is probably a factor of the book being marketed as a young adult novel—a genre that rarely receives rigorous academic attention—Dhondy was nevertheless positioned as the Indian-born writer who might help to broaden the racial scope of young adult literature: he was pitched as the man who would take the spear in his black hands. In 1980, for example, David Rees wrote:

> Perhaps what has been lacking until now, at least in England, has been a major contribution to children's literature from coloured writers themselves; there are doubtless some very good sociopolitical explanations for this. Books written by white people, however sensitive their portrayal of coloured characters may be, do not portray any real idea of what it is like to be non-white in a crowded modern American or British urban environment.[50]

This, of course, brings us right back to the practice of strategic essentialism and its call for "coloured" authors for "coloured" readers; "coloured" subjects for "coloured" scholars. *Black Swan* clearly de-centers the canon with neither the center nor the margin in a firm, set, or even predictable position. The novel asks its reader to interrogate the narratives that create neatly centered racialized (both white *and* black) histories.

Moreover, the novel leaves ambiguous whether Shakespeare's plays were written by Lazarus/Henry and Marlowe, or even whether this change in authorship alters the meanings/values of the plays. For example, it is unclear exactly why the diaries are hidden by Mr. B and sought by those who follow him. Is the value only that they contain the secret Swiss account number that contains the stolen millions, in which case the race of "Shakespeare" would be inconsequential? Or, are they valuable because they reveal that some of Shakespeare's plays were written by a black man? Herbert, an old Caribbean acquaintance of Mr. B's who follows him in the hopes of attaining the diaries, reveals that he is a student at "the Poly," studying "English literature, as it happens. Special subject? Not Caribbean literature, Elizabethan playwrights."[51] Does this fact reveal that a reevaluation of authorship renders the texts more relevant to black readers, like Herbert? Or is this merely proof that Herbert believes the clues to the Swiss bank account are hidden in the diaries so he must have a clear mastery of Elizabethan texts? As Forman's diaries delineate which Shakespearean texts are written by Lazarus/Henry (*Titus Andronicus*, the three parts of *Henry VI*, *Comedy of Errors*, *Two Gentlemen of Verona*, and *Othello*), which are written by Marlowe (*Richard II*, *Romeo and Juliet*, *Troilus and Cressida*, *Measure for Measure*, *Macbeth*, and *Cymbeline*), and which are written together (*Julius Caesar*, *The Rape of Lucrece*, and the sonnets), are we to reevaluate these texts based on the race of the author(s)?

At some point, Rose speculates that "the plays that Marlowe wrote may not be thought as good as those written by Lazarus."[52] But the novel renders this type of speculation as, well, speculative because authorship as a category is completely undermined. The stories are important, and the authors are important, but the relationship between them is unresolved. In the end, when Mr. B leaves Rose to be the "defender" of Forman's diaries, she sends them off to his old publisher. The publisher replies to Rose, "you have done a very good re-creation of his style. It is, in our opinion, an original story and you should consider publishing it under your own name."[53] *Black Swan* forces the reader to ponder what an author is and what an author's race represents; it asks its reader to question what an authority is.

SHAKESPEARE'S ESSENTIALISM

Black Swan also encourages the reader to return to Shakespeare's texts to ponder further the questions posed about authorship, authority, and race. While many others have made this kind of move from allusion to source to debate whether Shakespeare's plays are tolerant or prejudiced, racialist or racist, universal or particular, at this moment I am more interested in examining the way Dhondy fashions Shakespeare's plays as figuring essentialist thought. *Black Swan* asks the reader to interrogate if/how the identity and race of Shakespeare impact one's understanding of the plays, but it also asks if this impact is different for different plays.

For example, the novel promotes *Othello* over *Titus Andronicus* in an unambiguous way. About *Othello*, Forman writes in his diaries, it "is the greatest test of the sin of jealousy ever offered in poem or play or indeed in sermons or in the holy book itself."[54] Written by Lazarus/Henry to Marlowe as an expression of his jealousy and grief over Marlowe's rejection of him, *Othello* is presented as an expression of Lazarus/Henry's personal story. It should come as no surprise, then, that not only does Lazarus/Henry play the part at the Globe, but also he kills himself onstage while speaking the famous lines: "When you do these unlucky deeds relate / Speak of me as I am" (*Othello* 5.2.350–351). In Dhondy's novel the joke that Soyinka tells—that only "a man from beneath the skin" could tell Othello's story—becomes reality: to "speak" of Othello as he is, is to speak of Lazarus/Henry. The novel implies that Lazarus/Henry's feelings of abjection are more fully fleshed out through his authorship and performance of *Othello*. We, the readers of Forman's diaries/Dhondy's novel, should be able to speak of Lazarus/Henry *and* Othello as they are, and "Nothing extenuate," after absorbing the notion that *Othello* is the unique expression of a black man living in a racist white world.

Dhondy constructs Lazarus/Henry's authorship of *Titus Andronicus*, however, in a completely different way. Shortly after Lazarus/Henry is initially employed by Lord Strange's Men as a "shake-scene"—that is, a property hand, but also a clever reference to Robert Greene's name for Shakespeare, the "upstart Crow" he mentions in his own narrative about the early theatre[55]—*Titus Andronicus* is performed with Lazarus/Henry disguised in the role of the clown. Dhondy does not allow Forman to say anything positive about the play; instead, it is discussed as provoking riots and appealing to the lowest orders of Londoners. The play is described as Lazarus/Henry's first stint at playwriting, his first unacknowledged authorial endeavor. One is left to assume that Forman's assessment of the play as amateurish, "bloody and full of hanging and men eating men," is a result of Lazarus/Henry's lack of prior writing experience.[56]

Of course, this type of critical assessment of *Titus Andronicus* was standard—T. S. Eliot famously called it "one of the stupidest and most uninspired plays ever written"[57]—until Jonathan Bate's influential, and now seminal, reassessment of the play in 1995.[58] Before this late twentieth-century recovery, *Titus Andronicus* was long considered both un-Shakespearean (perhaps not written by the Bard at all) and amateur Shakespeare (perhaps written when he had neither a good eye nor a good ear for dramatic poetry, structure, and/or decorum). Dhondy clearly taps into both of these critical traditions by having the inexperienced and non-Shakespearean Lazarus/Henry authoring forth *Titus Andronicus*. This play, the novel implies, does not reveal anything about Lazarus/Henry except his lack of polish and training. While *Othello* is supposed to reveal a deep psychological trauma, *Titus Andronicus* is only supposed to reveal authorial naiveté and inexperience.

And yet, *Titus Andronicus* has more to say on the subject of racial essentialism than does *Othello*. It is after all, Aaron the Moor who triumphs over the white sons of the Queen of the Goths with the following lines:

Coal-black is better than another hue
In that it scorns to bear another hue;
For all the water in the ocean
Can never turn the swan's black legs to white,
Although she lave them hourly in the flood.
(*Titus Andronicus* 4.2.98–102)

As many have noted, the reference to the swan's inability to wash her black legs white comes from an ancient proverb that probably originated in Aesop. The proverb relates the essence of laboring in vain, of working for nothing, and of futility itself. For example, the Latin form of the proverb reads, "abluis Aethiopem: quid frustra" (you wash an Ethiopian: why labor in vain), and the English form commonly appears as "to wash an Ethiop white."[59] Of course, Aaron the Moor employs this familiar proverb as a way to celebrate the proof of paternity his indelible *and* essential color affords him. He is able to recognize his illegitimate and biracial child because the "thick-lipped" (4.2.174) child's color offers the certitude of *kinship*, in all its multivalent meanings: biological, temperamental, emotional, and perhaps even moral.[60] As Alden and Virginia Vaughan argue, the characters in *Titus Andronicus* "repeatedly fuse Aaron's physical blackness with his moral corruption," and Aaron appropriates this conflation, celebrating the kinship that this baby's color creates.[61] For Aaron, then, blackness and an essentialized sense of racial identity go hand in hand. A black man would author forth an essentially different baby and, we must assume, a different type of *play*.

Shakespeare employs the proverb for futility through Sisyphean washing in several other plays as well. In some, the proverb is employed to express a stain that cannot be removed, like a mark that reveals one's moral depravity. For instance in *Much Ado about Nothing*, Leonato, believing Claudio's claims that Hero has been unfaithful, laments the fact that the essence of his beloved daughter is "smirched" and permanently "mired" (4.1.132). Precisely because he is certain of her paternity—he readily claims her as his own—Leonato mourns her descent into a "pit of ink" which symbolizes her foreignness to him.

But mine, and mine I loved, and mine I praised,
And mine that I was proud on, mine so much
That I myself was to myself not mine,
Valuing of her—why she, O she is fallen

Into a pit of ink, that the wide sea
Hath drops too few to wash her clean again
(*Much Ado about Nothing* 4.1.135–140)

Although Leonato's rhetoric makes it seem as if Hero was unstained before she fell into the "pit of ink," the stain is now permanent, something that cannot be washed away. Even though he readily, and repeatedly, calls Hero "mine," the ink into which she falls makes her both stained and wholly other.

Similarly, the murderous characters in *Hamlet* and *Macbeth* wonder if there is water enough to wash the blood from their guilty hands. King Claudius, kneeling in prayer, asks:

What if this cursed hand
Were thicker than itself with brother's blood,
Is there not rain enough in the sweet heavens
To wash it white as snow?
(*Hamlet* 3.3.43–46)

King Claudius's rhetoric resembles Leonato's not only in its use of the proverb, but also in its coloration of the stain as the opposite of white. Whiteness is constructed as the pure and unstained, and the stain is figured as that which not only defiles the pure but also reveals the impurity of the marked one. Here the desire to "wash it white as snow" is the figure of impossibility. Finally, after killing Duncan in *Macbeth*, Macbeth asks his partner in crime, Lady Macbeth, "Will all great Neptune's ocean wash this blood / Clean from my hand?" (2.2.58–59). Lady Macbeth, of course, eventually answers this question in the negative as she goes mad attempting to wash her hands white: "Out, damned spot; out, I say" (5.2.50). Again, the stain that cannot be washed away symbolizes a moral depravity that is revealed *and* essential. In these examples, the proverb of washing reveals the futility of attempting to undo past crimes. The stain on the individual cannot be washed away, and the stained individual cannot be cleansed regardless of the abundant water supply.

The proverb, however, is also used as a way to celebrate essential characteristics. In this sense, the proverb is not about the futility of attempting to wash away a stain; but rather about the futility of attempting to alter, denigrate, or forcefully change a *royal essence*. For example, in *Henry V*, the Welsh captain Fluellen celebrates Henry's strength as something that stems from his Welsh blood. This "plood," as Fluellen calls it in his Welsh pronunciation, is something that can never be altered or washed away:

All the water in Wye cannot wash your majesty's Welsh plood out of your pody, I can tell you that. God pless it and preserve it, as long as it pleases his grace, and his majesty too.
(*Henry V* 4.7.97–100)

Unlike the stains that Leonato, Claudius, and the Macbeths fear cannot be altered, Fluellen presents a positive essentialist portrait of power. His King Henry is Welsh within even if the outward shows do not reveal this essence. This essential nature, however, is unchangeable in Fluellen's estimation, and, thus, provides the source of their affiliation and brotherhood (and Fluellen's loyalty as well).

Similarly, in *Richard II* after King Richard learns that his cousin Bolingbroke has raised a rebellious faction against him, Richard proclaims his identity as essential in the following manner:

Not all the water in the rough rude sea
Can wash the balm from an anointed king.
The breath of worldly men cannot depose
The deputy elected by the Lord.
(*Richard II* 3.2.50–53)

Because Richard views his position *and* identity as forged by God, he uses the proverb for futility ("Not all the water . . . / Can wash") to communicate the indelible nature of his identity as the "anointed king." Likewise, Richard interprets Bolingbroke's treasonous activities as deeds that go against the will of God; thereby Richard rhetorically opposes his own heavenly anointing with that of the earthly "breath" of all other men. Continuing this logic in the deposition scene, Richard likens Bolingbroke's ministers to Pilate, Jesus's judge, who famously washed his hands of responsibility when Jesus was sentenced to death. Richard warns the traitors:

Though some of you, with Pilate, wash your hands,
Showing an outward pity, yet you Pilates
Have here delivered me to my sour cross,
And water cannot wash away your sin.
(*Richard II* 4.1.229–232)

Just as Richard constructs his own identity as essential, so too he figures the guilt of his detractors as fixed. Therefore, no amount of washing will cleanse away their sins: they are not superficial, but rather essential. For Richard, as for Aaron the Moor in *Titus Andronicus* and Fluellen in *Henry V*, the ancient proverb provides the vehicle to express the power *and* comfort of an essentialized notion of identity. One might even call this a type of *strategic essentialism* because Richard claims that he is essentially different from those who attempt to oppose him, and no amount of scrubbing or whitewashing can alter the essence within.

In Dhondy's novel, however, these types of throughlines between texts are not explored. Lazarus/Henry is figured in the novel as the author of both *Titus Andronicus* and *3 Henry VI*, but Forman/Dhondy dismisses both as early experiments in writing under the "Shakespeare" name. *Richard II* fairs slightly better in the novel with an interesting rumination on the nature of identity. For example, Forman grapples with questions of identity through his discussion of the controversy surrounding the play (e.g., Shakespeare is rounded up to be interrogated by the Knight Marshall's men), and Dhondy allows the reader to grapple with these questions through his discussion of Marlowe's psychology. Marlowe, who is figured in the novel as a solipsistic, renegade spy who fakes his own death to save his own life, is exactly the type of person who would write such a play, the novel implies. He alone would be audacious enough to question the proper succession of kings; he alone would tackle the essentialist notion of the King's identity; he alone would be interested in essentialism.

Forman's engagement with *Richard II*, of course, is radically different from his engagement with *Titus Andronicus*. One is "bold," while the other is merely "bloody." Despite the fact that *Black Swan* is a novel invested in pressing notions of authorship, authority, and strategic essentialism, *Othello* becomes the only vehicle through which Dhondy explores them for Lazarus/Henry. Although Dhondy explores the relationship between authorial race and strategic essentialism, *Othello* is presented as the only play through which Lazarus/Henry explores his own essential nature. While there are many Shakespearean plays that explore the nature and value of essentialism as demonstrated above, in popular culture only *Othello* is thought to do so in terms of race. So Dhondy figures Lazarus/Henry as *essentially* Othello. Of course, Dhondy is not alone in promoting this most reductive essentialist connection. A quick glance at BlackPlanet, the largest online social networking Web site for black Americans, reveals over 200 members who have chosen "Othello" as their username![62] One is left to wonder if this means that the appropriators of the "Othello" moniker are black men who love white women, black men who desire to commit murder, black men who are educated, black actors, and/or black Americans who love Shakespeare? Whatever the answer, the use of "Othello" as their self-selected username is supposed to "speak of [them] as [they are]," but this is much more ambiguous and *less essential* than they might assume.

I could not help but wish that Dhondy had Lazarus/Henry write *Titus Androni-cus*, *Richard II*, and *Henry V* because they all reveal how tragic figures attempt to proclaim essentialized identities for themselves in moments of crisis; they all reveal that there is something compelling about a claim to a fixed and unalterable identity; and they all reveal that it is difficult to combat such claims. As a text which necessarily de-centers the literary canon by questioning the very nature of authorship and authority, *Black Swan* seems to be influenced by the scholarship of its era, the new historicism of the 1990s. While many scholars have noted the sim-ilarities between the lines in *Titus Andronicus* and *Richard II*, few have pursued the similarity of the concept that undergirds them. Since the rise of new historicism in the 1980s, critical attention has favored the way Shakespeare's texts reveal the many and various ways identities are socially constructed. Whether they are con-structed by the legal, religious, or military limitations/freedoms of the state; the social, cultural, and educational limitations/freedoms of the community; or the ambitiousness of the individual, identities in Shakespeare's plays are assumed to reveal a type of early modern *self-fashioning*, to borrow Stephen Greenblatt's famous phrase. That is, identities are not assumed to be fixed or essential, but rather mobile and fungible.

Greenblatt argues that Shakespeare was a "master improviser," one who "pos-sessed a limitless talent for entering into the consciousness of another, perceiving its deepest structures as a manipulable fiction, reinscribing it into his own narra-tive form."[63] In this formulation, improvisation is linked with an ability to under-stand, digest, and transform various identities to dramatic forms. Thus, essential differences are an impossibility because improvisation necessarily reveals the con-structed *and* performative nature of all identities. More recently Emily Bartels has focused specifically on the "the Moor" as the emblematic figure for improvisation: "the Moor presses on the boundaries of culture, exposing 'all the world' as a work in progress, improvised, for better or for worse, from the unpredictable variables of exchange."[64] Seeking to rectify the lack of attention to issues of race in early new historicist work, Bartels pinpoints improvisation as "essential" to the Moor "not because, as a signifier, 'Moor' is unstable and unreadable but because, as a sub-ject, 'the Moor' does not have a single or pure, culturally or racially bounded identity."[65] In this critical tradition, then, the plays provide evidence of a changing Renaissance world in which the nature of identity is also in flux and therefore so-cially constructed.

I *do not* disagree with this critical tradition. To highlight the ways identities are forged on various social grounds is both historically accurate to the Renaissance moment we examine and politically relevant to the twenty-first century moment in which we live. This type of argument, after all, riles conservative critics—like

D'Souza and Cheney—precisely because it provides ammunition for calls for increased government funding for low-income families, schools, the arts, and so forth. In other words, if one believes that identities are socially forged, then the onus to support the social programs that benefit this identity formation falls squarely on the state.

And yet, I wonder if this type of argument places too much weight on a type of historicized reading of identity that renders essentialist notions as old fashioned and out dated (like "Old John of Gaunt" in *Richard II*). In Shakespeare's plays, after all, both Aaron and Richard meet tragic ends, but their claims about the essential nature of their identities—the one's that cannot be washed away with any amount of water—are never fully negated. Both characters are defeated, but the plays reveal extreme ambivalence about how to interpret their claims. In *Titus Andronicus*, for example, the fate of the biracial child, with whom Aaron experiences a kinship based on essentialized notions of race, is unscripted both literally and figuratively at the end of the play. Is the biracial baby dead by the conclusion of the play despite the fact that Lucius promises to protect him? Does he survive because he adopts a more Roman notion of identity, one that promotes racial improvisation? Does he live, perpetuating the idea that his race is essential and essentially different from that of the Romans? Shakespeare leaves this fundamental issue unresolved, and it exemplifies in miniature the irresolution of the play's ending.

Likewise in *Richard II*, King Henry IV, who is often celebrated along with his son Henry V as the embodiment of the power of improvisation and performance, ends the play with questions about the nature of Richard's power. He promises to make a "voyage to the Holy Land / To wash this blood off from my guilty hand" (*Richard II* 5.6.49–50). Despite the fact that Henry IV is ever attentive to the importance of performance, at the end of the play he worries about the blood that reveals the guilt of his actions *and* the blood inside of him that does not have God's *gild*ing (anointing). At the end of the play, one is invited to wonder if there is water enough in the Holy Land to wash the guilt off his hands *and* to put the anointing on them. That is the legacy Richard leaves behind, a legacy that creates doubt within the heart and mind of King Henry IV, a legacy that renders improvisation unscripted and impoverished.

LEGACY OF STRATEGY / STRATEGY OF LEGACY

The notion of legacy lurks behind many of the arguments in this chapter, and it is an important element to analyze when approaching the topic of strategic Shakespeares. If nothing else, *Black Swan* is a novel about father figures, one's heritage, and the relationship between, and legacy of, both. Rose Hassan, after all, has no idea whether her Afro-British father, Merry Hassan, is dead or alive (possibly "[i]n Africa," Rose muses at one point).[66] At the beginning of the novel, Dhondy explains:

> There was nothing left of Merry Hassan in their London flat. Maybe a photo-graph or two in mom's old album, his name which they both carried and the ghost of his blackness. The fact of color, differentness, which Rose inherited in her complexion. It was a constant reminder of her missing dad. He had of course left her a legacy, if indeed he was dead, of his color.[67]

As a biracial child, Rose thinks of her dark skin color as her father's "legacy." What is missing, the novel implies, is the knowledge and understanding of what she is supposed to do with this legacy. Thus, her relationship with Mr. B is one of transference: she needs a father who will explain the meaning of her race's legacy, and he needs a child for whom he can control that meaning. Yet, what does it mean to describe one's "color" and one's "complexion" as a "legacy"? On the one hand, a legacy is a gift of property or money left in a will—a bequest. On the other hand, a legacy is something that is transmitted from the past by an ancestor or a predecessor. Is Rose's color supposed to be a gift? If so, what exactly are the benefits of this gift? Or, is her color merely something transmitted from her ancestors—something that comes from an ancient African past? If so, is this legacy merely an accident of biology and genetics? With either definition the reader must ask what role Shakespeare plays in this legacy of color. Is the legacy-as-gift Rose's knowledge that a black man penned these canonical texts? Is Rose's gift, then, a literary father with whom she is now connected? Or, is the legacy-as-ancient-transmission the knowledge that the race of the author alters not only the way one writes a text, but also the way one reads it—the information with which one is imparted? Is Rose's inheritance a deeper understanding of "Shake-speare's" plays (all of them? some of them? *Othello* only?)?

While *Black Swan* does not answer these questions definitively, some scholars have weighed in on the legacy of a black Shakespeare. When musing about the possibility that "Shakespeare [was] a brother," Henry Louis Gates, Jr. used to end his joke with the caveat that there "would be a critical reevaluation of his work: critics would start to say, 'I've been thinking about that Shakespeare guy, and he's not all he is cracked up to be. Take *Hamlet*, for example: all those clichés.'"[68] For Gates, the joke rests on the notion that formalist approaches to literature only go so far for critics—that notions of racial difference impede a more fully embraced formalist evaluation of literature. If not assumed to be the products of a white author, Shakespeare's plays would garner more criticism. Furthermore, if perceived

racial differences did not impede these valuations, Gates implies, many of the
poets and poems in his *Norton Anthology of African American Literature* would
already be canonical: they would already be included in the *Norton Anthology of
American Literature.*

Marjorie Garber expresses a similar belief that the limits of traditional humanism are tested when the author is not a white male. To the question, "What
would happen if it were *in fact* discovered that Shakespeare was a black woman, not
through a ventriloquizing voice lamenting an archetypal 'outcast state' but through
some diligent feat of archival research," she responds without hesitation, "What
would happen would be a massive campaign of disavowal."[69] For Garber, like Gates,
Shakespeare comes to "stand for a kind of 'humanness' that, purporting to be
inclusive of race, class, and gender, is in fact the neutralizing (or neutering) of
those potent discourses."[70] Shakespeare's authority, Garber implies, stems precisely from his assumed gender (male) and race (white). The legacy of an authorial
revision for Shakespeare necessarily involves, then, a reevaluation of his value,
cultural capital, and universality.

Stephen Henderson, in his famous theoretical essay on the nature of black poetry, "The Forms of Things Unknown," takes a slightly different angle on the
nature of authority. When discussing the thematic links that unite black poetry,
Henderson begins by discussing the theme of blackness and noting that not all
black poets "communicate" their race directly within their poetry. The critic,
however, may choose to go "outside the poem itself" to discover the poet's race,
which he advocates as an important analytical avenue to pursue.[71] Henderson
tests the "validity" of this practice by citing Shakespeare's sonnet 130 in its en-
tirety ("My mistress' eyes are nothing like the sun").[72] He concludes:

> This, of course, is Shakespeare's sonnet No. 130. But, if we discovered one day
> that it had been composed by an African at Elizabeth's court, would not the
> thematic meaning change? Perhaps formalist critics would not publicly admit
> the point, but a culturally oriented critic would. So, knowledge of the author's
> race altered our point of view, i.e., going outside of the poem changed our
> perspective on it.[73]

Unlike Gates and Garber, Henderson does not address the potential "disavowal"
that might occur if Shakespeare were proved irrefutably nonwhite. Instead, he
highlights what lies beneath both of their assessments: that literary-critical approaches are formed, informed, and validated by the knowledge of an author's
race. In other words, a formalist critic, one who clings to the belief that only the
formal elements of the text are relevant to one's analysis of it, would find his/her

adherence to formalism challenged if Shakespeare were revealed to be "an African at Elizabeth's court." Henderson argues that while formalist critics might protest their desire to go outside the text, they nevertheless will when/if canonical authors are not all white males.

The "of course" in Henderson's statement makes one wonder whether he assumes a readership that is familiar with the sonnet's authorship from the first line cited or a readership that is surprised to learn that it is not the product of a black poet. As John Carpenter notes in his essay on Shakespearean allusions in the Black Arts Movement, Henderson constructs a clear binary between black and white cultural productions that is based on essentialist ideas even as he borrows and transforms a Shakespearean allusion in the title of his essay.[74] In other words, Henderson privileges the "Black poet" as someone who knows how to cite, adapt, and transform anything into "Black poetry." While Henderson assumes that Shakespeare is not capable or "successful in absorbing Black expressive patterns," he assumes that the black artist is capable of not only absorbing but also transforming white, Western artistic forms: "there is a Black poetic mechanism, much like the musical ones, which can transform even a Shakespearean sonnet into a jazz poem, the basic conceptual model of contemporary Black poetry."[75] Thus, the legacy of a black poetic tradition, Henderson implies, is the development of a powerful appropriative tool that can make anything artistically *and* essentially black. In this evaluation, Henderson has no desire to claim Shakespeare as black because he views black cultural production as better than Shakespeare. Although approached from a different angle, this statement is not that far from the epigraph to this chapter by John H. Bracey, Jr. In both, black cultural production is assumed to be better than white cultural production; nevertheless, Shakespeare's position within these statements is central because his name represents the ultimate symbol, marker, and place holder for great art.

In his brilliant book, *Citing Shakespeare*, Peter Erickson writes about the differences between Harold Bloom's notion of "influence" and Harry Berger's notion of "allusion." According to Erickson, "In Bloom's case, the direction is from the precursor to the successor artist, thus enhancing the former's primacy. Berger dismantles this hierarchical relation by reversing the directional flow and thereby restoring creative agency to the later artist."[76] Adding an attention to race to Berger's theoretical and methodological model, Erickson traces the way Shakespeare is cited in various contemporary literary and artistic creations by black artists. He concludes with the statement, "Contrary to conventional wisdom, I argue that the more it changes, the more it is not the same thing. Quotation is transformation; citing means making changes."[77] The citation for Erickson is the moment of dialogue and transformation, but I wonder if the essentialist claim that "Shakespeare was black" is also a moment of encounter that enables change. Are legacies formed and reformed through these essentialist claims in the same way that "literary and artistic referentiality involves being in a conversation in which making changes is the only way"?[78]

To date the legacy of strategic essentialist claims that "Shakespeare was black" is not one of dialogue, transformation, and/or change. The statements by Soyinka and Angelou that claim that Shakespeare was "Arab" and "black" have not changed the centrality of Shakespeare as a white male author *and* the universal playwright. That strategic move is too easily dismissed as "a figure, an allegory," to borrow Garber's words again, which conservative critics happily employ to re-center Shakespeare within the canon as speaking to all races and peoples in all times.[79] The strategy of creating a de-centered and colored legacy from Shakespeare to artists of color ends up not being strategic at all. It is too easy to spot and dismiss, just as were the naked "gesture politics" that Spivak critiqued so fervently during the culture wars.

As contrary as this may sound, I see a strategy of legacy emerging, instead, from statements that Shakespeare could be confused for black *and* improved by blackness: in Bracey's terms, Shakespeare "sounded like a black way of speaking"; in Henderson's terms, "there is a Black poetic mechanism, which can transform even a Shakespearean sonnet." These statements are clearly essentialist in their formulation of blackness. Blackness is the norm, the center, and the apex which improves whatever it touches—even Shakespeare. Moreover, these statements are strategic in the way they figure everything outside of blackness and black cultural production as the deviation and the margin: things that need to be improved by blackness. Thus, for Bracey, "It never occurred to us that a white man could write that good." The humor is obvious—who really believes Shakespeare sounds "black"— but the claim is disarming. How can a conservative critic rebuff the claim without destroying the fiction of Shakespeare's universality? If his works are truly universal, can they not be confused for the cultural production of another race? Is not *universal* precisely the provenance of any and all races? And if Shakespeare's works can be confused with the cultural production of another race (because it is "universal"), can they not be improved upon by making them more closely aligned with that race's cultural production? Strategically, Henderson will not admit that there are those who would not want to "transform" Shakespeare's sonnets. Instead, he holds a "Black poetic" production as the essential core that has the power to gild everything "whereupon it gazeth," *even* Shakespeare (sonnet 20, line 6).

The legacy that *Titus Andronicus*, *Richard II*, and *Henry V* impart is that strategic essentialism may not guarantee a happy ending, but the logic and rhetoric are incredibly difficult to disprove. One can never be sure that Aaron, Richard, and Henry are not essentially different in ways that cannot be washed off, like makeup, dirt, or a crown. In fact, the logic and rhetoric of essentialism can haunt the most ardent disbeliever into, if not absolute belief then at least, tortured acquiescence. This is the strategic line to which *Black Swan* leads its reader. We are invited to think about the ways a black Shakespeare would sound and be read differently. Do the plays attributed to Lazarus/Henry sound different from, or better than, those attributed to Marlowe? The limitations of *Black Swan*, however, are similar to the limitations of statements like, Shakespeare was black, Arab, a woman, or ambiguously other (Catholic?). These statements can be dismissed as eccentric or treated in a condescending fashion as merely allegorical. This, I think, explains the ways the reviews of *Black Swan* consistently replace Shakespeare's white centrality by erasing the centrality of Lazarus/Henry's, Mr. B's, and Rose's blackness.

To cross the line into a more effective realm for strategic essentialism, one must truly displace the margin and the center rather than merely coloring the center. If Shakespeare's works can be confused with black cultural productions, then the center and margin are indistinct and indiscrete. While statements like Shakespeare was black, a woman, a Jew, or Other are essentialist, they are not strategic. Rather, the strategic "conversation in which making changes is the only way," to cite and alter Erickson, begins when we recognize the significance of statements such as, Shakespeare sounds as good as a black artist, female artist, and so forth. In these strategic essentialist statements the notions of center and margin are fully displaced by a destabilizing rhetoric that renders racially-coded cultural hierarchies obsolete. There can be neither center nor margin when they are constantly confused for each other. This type of strategic essentialism is rarely embraced by popular American culture. Instead, the logic and rhetoric of multiculturalism have been embraced, and this is the topic for the next chapter.

FIGURE 4.1 Peter Macon (Macbeth) and Robin Goodrin Nordli (Lady Macbeth) in the Oregon Shakespeare Festival's 2009 production of *Macbeth* (directed by Gale Edwards). Photo by Jenny Graham.

[N]ot-for-profit American theatre considered the keystone of its very identity . . .
non-traditional casting. . . .
—ROBERT BRUSTEIN[1]

In fact, by the 1990s, interracial casting is a non-issue in many productions. . . .
—AMY S. GREEN[2]

In my view, the 1990s debate over race-based casting and race-blind casting has
clearly been decided in favor of the latter. . . .
—RICHARD BURT[3]

4

Multiculturalism

THE CLASSICS, CASTING, AND CONFUSION

IN EARLIER CHAPTERS I analyze key terms (universal and colorblind) and con-
cepts (essentialism) that circulate around popular American treatments of Shakespeare, but I do not address them in terms of theatrical performances, opting
instead to focus on the employment of Shakespeare in other artistic media (film
and a young adult novel). At this point, it is time to turn to the theatre itself to
analyze Shakespeare's position within the conversations and debates about contemporary racial constructions because the theatre puts into practice what can
often remain a theoretical debate elsewhere. Thus, I begin with epigraphs by Robert Brustein, Amy S. Green, and Richard Burt about the state of late twentieth-
century American racial casting because they address the specific practice of
casting without regard to race. While they agree that the prevalent form of casting
after the 1990s is one that does not take race into consideration, they employ radically different terminology for this practice, leading one to realize that it is not
one but multiple sets of casting practices: Brustein calls it "non-traditional
casting"; Green calls it "interracial casting"; and Burt calls it "race-blind casting." I
will address this issue slightly later in the chapter because I begin with the definitions and practices of the multicultural classical theatre.

If multiculturalism is described as "the simultaneous existence and egalitarian
recognition of separate cultures side by side,"[4] then multicultural theatre "holds
that many ethnically distinct writers, plays, and institutions can coexist within

the same artistic arena at the same point in time."[5] While the practice of multiculturalism in theatre companies varies, the theoretical backbone asserts that a diversity of stories, actors, and audiences will necessarily enrich American drama.
In fact, books that pair "multicultural" and "acting" or "theatre" in their titles
often offer anthologies of performance scenes and monologues that address issues of race for actors of color by writers of color.[6] Thus, the push for multicultural
theatres in the late twentieth century was a push for theatres that presented material by artists of color performed by actors of color for audiences of color.

Both the ideology behind multicultural theatre and the actual practice of it
proved controversial, especially during the culture wars of the 1990s. Robert Brustein, the Founding Director of the American Repertory Theatre in Cambridge,
Massachusetts, famously decried that "multiculturalism" would "doom us to a
future of racial type casting" and usher in a "new separatist movement of self-
segregation."[7] For Brustein, the only way to combat the negative effects of multiculturalism is a staunch support of nontraditional casting that is blind to an actor's
race. "Limiting actors to their own racial or ethnic groups is precisely the sort of
thing that the resident theatre is dedicated to changing," Brustein writes.[8] On the
other side of the debate, the black playwright August Wilson argued, "We do not
need colorblind casting; we need theatres. We need theatres to develop our
playwrights."[9] Urging a multicultural approach that would support, fund, and produce plays about life in black America, Wilson declared, "They [white Americans]
refuse to recognize black conduct and manners as part of a system that is fueled by
its own philosophy, mythology, history, creative motif, social organization, and
ethos."[10] I draw our attention to this debate to demonstrate how frequently multiculturalism was pitched against nontraditional casting in the 1990s. Regardless of
one's stance within this debate, it is obvious that this definition of multiculturalism is not the one evoked when classical theatre companies bill themselves, their
approaches, and their audiences as such. So what exactly is a multicultural *classical*
theatre?

Sometimes classical theatre companies announce that they are "multicultural"
in their very own makeup, a euphemism that frequently means that the actors in
the company are not all white.[11] Other companies advertise themselves as offering
a "multicultural approach to Shakespeare," which one can assume means that the
production's mise-en-scène is not all English Renaissance costumes and settings.[12]
And still other companies focus on their "multi-cultural audience," another euphemism that often signals that the audience is not all white, not all wealthy, and not
all over fifty years of age.[13] Writing about the change in the artistic direction at
the Stratford Shakespeare Festival in Canada, Peter Parolin outlines the aspects
that appear to be remaining the same. He writes that the continuity includes "an

aggressive mixture of classical and contemporary fare" and "a commitment to reflect Canada's multicultural, multiracial society."[14] These aspects, I think, are characteristic of the twenty-first-century classical repertory company; that is, a company that produces shows in rotation with a set of residential actors and invited visiting directors. Thus, a multicultural classical theatre usually achieves its multiculturalism through the pairing of the classics with contemporary plays (some by playwrights of color), the inclusion of actors of color into the repertory company, and an outreach to a diversified audience membership.

In this chapter I analyze each of these components—the productions, the actors, and the audience—to examine how well multiculturalism and Shakespearean classics are paired in contemporary American theatre. While the pairing is as least as old as Joseph Papp's nontraditional Shakespeare productions of the 1950s at the New York Shakespeare Festival, multicultural classical companies in the twenty-first century still advertise themselves as doing something new. Why is it still considered and advertised as new? It is important to ask how the competing definitions and ideologies of multiculturalism prevent the creation of a longer historical narrative about multicultural classical productions. Thus, I will constantly query the terms and theories that are employed to support these theatre companies. Towards the end of the chapter, however, I offer some specific strategies and techniques that I hope will advance the dialogues about, and the practices of, the self-proclaimed multicultural classical theatre company.

THE LOGIC AND RHETORIC OF MULTICULTURAL CLASSICS

At first glance a multicultural classical company does not appear to be wrestling with the same issues Brustein and Wilson so publically debated because these companies do not appear to be pitting the classics against contemporary race plays;[15] rather, they appear to be uniting them seamlessly. Many companies proudly market their multiculturalism as a selling point—as something that will draw in larger and more diverse audiences, as something that makes their company especially relevant—and this rhetoric often taps into the discourse of universalism (which I address at length in chapter 2). Groups as diverse as the International Centre for Theatre Research (CIRT), the Southern California Shakespeare Festival, and the East L.A. Classic Theatre describe *and* justify their multiculturalism (or in CIRT's case interculturalism) in terms of the universality of Shakespeare's plays, themes, and characters. I briefly discuss the rhetoric these companies use to describe their approach to Shakespeare not because they are extraordinary, but because the rhetoric is highly representative of the ways multicultural classical companies frame their ideologies, approaches, and practices.

For instance, Peter Brook describes his 1990 CIRT production of *The Tempest*, with the African actor Sotigui Kouyaté as Prospero, in this way:

> I looked around for a play that would suit our international group, that would have a quality that could inspire the actors and simultaneously bring something of value to the audience, something related to the needs and realities of our era. Such reasoning has always led me straight to Shakespeare. Shakespeare is always the model that no one has surpassed, his work is always relevant and always contemporary.[16]

Staging *The Tempest* in a nontraditional way that highlights several "non-English cultures,"[17] Brook links his intercultural production with its ability to "inspire the actors" and bring "value to the audience" precisely because it is "related to the needs and realities of our era." In Brook's rhetoric, Shakespeare is already "always relevant," but a late twentieth-century audience may not realize this. Therefore, his production is meant to draw them in through methods that are more easily identified as relevant and valuable precisely because they are diverse and "non-English." Brook's rhetoric makes CIRT's intercultural approach and the Shakespeare text mutually beneficial *and* mutually benefitting—a perfect example of a symbiotic relationship.

Similarly, the Southern California Shakespeare Festival (SCSF) announces that its own mission is to provide "the Inland Empire with a professional theatre company of multicultural actors and students that will reach [its] audience."[18] In seeking to "enrich the diverse community," SCSF also declares that it "endeavors to explore the eternal human questions [and] to enlighten and excite contemporary audiences with the timeless relevance of Shakespeare's literature." On the one hand, the assumption seems to be that the contemporary audience in Inland Empire, the third largest metropolitan area in California that includes Riverside and San Bernardino counties, will not recognize the timelessness of Shakespeare's plays without a multicultural approach. On the other hand, SCSF promotes its multiculturalism as exemplifying the "eternal human questions" and "timeless relevance of Shakespeare's literature." While this type of logic might be viewed as tautological, it is clear that SCSF seeks to convey that its multiculturalism is a substantial bonus for the company and the community.

And finally, the East L.A. Classic Theatre (ECT) was established in "1992, when a group of multi-cultural arts professionals . . . launched the company as a forum where classically trained Latino and minority artists could investigate the classics in culturally specific productions and adaptations."[19] The company is most well known for its "mariachi style" *Much Ado about Nothing*, which has toured many schools in southern California as part of the National Endowment for the Arts "Shakespeare for a New Generation" initiative (which I discuss at length in chapter 6). In its "Shakespeare for Youth Productions," ECT offers workshops for "students at underserved schools in socio-economically marginalized neighborhoods and minority communities," and the "experience can include preparatory and post-play workshops that examine storytelling techniques, universal human themes, and the roles of literacy, self-expression, and education in the achievement of one's life goals."

So once again we see a theatre company announcing itself as being invested in both "culturally specific productions" and the "universal human themes" of Shakespeare's plays. Not only is this rhetoric not presented as being in conflict with itself, but also it is presented as bolstering both cultural specificity and universalism seamlessly. The logic is thus: Shakespeare is universal; multiculturalism is relevant; and therefore multicultural Shakespeare is universally relevant. Unlike the debate that Brustein and Wilson articulated that pitted multicultural theatre against classical theatre, multicultural classical companies often create a rhetoric that unites them. In multicultural classical companies, cultural specificity, temporal relevance, and timeless universalism are constructed together to form a sturdy triumvirate of theatrical necessity. Furthermore, the sense of necessity is often achieved through declarations of their own uniqueness and immediate relevance.

AMERICAN SHAKESPEARE = MULTICULTURAL SHAKESPEARE: CONCEPTUAL DIRECTING = NONTRADITIONAL CASTING

While theatre companies like CIRT, SCSF, and ECT often promote themselves as offering something new through their highly relevant multicultural Shakespearean productions (they do this, of course, out of necessity in the hopes of creating and sustaining a younger audience, but more on this later), the history of Shakespeare in America is also the history of multiracial, multiethnic, and multicultural productions. Lawrence Levine sketches the separation of Shakespeare from popular and populist nineteenth-century American theatre,[20] but Amy Green links the "beginnings of an unapologetically American approach to producing the classics" as arising from Works Projects Administration/Federal-Theatre-Project-funded productions of the 1930s.[21] As Green makes clear, the FTP's

> mandate to serve the diverse needs and talents of its separate regional and
> racial units, provided fertile ground for experiments with classical texts

(large casts, no royalties). The Negro units in particular presented a direct challenge to tradition. Black actors, professionals who had been denied opportunities to perform major classical roles in the commercial theatre, were eager to prove their mettle.[22]

Charting the way American productions began to challenge the "tradition" of overly Anglicized Shakespearean productions, Green locates the FTP's funding of regional and racial units in the 1930s as creating a space for American experimentation with classical theatre. Orson Welles's FTP-funded 1936 production of *Macbeth* at the Lafayette Theatre in Harlem is a prime example. With an all-black cast, a Haitian setting (with African drummers), and an all-black audience (supposedly numbering 10,000 outside the theatre), Welles's production initiated several of the ways Shakespeare would become American *and* multicultural in the twentieth century.[23] As Green saliently notes, "Race reversal has since become a common strategy among directors seeking to *Americanize* classic plays."[24]

By 1959 when the Ford Foundation awarded its first major grants for the construction of new regional theatres, many of the companies declared their missions as bringing an American touch to theatre, including the classics. While the Ford grants to theatre companies began with five hundred thousand dollars in

FIGURE 4.2 Premiere of the Federal Theatre Project *Macbeth*, Harlem, 1936. Library of Congress, Music Division.

1959, in 1962 the grants "had risen to nine million dollars [and] by the mid-1980s, their cumulative contribution amounted to sixty million dollars."[25] In turn, these companies became multicultural and promoted multiculturalism as part of their contribution to the creation of a uniquely American theatrical tradition. Think, for example, of the New York Shakespeare Festival; the Oregon Shakespeare Festival; the Guthrie Theatre in Minneapolis, Minnesota; and the Arena Stage in Washington, DC, all of which received funding from the Ford Foundation, and all of which proudly created multicultural approaches to the classics.

As directors, producers, and theatre companies in general began to experiment with rewriting and reinventing the classics on the twentieth-century American stage, conceptual directing and nontraditional casting sprang into existence together. Amy Green identifies three waves of American experimentation with classical texts. The first wave, she argues, introduces American pronunciation and non-period dress. The second wave, which I will focus on the most, she identifies as being dominated by "simile makers," a term she adapts from Robert Brustein, which signifies a director who transplants the classics to new locations, including non-European ones. And the third wave is postmodern in its desire to rearrange not only the settings, but also the plots, characters, and narrative structures with an emphasis on "contemporary theatrical imagery and technology over traditional linguistic and thematic content."[26]

It is the simile maker as one type of conceptual director on whom I will focus now because his/her approach to directing has impacted self-professed multicultural classical companies the most palpably. The "conceptual director [is] dedicated to reinterpreting and refreshing existing works, primarily the classics, and so mak[es] them more immediate to the present day."[27] Conceptual directing, then, assumes that while classical theatrical pieces are important and necessary in the modern world, they may need to be reinterpreted and refreshed to make them both accessible and relevant. Putting the phrase "simile directing" into play in 1988, Robert Brustein explains that:

> Directors who are fond of similes assume that because a play's action is like something from a later period, its environment can be changed accordingly. . . . Simile directing is a prose technique. Its innovations are basically analogical—providing at best a platform for ideas, at worst an occasion for pranks.[28]

The conceptual director as simile maker, as both Green and Brustein define him/her, is someone who is interested in making connections between Shakespeare's early modern plays and the twentieth-century American world. And many of these directors, following the immense popularity and success of Joseph Papp's New York Shakespeare Festival (NYSF), make nontraditional casting part and parcel of their reworking, reinventing, and Americanizing of the classical play. While not all conceptually derived productions employ nontraditional casting, conceptual directing and nontraditional casting helped to give birth to each other. It is hard to conceive of the popularity of conceptual directing without the birth of nontraditional casting, and it is hard to conceive of the popularity of nontraditional casting without the birth of conceptual directing. The push for a unique and modern approach to classical theatre enabled the creation of these two cornerstones to contemporary American theatre.

NONTRADITIONAL CASTING(S)

Despite the fact that conceptual directing held sway on much of the late twentieth-century American stage, and despite the fact that nontraditional casting is now often considered the norm (look back at the epigraphs for this chapter), nontraditional casting did not cohere into one consistently defined practice. So what exactly is nontraditional casting? In the most reductive sense, nontraditional casting is the practice of casting actors of color for roles that were originally conceived as white and written for white actors. Although Joseph Papp and the NYSF began staging nontraditionally cast productions of Shakespeare in the 1950s, it was not until the late 1980s that the Non-Traditional Casting Project enumerated four different types of nontraditional casting (NTCP was renamed in 2007 as the Alliance for Inclusion in the Arts). I will take some time to go over these models because they demonstrate how varied nontraditional casting is, but I want to make it clear from the outset that these terms are not ones that are widely understood or used in theatre companies. While I will come back to this point a little later, I begin with the terms spelled out by NTCP because they reveal some of the internal conflicts within nontraditional casting. There are four models:

COLORBLIND CASTING: a meritocratic model in which actors are cast without regard to race; the best actor for the best role

SOCIETAL CASTING: a socially informed model in which actors of color are cast in roles originally conceived as being white if people of color perform these roles in society as a whole

CONCEPTUAL CASTING: a conceptually conceived model in which actors of color are cast in roles to enhance the play's social resonance

CROSS-CULTURAL CASTING: another conceptually conceived model in which the entire world of the play is translated to a different culture and location[29]

Thus, nontraditional casting is the umbrella category for alternative casting models. Under this umbrella, however, are four radically different approaches to casting *and* four radically different conceptions of the semiotic meaning of racial difference onstage. When I refer to the semiotic significance of race, I mean if and how an actor's race is endowed with any meaning within a performance—whether realistic, symbolic, or otherwise. That is: What does the audience see with regard to race? How does the audience make sense of it? And how does the audience interpret it within the larger scope of the theatrical visit when an actor of color is employed in a Shakespearean production? Although it was initially assumed that nontraditional casting would be a kind of magical panacea to cure the ills of racism and exclusion, it has become clear that the various models of nontraditional casting can actually replicate racist stereotypes *because* we have not addressed the unstable semiotics of race (when we see race; how we see race; how we make sense of what race means within a specific production).

Colorblind casting assumes one can and should be blind to race. It also assumes that theatre is a location that can enable a society to change long-held views of race. As a model that prides itself on its meritocratic roots (the best actor for the best part), colorblind casting also assumes that an actor's color has no semiotic value onstage unless it is invested with one by the director. For example, in 1977 La Mama Experimental Theatre in New York advertised itself as having an interracially cast production of *Macbeth*, starring Tom Kopache as Macbeth and Barbara Montgomery as Lady Macbeth. This particular production emphasized the "sensuality, lust, and greed of the main characters," and Montgomery played Lady Macbeth with "an embodiment of sexuality and passion with a sense of evil that makes even the witches cower."[30] Because Montgomery's race was never discussed within the production itself, the significance of the publicity's insistence on the "interracial" quality of the production was disturbing to some. Ellen Foreman, for example, asked, "Was it intentional to link sexuality and evil with blackness? For what other purpose is the interracial aspect stressed?"[31] Foreman wanted to read the play as cast without attention to race, as a colorblind production, but the publicity materials made her wonder if in fact the production was extremely, and offensively, color conscious.

Societal casting, the second casting method identified by the Non-Traditional Casting Project, offers a radically different approach to casting actors of color. In this approach actors of color are cast in roles that might stereotypically be associated with them even if those roles were not originally written in that fashion. For example, we know that the witches in *Macbeth*, who are described as being "weyward sisters" with "beards" (1.3.30 & 44), were written for white male actors in drag. Today, however, if *Macbeth* is cast nontraditionally, it is more often

than not a witch who is played by an actor of color. Describing the impetus
behind creating the African-American Shakespeare Company in San Francisco,
California, Bonnee Stingily relates "a joke often repeated in the African-American theater community [that] seemed to describe their fates: 'The only way we
will get to do Shakespeare is as one of the three witches in *Macbeth*.'"[32] Black
witches make sense because of the stereotype of the "magical negro," a stereotypical, stock character employed in many genres of contemporary popular culture, a figure who has other-worldly or earthly connections, a figure who has no
past, a figure who helps to save a white protagonist: a kind of *negro ex machina*.[33]
Writing about her own experience being cast as a witch in *Macbeth*, Lola Young
bemoans the

> consistency with which I was chosen to play the witch every play-time. That
> childhood re-memory was re-invoked, when as a professional actor during
> the mid-1980s I was cast as one of the three witches in a production of *Mac-
> beth* at the Young Vic in London. That experience was not without its contra-
> dictions since for many years, Blacks have demanded the right to play as wide
> a range of characters as "white" actors are allowed to, and here I was stuck
> playing the witch again, albeit in Shakespeare.[34]

Unlike colorblind casting, societal casting does not assume that audiences can,
will, or even desire to be blind to race in performance. Likewise, societal casting
also assumes that an actor's race always has semiotic meanings in performance,
ones informed by stereotypes. This model of casting assumes that certain social
constructs are entrenched and therefore can be employed and capitalized upon in
performance.

Conceptual casting, as defined by the Non-Traditional Casting Project, also
does not assume that audiences are completely blind to race in performance. In
this model of nontraditional casting, an actor's race might be highlighted to draw
parallels between the early modern and (post) modern periods. I can imagine a
production of *Macbeth* in which Macbeth is the only person of color in the society. His racial difference could be employed to explain how he seems both inside
and outside of the social structure: he shall be king but beget none because of the
cultural strains on his interracial union. His dire ambition, his desperate need to
conquer, and his utter isolation in the face of both success and failure could all be
interpreted through the lenses of race and racism in a production that cast a
black Macbeth within and against an all white society. This type of casting is
conceptually based because it seeks to reflect themes within the play through a
more modern prism. It is not merely about ambition and greed, but about the

strange psychological desires, pressures, and breaks that racialized individuals suffer within racist, patriarchal, hegemonic societies. This production could potentially provide a powerful counterpoint to *Othello* by showing the psychological damage of racism without pandering to the stereotype of the uxorious black man. The Oregon Shakespeare Festival's 2009 production of *Macbeth* came close to employing this conceptual model by casting the black actor Peter Macon as Macbeth. In the previous 2008 season Macon played Othello, so an audience member with this knowledge might reasonably interpret Macon's Macbeth through this conceptual lens.

Nontraditionally cast productions of *Macbeth*, however, more frequently employ the final casting model, cross-cultural casting. The final model under the nontraditional casting umbrella works by translating an entire play to a different cultural location. Thus, Orson Welles's so-called "Voodoo" *Macbeth* from 1936 transported medieval Scotland to nineteenth-century Haiti. Welles employed an all-black cast to emphasize the play's cultural translation. Like societal and conceptual casting, and unlike colorblind casting, cross-cultural casting does not assume that an actor's race is rendered meaningless onstage. Rather, cross-cultural casting assumes that an actor's race carries a wealth of semiotic meaning that can and should inform a production's cultural, historical, and perhaps even political landscape. Cross-cultural casting is the most closely related to Brustein's notion of conceptual

FIGURE 4.3 James J. Peck (First Murderer), Peter Macon (Macbeth), and Trevor Hill (Second Murderer) in the Oregon Shakespeare Festival's 2009 production of *Macbeth* (directed by Gale Edwards). Photo by Jennifer Reiley.

directing as simile-making; it merely makes race, culture, and ethnicity the center of the translation.

The application of nontraditional casting, however, does not ensure a semiotic stability for the actor of color. The four casting models—colorblind, societal, conceptual, and cross-cultural—provide radically different approaches to, *and* understandings of, the semiotics of race in performance. While societal, conceptual, and cross-cultural casting all assume that race has semiotic values and meanings in performance, these approaches do not necessarily present a unified vision of how race is seen and interpreted in performance, or even how race should be seen and interpreted in performance. An audience member, then, who attends a nontraditionally cast production may feel confused or left adrift to navigate the complicated, and often contradictory, approaches to nontraditional casting.[35] Audiences often find it difficult to determine which model is being employed and why.

Likewise, it is clear that there is a great deal of confusion among critics, who employ a panoply of terms for practices that are not clearly identified by the theatre companies. Think for a second about the epigraphs cited at the beginning of this chapter. While Robert Brustein, Amy Green, and Richard Burt all seem to agree that a traditional race-based casting model should, and does, cease to exist by the end of the twentieth century, their terminology for a new model neither admits that there are divergent and competing models nor is consistent in terminology. Brustein's "non-traditional casting" is vague and not practically specific. Although it appears as if he endorses the generic phrase that Harry Newman put into circulation in the 1980s, it is not clear exactly what *practices* Brustein includes and/or excludes from "non-traditional casting."[36]

Similarly, Green's "interracial casting," like the phrase "integrated casting," does not explain how race will, or should, function semiotically onstage in such a production.[37] While the word "interracial" is descriptive, indicating that there is more than one race represented on the stage, it does not explicate if and how a representation of diversity achieves meaning, let alone if and how it should achieve meaning in a theatrical production.[38]

Burt's use of the terms "race-based" and "race-blind casting" actually represents one of the more popular current constructions of nontraditional casting: a construction that juxtaposes a casting model in which race is considered semiotically relevant with one in which race is not. Take, for example, Ralph Berry's bald declaration: "There are now two casting conventions on the stage, 'colour-blind' and 'colour-conscious.'"[39] While "colour-blind" clearly lines up with the first type of nontraditional casting identified by NTCP, "colour-conscious" seems to collapse the latter three categories into one. And while it is true that an attention to, and a consciousness about, color and race inform these latter models, they do not construct, perform, and present this consciousness in exactly the same ways. The semiotics of race are not the same in all color-conscious productions even when they are aligned under this designation.

Following Zelda Fichandler's query into what it would mean to "assign roles freely," many have also used the phrase "race-free casting."[40] Richard Schechner's 1989 *TDR* essay, for example, is entitled "Race Free, Gender Free, Body-Type Free, Age Free Casting." And while Schechner admits that "American audiences are not color or gender blind anymore than they are body-type or age blind," he argues for a freedom from these categories, for "an extreme flexibility that allows for situation-specific decisions regarding when to use, when to ignore, and when not to see race, gender, age, and body type."[41] If one considers race and gender as social constructions, Schechner argues, then theatre can be a space in which these constructions are wrested from their traditional performances. In this formulation, then, nontraditional casting offers a way to free the actors and audiences from potentially outmoded social constructions.

THE PRODUCTION OF MULTICULTURAL CLASSICS

While terms like multicultural, nontraditional, interracial, integrated, color-blind, race conscious, and race free are often used interchangeably, they signify dramatically different approaches to how one constructs the semiotics of race, color, and ethnicity onstage. So why is it that self-described multicultural and/ or diverse theatre companies do not engage in more systematic discussions about their casting models and approaches? As I briefly mentioned earlier, the terms and models devised by the Non-Traditional Casting Project and spelled out by Clinton Turner Davis and Harry Newman in the collection *Beyond Tradition* are not ones that are recognized, let alone employed, by theatre practitioners when they conceive, describe, or promote their productions. It is rare for theatre companies to identify in either their mission statements or programs notes the exact type of nontraditional casting they employ in general or for a particular production (indeed, I have not been able to find any that do this explicitly).

Theatre companies like the African-American Shakespeare Company and the East L.A. Classic Theatre declare that they offer "culturally specific productions," which actually seems to be another phrase for what NTCP called "cross-cultural casting," but that is about as specific as theatre companies get in their mission statements or program notes. So it is important to investigate who within the organizational system of a theatre company decides how its multiculturalism will be put into practice. While the obvious answer is that the artistic director must be responsible for conceiving, articulating, and shaping this vision, this answer is too simplistic because it does not take into account the myriad minor networks that actually create each production, season, and hence the larger company ethos.

Let me briefly discuss a repertory company that I admire immensely, the Oregon Shakespeare Festival (OSF), to exemplify the smaller networks that create the company's multicultural approaches. Aside from Joseph Papp's New York Shakespeare Festival, I would venture to argue that OSF has a more diverse acting company than any other large classical repertory company. One of the oldest classical repertory companies in the United States, OSF truly embraces and demonstrates multicultural approaches to the classics. In fact, in 2005 the associate artistic director at OSF at the time, Timothy Bond, made the pronouncement: "We don't do 'colorblind' productions. We don't use that term here [at OSF]. To me, 'blind' means you can't see something. First of all, we can all see it. Second of all, I want you to see it."[42] Bond also declared that OSF practices "'new-traditional' or just 'inclusive' casting," and that he personally is interested in "intimate cross-cultural approaches to the texts."[43] This is an extraordinarily candid, focused, and well-articulated vision for OSF's multiculturalism, especially when compared to statements made by other artistic directors at the time.[44]

Likewise, Bill Rauch, the current artistic director at OSF, has stated on numerous occasions that the diversity of the company, its productions, and its audiences are cornerstones of his vision for the future of OSF. Although Rauch has not articulated as clear a vision as Bond did in 2005, Rauch promotes that he is "eager to widen the scope of OSF's classical repertoire."[45] For example, Rauch launched an ongoing series of classical plays from outside the Western canon to be played as part of the repertory. As he states in the program note for the 2009 season, OSF's *"Cultural Connections* programs continue to expand our audience and company so that we increasingly reflect the full diversity of contemporary American society."[46] And in the 2009 season, approximately forty-five percent of the actors in OSF's repertory company were actors of color, in addition to two deaf performers, which is an astonishing percentage for a company that was not initially created to be a multicultural or diverse one.

And yet, OSF does not articulate or specify in any official capacity how the company envisions race, color, and ethnicity working on its stages. While it is clear that the races presented onstage will not be all white, it is not clear what types of multiculturalism or nontraditional casting they endorse, practice, or reject. Because of the absence of this official direction, one can detect smaller structural networks within the organization that challenge a unified ideology and practice of multiculturalism. Like most repertory companies, OSF invites visiting directors to direct the company's individual plays. For example, the artistic director invites visiting directors to work for the company. Together with the upper artistic administration (usually the artistic director, the associate artistic director, and the associate producer), they choose a play to produce in an upcoming season. The visiting director will then start developing his/her vision for the production, but usually he/she is not involved in the casting process. Thus, most visiting directors will have at least a full year to work with the production team at the company, but he/she will not know who is cast until about half way into that year. In other words, the visiting director cannot fully take race, color, or ethnicity into consideration as part (or not part) of his/her initial vision because he/she has no voice in the casting process. Furthermore, visiting directors usually only have a five-week rehearsal period with the cast so that any conflicts between their initial vision of the direction of the production with regard to race and the actual cast have to be resolved quickly.

While this is not an insurmountable problem, it does create a scenario in which it is easier for visiting directors not to invest too much time and thought into their vision for the semiotics of race in the production. Then once the production goes up with whatever vision (or lack thereof) he/she has with regard to the semiotics of race, the visiting director is not around to comment upon, receive input about, or alter the direction of that vision: the show will run for months (some for as many as ten months) without him/her in residency. Again, while this is not necessarily a crippling structure, especially as the stage manager oversees the continuity of the production, it does not provide an incentive for the visiting director to put a lot of energy into how race fits, and should fit, into his/her concept for the production.

In the 2009 season at OSF there were eleven plays in production. Eight of them were directed by visiting directors, and three were directed by resident artists (two by the artistic director himself). This means that there were numerous different casting models employed, and sometimes these models seemed in conflict with each other. For example, it was clear that at least two of the productions featured colorblind casting, in which the races, colors, and ethnicities of the actors were not supposed to be semiotically relevant within the production itself. In *Henry VIII* (directed by John Sipes), two veteran black OSF actors Derrick Lee Weeden and Tyrone Wilson played Lord Chamberlain and Sands respectively, and their blackness did not appear to carry any meaning (literally, symbolically, or otherwise) within the production. I hedge this statement, however, because there was nothing in Sipes's director's note about casting and/or race. Likewise, *The Music Man* (OSF's first musical, directed by Bill Rauch) seems to have been cast in a colorblind fashion with the black actress Gwendolyn

Mulamba cast as Marian Paroo. Again, Rauch's director's note does not mention the casting model employed. Nevertheless, he does discuss the importance of the "cultural specificity" of the play's setting in Iowa, 1912. If one is familiar with the cultural specificity of American segregation in 1912, however, then one can only assume the production is colorblind.

At the other end of the spectrum, OSF's *Macbeth* (directed by Gale Edwards), starring Peter Macon, offered an extremely color-conscious production. Designed with a postmodern aesthetic, the play's integrated cast, with black, white, Asian, and Hispanic cast members, fit seamlessly (see Figure 4.1). This is no utopian, race-free fantasy world, however, as exhibited by Malcolm's emphasis of the phrase "black Macbeth," indicating his belief that Macbeth's moral failings might be revealed by his black skin (4.3.53). With the black actor Kevin Kenerly playing Macduff, this production did not align blackness solely with waywardness. Nevertheless, it was clear that Macbeth's character was racially and culturally black, that Macon's race both informed the character and had semiotic relevance within the production. Finally, OSF's production of Wole Soyinka's *Death and the King's Horseman* (directed by Chuck Smith), the second production in the company's world classics series, was extremely color-conscious with all of the actors cast according the races of the characters (with blacks as Africans and whites as Brits).

So an audience member seeing plays in rotation at OSF is implicitly asked to switch between extremely different casting models and extremely different interpretations of the semiotic meaning and value of an actor's race, color, and ethnicity onstage. While it is not inherently a problem to ask audience members to switch between different casting models, it can become problematic if the switches are not governed by a coherent vision or ideology. As should be clear from these few examples, the variations in casting models between shows in one season at OSF is not governed by a clear ideology or even a systematic process. Instead, the variances occur because of smaller structural networks. While I have highlighted the smaller networks around directing, I could have discussed just as easily the networks around production design or marketing because all of these networks affect the models for interpreting the semiotics of race onstage. In addition, the collapse of these various models under the rubric of multicultural, diverse, or even simply nontraditional does not help to advance our understanding of how the semiotics of race, color, and ethnicity work, or, more importantly, how they should work in this repertory company, in this company in the future, or even in the ideal world. I will return at the end of this chapter to some strategies and techniques that I believe will advance the dialogues and practices of multicultural classical companies, but first I address another facet of the multicultural theatre company: the actor's race.

MULTICULTURAL CLASSICS AND THE ACTOR

Even when actors of color celebrate the fact that they are now more marketable to multicultural theatre companies, they complain about the lack of clear direction and open dialogues about the how their races should, or should not, play into the director's vision for the production. Dion Johnstone, a black actor who is regularly employed by the Stratford Shakespeare Festival of Canada, discusses the way non-traditional casting can sometimes be invoked as a cover to evade discussions about race:

> I found sometimes colorblind casting can mean that "we're going to dress you up in Elizabethan costumes, and your color doesn't matter." . . . But the fact is I'm black. . . . I am the only black member of this company, and when I go up on the stage, people are going to see that, and especially when young kids who are black come to see it, I don't want them to see the paradox where it hasn't even been thought about, where I'm by default playing a white person. . . .[47]

As Johnstone makes clear, his race and the semiotic significance of his race in any given production at Stratford are rarely discussed by the visiting director, the artistic director, or the company as a whole. In his estimation, then, colorblind casting becomes a type of whitewashing in which race does not have to be addressed at all. Elsewhere I have written about the difficulties the black British actor Clarence Smith faced when he played the King of France in the Royal Shakespeare Company's 1991 colorblind production of *King Lear*. When Smith was heckled onstage by a French woman who was protesting the fact that a black man was playing the King of France, "the RSC persisted in insisting that race should not be a factor for discussion, even when Smith wanted to initiate one."[48] While these examples represent types of extremes, they are also indicative of the lack of dialogue within multicultural theatre companies about what an actor's race does, may, or should signify in any given production. Of course, these dialogues are not solely important for actors of color. White actors also need to think about how the semiotic value and significance of their own race is interpreted onstage not simply because their whiteness may be rendered more visible in a multicultural production, but also because whiteness has a fluid semiotic meaning in performance (like blackness, Asian-ness, Hispanic-ness, etc.).

So how are actors trained in universities and actor training programs with regard to race in performance? What are actors taught about nontraditional casting models? What are they taught about the semiotics of race in performance?

As Roberta Uno notes in the preface to *Monologues for Actors of Color*, debates about how to train actors of color came to a head in the 1990s:

> A symposium entitled "Training the Actor of Color," convened by the Tisch School of the Arts of New York University in 1994, brought this question to the foreground when actors of color in the audience spoke about their peripheral existence in major training programs. One observed that . . . reading lists and course assignments typically draw from a very narrow and Eurocentric canon.[49]

The content of this quotation along with the title of Uno's book reveal one of the major reasons for these debates: actor training in the United States, which is a twentieth-century phenomenon, has focused almost entirely on white canonical texts written for white actors. If one casually glances into manuals or advice books written for young actors or even collections about actor training methods, one rarely encounters discussions about an actor's race, multicultural theatre, or non-traditional casting, let alone racialized performances or the semiotics of race in performance.[50]

Thus, starting in the 1990s, many practitioners and scholars advocated for the inclusion of material by and for artists of color within actor training programs. Douglas Turner Ward's thoughts on the matter are fairly typical:

> The training of black actors today in academia and in acting schools is ass backwards. . . . I mean most of the schools don't even use black material. Could you imagine a bunch of actors going to college for four years and not even studying a piece of their own material? Not one character that might be remindful of their own experience or somebody they might know? And yet they're asked to do everybody else's characters.[51]

While early twentieth-century theories for actor training emphasized a "universally applied method" for all actors regardless of race, culture, or background, the debates in the 1990s brought into focus the need for race- and culture-specific materials for actors of color.[52] During this period, some training programs like the one at San Francisco State University began "creating a multicultural component, featuring courses in multicultural and Latino theatre and producing plays with students from both the Theatre Arts and Ethnic Studies departments."[53] Likewise, many theatre programs in university settings began instituting new policies such as "a color-blind policy for casting and assignment of production responsibilities, and a rotation of plays that included a 'multi-cultural' production."[54]

Supporting this new multicultural push, books with monologues for actors of color for training, auditioning, and performing in showcases were produced widely.[55]

Nonetheless, the investment in multiculturalism has only gone so far in actor training programs. As Micha Espinosa and Antonio Ocampo-Guzman point out, despite the fact that there is an "increase of Spanish-only jobs in the Latino entertainment industry" in the United States, "[p]rofessional actor-training programs in the U.S. offer instruction exclusively in English."[56] Of course, bilingual training seems like an obvious aspect to be included in self-proclaimed multicultural training programs, but the older and more traditional training models and standards for speech and performance still prevail, making it particularly difficult to make the Latino actor feel welcome in many actor training programs. Conversations about diversity occur frequently within the professional training organizations, like the Association for Theatre in Higher Education (ATHE) and the Voice and Speech Trainers Association (VASTA), but actor training programs within universities and colleges still remain somewhat isolated from the debates in other departments about race and "cultural stereotyping and [their] nature, roots, and consequences."[57] As David Eulus Wiles candidly writes, "I have never encountered a theoretical critique of student selection and casting practices that addressed the impact of those practices on campus audiences and the department's own students. While I've certainly heard colleagues lament, sometimes bitterly, the absurd standards the mass media has for what constitutes acceptable physical appearance, particularly for women, those laments" have not addressed the casting practices at their own institution.[58]

While there is an increased awareness in actor training programs that an actor's racial, cultural, and ethnic background may affect what he/she wants to perform, these programs often do not address how he/she performs this background or how he/she should perform it in a consistent fashion. The close attention to the intimate cultural, psychological, and historical details that actors need to access in what Venus Opal Reese refers to as "embodiment" acting for multicultural productions ("Embodiment . . . has to do with how a history, told through cultural memory, reformation, and representation, impacts a community in which the individual is directly linked to the collective") suddenly disappears when actors are trained to perform in the classics.[59] For example, when Kaliswa Brewster, a young black actress from New York, attended the MFA program at the American Conservatory Theatre in San Francisco, California, she was eager to play roles written for black actors. While in her first year she performed in Lynn Nottage's *Intimate Apparel*, "by the second year the curriculum's focus had shifted to 'language plays'—Shakespeare, Molière."[60] Because the shift focused on "being exposed to heightened text," there was no longer any attention to exploring how race functioned in performance.[61] Thus, many actor training programs segregate the training for the performance of race and culture from the training for the performance of the classics. They simply do not address how an actor of color who is interested in the classics should approach them in his/her own skin and racial/cultural identity.

This is not to suggest that actor training programs do not train actors of color to perform the classics. On the contrary, there are numerous programs (usually outside of academic institutions) that specialize in exactly this training.[62] For example, Donna Walker-Kuhne writes about how the "Shakespeare in Harlem" program founded by The Public in 1994 was the result of discussions with community leaders in Harlem. Walker-Kuhne explains, "we established a free workshop in which Harlem-based actors could work with other African American actors on the physical and language demands of Shakespearean performance. We learned that the thought of performing Shakespeare intimidated many of them."[63] The emphasis here, as in Kaliswa Brewster's description of her training at ACT, is on performing the language, which is difficult for every modern actor. But the language is not the only difficulty these actors will face when performing Shakespeare, and these programs do not address the thorny issues of the current, desired, or changing semiotics of race onstage.

Thus, the debates from the 1990s have created a space for actor training for the multicultural theatre in the sense that the multicultural theatre is both plays by, for, and about people of color and classical productions with actors of color. While training programs have made some strides to broaden their training approaches to be able to discuss the complicated histories, cultures, and traumas represented in plays about contemporary race issues (again, Venus Opal Reese's model of "embodiment" acting is a good example), these advances do not cross over into the training of the classics. In fact, the advent of the multicultural classical company has not advanced discussions and debates in training programs about the specifics of the semiotics of race, color, and ethnicity onstage in classical productions in any palpable way. On the one hand, there are actor training programs that encourage actors of color to perform roles and characters that match their racial, ethnic, and cultural backgrounds ("I really hungered for a chance to thrive with some literature written for me").[64] On the other hand, there are classical theatre companies that offer actors of color classical training and, as Michael Kahn proclaims, "the opportunity to exercise that training."[65] But neither the twain shall meet. As young actors of color repeatedly make clear, the options in training programs appear to be multicultural approaches with material specifically designed for actors of color or colorblind approaches in which race is deemed completely irrelevant.[66]

MULTICULTURAL CLASSICS AND THE AUDIENCE

So where does this leave the audience? How is the composition of the audience figured into the construction of the self-proclaimed multicultural classical company? A common declaration in the mission statements, Web sites, and programs of these companies is that they are bringing Shakespeare to the people. Writing about audience development, Betty Farrell claims, "Many cultural organizations believe that their first order of business is to dispel the notion that they are elitist institutions—or, in the words of Lonnie Bunch . . . 'a venerable institution that few people actually want to visit.'"[67] For instance, Richard Monette, the late artistic director of the Stratford Shakespeare Festival of Canada, proclaimed, "If I had done nothing else in my tenure to be proud of, I would be proud of the fact that I have been a 'people's director' who did everything I could to make audiences feel as much at home in the theatres of the Stratford Festival as I do myself."[68] Rebuffing the critique that the festival created "vulgar" productions devoid of artistic merit, Monette returned to the Latin definition of *vulgus* as meaning the common people: "I can think of no higher accomplishment for a classical company than to be vulgar in the true sense of the word."[69] It is this notion—that a classical company needs to attract, reach, and retain the common people as members of the audience—that is commonly repeated by these companies.

Some companies stress that they are creating a more populist audience for the future. Shakespeare in Action, the Toronto-based company, for instance, declares in its mission statement that the "goal is to inspire a love and appreciation for the spoken word and to build a future audience through [its] innovative . . . productions." Moreover, the company's statement of philosophy announces, "It is our belief that Shakespeare can and should be accessible to everyone, regardless of age, race, education, or socio-economic background."[70] Similarly, the Walltown Children's Theatre in Durham, North Carolina, a recipient of the National Endowment for the Arts "Shakespeare in American Communities: Shakespeare for a New Generation" grant (about which I write more in chapter 6), announces that "part of the company's mission is to make theater and other performing arts accessible to North Carolina's growing Hispanic population."[71] In these types of statements, there is often an implicit logic that links making the classics accessible with generating diverse, new, and future audiences. The African-American Shakespeare Company, however, renders this logic explicit in its mission statement. For AASC, part of the mission is "to unlock the realm of classic theatre to a diverse audience who have been alienated from discovering these time-favored works in a style that reaches, speaks, and embraces their cultural aesthetic and identity." In addition, its mission is to make the classical production "ring relevant to diverse contemporary audiences."[72] While AASC's mission statement does not mention accessibility, its focus on cultural and temporal relevance identifies "diverse" audiences as traditionally "alienated" ones.

The fact that so many classical theatre companies describe as one of their goals the diversification of their audience, coupled with the fact that the NEA has created a grant that is specifically about creating "Shakespeare for a New Generation," is a good indication that the new, desired, and more diverse composition of the audience is still a work in progress. Although published in 1994, Amy Green's statement still rings true all these years later:

> It would be naïve, however, to conclude that these productions have in fact brought large numbers of otherwise alienated audience members into the classical theatre. That wide-reading, truly diverse audience is still more wish than reality.[73]

But why exactly is it still "more wish than reality" when many classical companies have embraced the notion that "the inclusion of diverse people, ideas, cultures and traditions enriches both our insight into the work we present on stage and our relationships with each other"?[74]

Donna Walker-Kuhne, the president of Walker International Communications Group, a consulting firm that specializes in audience development and arts marketing, defines audience development as the

> cultivation and growth of long-term relationships, firmly rooted in a philosophical foundation that recognizes and embraces the distinctions of race, age, sexual orientation, physical disability, geography and class. Audience development is also the process of engaging, educating and motivating diverse communities to participate in a creative, entertaining experience as an important *partner* in the design and execution of the arts.[75]

Walker-Kuhne identifies several obstacles that have prevented organizations from achieving their desired goal for a diversified audience, such as the failure to treat communities of color as partners in the creative endeavor. In writing about her early experiences working for The Public Theatre in New York, Walker-Kuhne notes that several cultural organizations in Harlem were "suspicious" because "they had been contacted by other 'white arts institutions' under the pretense of working together, and that after sharing their mailing lists with those institutions, they never heard from them again." One executive director even "stood up and announced that she would not participate in 'cultural appropriation.'"[76] In other words, organizations firmly rooted in communities of color have not always felt that their relationship with budding multicultural arts organizations is actually a *relationship*—that is, one in which both sides participate and benefit.

It is not surprising, then, that Walker-Kuhne constantly returns to the notion of a partnership in which both parties have a voice. She notes that "Audience development requires a strategic plan that is holistically integrated into the fabric of your arts institution. The strategic plan must be grounded in the history of the institution, as well as the history of the audiences you are seeking to attract."[77] Although Walker-Kuhne does not specifically discuss the casting models employed by multicultural classical companies, it seems clear that discussions, debates, and negotiations with community partners about the semiotics of race might help to strengthen both the companies' productions and the communities' comfort with and investment in these theatrical organizations. If, as Walker-Kuhne stresses, "Audience development is the merging of marketing techniques with relationship-building skills" by "building a consensus and understanding among people through personal interaction, dialogue *and* participation in the arts," then it is not simply enough to discuss and debate what plays should be produced and what actors should be included (or excluded).[78] Rather, it is vital to build a "consensus and understanding" about how race, color, and ethnicity should be employed to convey meaning (or not) onstage.

This is not to suggest that the consensus will be universal, or that every multicultural classical company will come to the same conclusion about what casting models work for that particular organization and that particular community. Rather, I think there will be as many models employed as there currently are today (perhaps even more if new ones are developed through these dialogues) because no two communities have exactly the same relationship with the semiotics of race. In the end, however, a community that has been involved in the creation of these casting models will be informed, interested, and invested in their local (or not so local) multicultural classical company. This would provide a giant leap forward in making Shakespeare new, popular, populist, and relevant: "Shakespeare for a New Generation."

A HOLISTIC MODEL: A STRATEGY FOR THE FUTURE

I imagine that some artistic directors and directors might be horrified by the suggestion that artistic decisions regarding race and casting should be made in consultation with the desired new community of audience members. While I agree that artistic integrity is important (directors, after all, have studied and developed their craft through years of training and practice), I am not convinced that either the artistry or ideology behind the semiotics of race onstage has been fully explored by most directors. The lack of a clear and consistent rhetoric about the various casting models, I think, points to this fact. Thus, in this section I briefly outline a holistic model for nontraditional casting because I think it will provide a way for multicultural classical companies to sharpen their notions of what exactly multiculturalism means in their organization. Of course, I am borrowing the notion of a holistic approach from Donna Walker-Kuhne's advice that audience development requires a strategic plan that is "holistically integrated."[79] As she says, "If your audience development efforts are to be successful, every executive in your organization, every member of your board of directors, every department in your organization—from the person who answers the telephone to the person who collects the tickets at the door—must understand and support the initiative."[80]

I am also appropriating the holistic approach from the vocal training program that Scott Kaiser has developed at the Oregon Shakespeare Festival. Because OSF has multiple stages (some indoor and intimate, and one outdoor that is modeled on a traditional Elizabethan stage), its company members have to be able to switch between "various styles of verse speaking," and "these skills are very specific by director, venue, and character."[81] As the director of company development, Kaiser works closely with 1) the artistic director to choose which shows should go on which stage, 2) the directors to determine how best to fit their vocal preferences for the specific stage in use, and 3) the actors to help adapt their vocal styles for the director's preference and the stage in use. Thus, this is a holistic model that demonstrates that no artistic decision is made in isolation; rather, there is always a negotiation between all of the parties involved. Nonetheless, it is coordinated by one person.

For a holistic approach to nontraditional casting within the multicultural classical company, the artistic director or a director of diversity initiatives (or a similar position) needs to function as the coordinator. The point is that this person needs to be in a position in which he/she is at the table for all of the major decisions because the casting models employed will affect every aspect of the company's season: the productions chosen, the directors hired, the actors cast, the marketing materials created (including posters, fliers, mailings, and production notes), the talkbacks planned, the outreach to schools and the community, the audiences targeted, and so forth. If a classical theatre company already has a director of diversity initiatives, then he/she is probably already a part of these discussions. What I want to emphasize is that he/she needs to ensure that the casting models employed—the company's approach to the semiotics of race, color, and ethnicity onstage—are a part of every discussion. While it is imperative that the director advocate for the diversification of the company, it is not enough to achieve the numbers (a target percentage, diversification beyond black and white, etc.). As part of advocating for the diversification of the company, the director must facilitate the dialogues about what this diversification means both offstage and onstage.

As many organizational behavioralists will advise, the first step should involve changing the culture and practice within the organization. The director of diversity initiatives should work to "[break] down silos within the organization by creating more channels of cross-departmental communication and collaboration."[82] As Betty Farrell notes, "Work groups, cross-divisional teams, meetings, and retreats are . . . longer-term strategies for changing the dynamic process through which an organization works."[83] For example, a group comprised of a vocal coach, an actor, a marketer, a production designer, the audience development specialist, a board member, and a lighting designer might have incredibly productive and insightful ideas about how the semiotics of race, color, and ethnicity should function on the company's stages. This group should not only function internally, however. It should also hold conversations within the community about 1) what casting models they think the company employs; 2) what casting models they think the company *should* employ; 3) how the company should convey what models it employs; and 4) ways for the company to further conversations both internally and externally about casting models and the semiotics of race onstage.

Although Walker-Kuhne is writing specifically about audience development, I would like to appropriate her quotation to speak to multicultural development more broadly: "[Multicultural] development means educating not only your audiences but also the artists whose work is ultimately the foundation on which the initiative rests. You have to take on the role of educators, creating systems that inform your artists and audience about your vision and that build support based on shared interests."[84] By bringing discussions about casting models and the semiotics of race to the fore, multicultural classical companies have the opportunity to shift what appears to be a long-term stalemate. Despite the fact that many American classical theatre companies promote themselves as being invested in diversity, in reflecting and including a diversity of people, most have not resolved what it means to be multicultural and classical at the same time. Although gains have been made in "rewrighting" Shakespeare through cross-cultural productions, through the pairing of Shakespearean productions with non-Western classics, and through the inclusion of multiracial casts (as Amy Green notes, "In our age of interpretation, directors of progressive and experimental bent take for granted their liberty to remake, rework, 'rewright' what venerable playwrights have wrought"), Shakespeare is still not widely considered vulgar, or, of, by, and for the people, all people.[85]

CONCLUDING THOUGHTS

At the First National Symposium on Non-Traditional Casting in 1986, the participants debated who was ultimately responsible for enabling nontraditional casting to flourish: agents, casting directors, producers, directors, actors, reviewers, or audiences. When one begins to parse the various constituencies involved, it becomes clear just how slippery and difficult it is to determine how color, race, and ethnicity are interpreted onstage and who helps to solidify that interpretation. Of course, the obvious answer to the question is that each individual involved in the process decides for him/herself *and* that everyone decides together. Everyone involved in a Shakespearean performance makes conscious and unconscious decisions about the semiotic significance, or insignificance, of race in performance, but the power to determine the ultimate semiotic relevance, or irrelevance, is completely contingent on the serial effects of the decisions made by everyone involved.

While it is important to analyze the dynamics of each of the elements within the production and reception of racialized performances, this type of discussion may mask a larger problem: the fact that there are very few sustained discussions between these varying constituencies about these very problems. Despite the fact that the Non-Traditional Casting Project initiated a more systematic approach to discussing nontraditional casting in 1988 through the publication of the *Beyond Tradition* collection, and despite the fact that August Wilson and Robert Brustein had public debates throughout 1996 and 1997 about nontraditional casting, the debates have remained more academic than practical. Very few theatre companies have had open discussions about the dynamics of race in performance. As I have written elsewhere, actors of color often remark that directors neither initiate nor facilitate discussions about the semiotics of race in their productions; frequently they do not share their visions for how race should be read and interpreted, nor do they create an environment in which cast members feel comfortable questioning that vision or offering their own visions.[86] In turn, theatre reviewers often do not write about the semiotics of race in performance because producers and directors have not offered any guidance on their own visions.

This silencing has had a chilling effect on the development of twenty-first-century theatre: one might call it a stunting effect. While it is clear that nontraditional casting practices are common enough now to be considered traditional, we still have not had widespread debates about the significance of these traditions.

Part of the silencing comes from the idealistic notion that theatre should be "that last bastion of illusion." Arguing for complete colorblindness in theatre (including a return to white actors playing Othello in blackface), the playwright Neil LaBute, writes, "This is not an argument about opportunity or imbalance; all I'm asking is that you let the theater, that last bastion of illusion—a place of magic and hope and imagination—remain exactly that. The stuff that dreams are made of."[87] While it is true that theatre offers a space in which illusion can and should flourish, Anna Deavere Smith's formulation of the relationship between the realities of constraining social constructions and the theatre's defiance of "the real" offers a slightly more nuanced take. After listing a series of "chains that come from our inhibitions about a multitude of things," Smith writes, "The chains are real. But the pure fact of the matter is that art defies the real. . . . [It] does not reiterate the real. Your passion must be greater than your chains or you cannot create art."[88] In other words, the "last bastion of illusion" that LaBute celebrates cannot be created without passion and dialogues about the *real chains*. These chains cannot be ignored; they must be cut through together.

As the developmental psychologist Beverly Tatum has written, our modern society's rhetoric about the value of colorblindness has had the nefarious outcome of silencing discussions about race. Addressing the way many parents are embarrassed by their young children's questions about racial difference, Tatum notes:

> The White mother, embarrassed by her child's comment [about racial difference], responds quickly with a "Ssh!". . . . Perhaps afraid of saying the wrong thing, however, many parents don't offer an explanation [for racial difference]. They stop at the "Ssh," silencing the child but not responding to the question or the reasoning underlying it. Children who have been silenced often enough learn not to talk about race publicly. Their questions don't go away, they just go unasked. . . . My students have learned that there is a taboo against talking about race, especially in mixed settings. . . .[89]

Tatum's warning about what is implicitly learned from silencing discussions about the causes and meanings of racial difference seems entirely too applicable to the problems facing twenty-first-century theatre. Too often questions about race have been met with a "Ssh!" by directors, producers, actors, and theatre critics: many have internalized that it is a "taboo" to raise questions. It has become common to cast Shakespearean plays in nontraditional ways, but the real questions and answers about if, and how, audiences see and understand the meanings of those performances have been silenced. As Tatum warns, however, the "questions don't go away, they just go unasked."

FIGURE 5.1 Ron Vawter in the Wooster Group's 1981 production of *Route 1 & 9 (The Last Act)* (directed by Elizabeth LeCompte). Photo by Nancy Campbell.

Mark Rylance doesn't like the label *authentic*. . . . Instead of *authentic*, the umbrella term for the conditions of preparation and performance Rylance enlists in [the Globe Theatre] project is *original practices*. . . . One objection to *authentic* is its hint of the ersatz. It has become an advertising label like *genuine*, used in hawking imitation art of theme park phoniness. So used, *authentic* actually means inauthentic. . . . The other objection to *authentic* is the reverse, that it claims too much. Today's audience and actors can never be Elizabethan, and from them all else flows. So Rylance says he considers *authentic* to be "confusing and arrogant.". . . In contrast, *original practices* is designedly plural.
—CHRISTOPHER RAWSON[1]

5

Original(ity)

OTHELLO AND BLACKFACE[2]

IN THE PREVIOUS chapter I analyzed the logic and rhetoric of multiculturalism in twentieth- and twenty-first-century classical theatre companies, and I concluded on a very practical note, providing a strategy for a more holistic approach to nontraditional casting. In organization, chapter 4 moved from an analysis of the theatre companies' logic into an in-depth discussion of their potential practices. In this chapter, I continue to examine a specific theatrical practice, but my analysis will be more deeply theoretically engaged because of the nature of the practice examined. While many American classical theatre companies advertise themselves as being multicultural, as I just demonstrated in chapter 4, there has been a recent wave of criticism that advocates for experimentation with an "original practice" that was employed on Shakespeare's sixteenth- and seventeenth-century stages: the application and employment of blackface. As Dympna Callaghan has argued, "Othello was a white man."[3] That is, he was originally created for, and performed by, the white Renaissance actor Richard Burbage. Despite the modern production history to the contrary—with its long line of famous black actors performing the eponymous role—the part and the play were not written for black or even dark-skinned actors. Instead, Othello was a white man in blackface makeup.

Recently, many theatre companies, including London's Globe Theatre, Shakespeare & Co. in Lennox, Massachusetts, and The Blackfriars in Staunton, Virginia, have been experimenting with original-practices productions: that is, productions that utilize original practices from the Renaissance stage. As the epigraph to this chapter makes clear, however, these companies distinguish between the notions of authenticity and originality. In fact, original practices are usually identified as an adherence to recreated Renaissance theatre spaces (including no artificial lighting), costuming, music, dance, and even single-sex casts. As Tim Carroll, the Associate Director of the Globe from 1999–2005, explained in 2003, there were, however, original practices that the Globe was not pursuing. In an interview, he declared that Elizabethan acting styles, pronunciation, and racial casting were three original practices he found unnecessary. Focusing on pronunciation, he explained, "It's deadly to suggest to actors that there is one correct pronunciation or dialect. None of those actors would have sounded then as they sound now; they came from all over England."[4] On employing black actors, he explained "it's a pure accident of history" that there were no black actors in the Renaissance.[5] Including actors of color on the twenty-first-century stage, he argued, is as natural as including American actors, like the Globe's Artistic Director, Mark Rylance.

Interestingly, Carroll and the Globe Company reversed views on original pronunciation only one year after these comments were made. Contradicting his earlier claims about original pronunciation, Carroll argued, "To be sure, some previously well-known words were less familiar, but in that they were in the same boat as the characters in their original-practice costumes: we might not recognize them, we might not understand or even like them, but we can see that they belong together, that they come from one world."[6] So where does this leave actors of color and the historical practice of blackface? Clearly actors of color do not "belong" in "the same boat as the characters in their original-practice costumes," while blackface does.

While Dympna Callaghan's claim that "Othello was a white man" serves as a provocative jumping-off point for a discussion about the distance between the early modern theatre and modern ones, other scholars and practitioners have advocated for a practical bridging of that distance on ideological grounds. For example, Elise Marks has posited that black actors who play Othello have been received more coolly by film and theatre reviewers than white actors because "only a non-African knows how to be the perfect African, at least for the emotional fantasy-use of a thrill-seeking white audience. A real black actor . . . has too much independent selfhood getting in the way."[7] Although Marks does not specify how this "fantasy-use" performance of blackness ought to be staged in practical terms, several other scholars and practitioners have advocated for a return to blackface productions of Othello. Despite the fact that these scholars and practitioners disagree on theoretical grounds, they nonetheless come to similar practical conclusions: that Othello should not be performed by a black actor and, thus, blackface must be a viable performance option if productions of *Othello* are to continue.

I list four examples at length because it is important to analyze how these scholars and practitioners grapple with the factors that impact the semiotic significance of blackface performances of Shakespeare. In chapter 4, I wrote at length about what I mean by the semiotic significance of race in performance. It is an understanding about if and how an actor's race is endowed with any meaning within a performance—whether realistic, symbolic, or otherwise. It explains how an audience interprets the meaning of an actor's race within the larger scope of the theatrical visit. The scholars and practitioners that I cite here offer radically different justifications for the employment of blackface, and these justifications impact their implicit understandings of the semiotic significance of race and color in performance.

For example, in 1997, Sheila Rose Bland, a freelance actor and director, argued that a modern performance of a

blackfaced Othello would be seen by the audience, both black and white, as "other"—an outsider—a caricature. This would alienate and cause discomfort to the audience. By casting "real" blacks to play Othello . . . Shakespeare's original intent in writing *Othello* may well have been cloaked. . . . To see an actual black man kissing an actual white woman on stage is a powerful image—but one that misrepresents an even more powerful image on stage intended by Shakespeare: to see a white man in blackface kiss a white man in woman's clothing.[8]

The following year, Hugh Quarshie, the celebrated black British actor, made a similar argument when addressing the University of Alabama Hudson Strode Theatre. Quarshie declared:

if a black actor plays Othello does he not risk making racial stereotypes seem legitimate and even true? When a black actor plays a role written for a white actor in black make-up and for a predominantly white audience, does he not encourage the white way, or rather the wrong way, of looking at black men. . . . Of all parts in the canon, perhaps Othello is the one which should most definitely not be played by a black actor.[9]

Likewise, Hugh Macrae Richmond has argued that "a more accurate title for the play would be *Iago*, acknowledging that, because of [the audience's] superior knowledge of [Iago's schemes], we can never identify fully with Othello's overtly mistaken point of view."[10] Because of this interpretation, Richmond questions the modern tradition of casting black actors to play Othello.

> The irony is that such casting invites a non-aesthetic identification with the actors as truly representatives of the historical victims of just such conde-scension, which is potentially at odds with the author's more objective intent, to display the tragic fact that racism may distort its victims' own behavior. . . . [W]e might identify less with the emotional extravagance of Othello if we know he is not acted by someone of actual African descent.[11]

More recently, Virginia Mason Vaughan has argued that "a major ingredient in the audience's fascination with the Moor is the pleasure of seeing the white actor personate a black man and knowing that this is what he or she is seeing."[12] Acknowledging the pleasure of this "double consciousness" of viewing,[13] Vaughan suggests:

> While I would not go so far as Sheila Rose Bland and describe Shakespeare's original Othello as a "minstrel show" with Iago in the role of Mr. Interlocutor, cues in the text do call attention to the Moor as an impersonation, sporadi-cally reminding the audience that the actor's blackness is a façade.[14]

Thus, Vaughan concludes her book by advocating for "the Globe, the reconstructed Blackfriars in Staunton, Virginia, and other experimental theatres [to] consider offering selected blackface performances."[15]

After reading these calls for a return to blackfaced performances of Shakespeare, one must ask what the relationships are between known original practices, assumed authorial intentions, audience reception(s), and modern productions. What is the relationship between an original practice (a white actor playing Othello) and the authorial intent (Shakespeare's design for a white actor as Othello)? What should be the relationship between the assumed authorial intent and a modern production? And what is the relationship between practice and reception when modern blackfaced versions of Othello are produced?

The scholars and practitioners cited above seem to swing between these dis-courses, alternating between investing intention, practice, and reception with the power to determine the semiotic significance of blackface in historical, cultural, political, and practical terms. For instance, Sheila Rose Bland is interested in "alienat[ing] and caus[ing] discomfort to the audience" by staging "Shakespeare's original intent."[16] This sounds remarkably similar to a modernist, Brechtian take on the importance of distancing the audience from the actors and actions depicted. Nevertheless, Bland clearly relies on a notion of authorial intent; she states that she is interested in returning to "Shakespeare's original intent." One should ask, however, if and how a theatrical practice reveals authorial intent.

Hugh Quarshie, on the other hand, focuses on the "white way, or rather the wrong way, of looking," thereby emphasizing the power of audience reception to determine the semiotic significance of blackface.[17] Nevertheless, he too conflates practice with intention when arguing that the role was "written for a white actor in black make-up." While Hugh Macrae Richmond places the modern audience's "non-aesthetic identification" with the black actor as Othello in opposition to the "author's more objective intent," practice and intent are still conflated in his discourse as well.[18] And finally, Virginia Mason Vaughan focuses primarily on reception—the "pleasure" that is experienced by the audience through the knowledge that the blackface enacted is an impersonation of blackness—but she also privileges "Shakespeare's original *Othello*."[19] It is unclear, however, if this privilege is achieved through the original practice, the authorial intent, or the audience's assumptions of intention.

Theorizing the performative nature of the employment of blackface in early modern England, one must grapple with the nature of mimesis. As Michael Davis writes, the relationship between the real object and the mimetic representation of it is "something like the relationship of dancing to walking. . . . Mimesis involves a framing of reality that announces that what is contained within the frame is not simply real."[20] Thus, tracing the use of black costumes, black makeup, and black vizards in medieval mystery plays and city pageants, critics like Eldred Jones, Elliot Tokson, and Anthony Barthelemy have argued that mimetic performance styles increased when an awareness of, and exposure to, Africans occurred through trade in Renaissance England.[21] As has been documented, Tudor and Stuart courts employed numerous blacks as servants and curiosities. In addition, new research reveals that the use of blacks as servants was more widespread throughout early modern England than was previously assumed.[22] While it is safe to conjecture that the increased presence of actual black men and women affected theatrical representations, the exact relationship between real black bodies and theatrically depicted ones is fraught and complex.

As Callaghan has argued, there were "two distinct, though interconnected, systems of representation . . . [with] the display of black people themselves (exhibition) and the simulation of negritude (mimesis)."[23] Callaghan goes on to argue that these "phenomena are the poles of the representational spectrum of early modern England" in that the black people in exhibitions had no control over their representation, while the white actors in blackface did. As Callaghan argues, "power resides almost entirely with the spectator" in cases of exhibition.[24]

In this chapter, I take seriously these disparate calls for the cessation of black actors as Othello, asking how audiences will receive the use of blackface in a modern Shakespearean production. Shakespeare stands in the center of this chapter's spotlight not only because Shakespearean scholars and practitioners have been extremely vocal about the history of, and potential return to, blackface performances, but also because the power of Shakespeare's cultural capital intensifies the frequency with which convention, practice, and intention are entangled and collapsed. Despite the fact that in our poststructuralist world it is unfashionable to approach texts and productions through the lens of authorial intention, the force of Shakespeare's cultural capital keeps intentionality active. Because of the tendency in popular culture to impart universally positive motives to Shakespeare, I am interested in analyzing the tensions between intention, practice, and reception when blackface is proposed for contemporary Shakespearean performances.

As reception theorists like Susan Bennett have argued, race must not be ignored when analyzing the production-reception contract: it is a factor that influences production and reception *and* the relationship between the two.[25] The relationship between production and reception is deemed a "contract" precisely because they are mutually informing and mutually informed. As I have written elsewhere, "reception is never simply determined by the production itself. Instead, reception is complicated not only by the immediate effects of the production (what is being staged, where it is being staged, when it is being staged, etc.), but also by a larger, multilayered history of viewing (which bodies have historically been made objects, which bodies have historically been made subjects, which bodies have historically been allowed to be spectators, etc.)."[26] Yet, an analysis of the performance of race in *Othello* highlights the unique warping effect of Shakespeare's cultural capital, and, thus, this chapter strays far from Shakespeare at times to emphasize the unusual power of this effect.

I begin with an examination of three recent examples of non-Shakespearean blackface performances to demonstrate the failure of intention to guarantee a particular kind of reception: one could call the desired reception "an opposition gaze," a way of looking and analyzing that challenges traditional semiotic meanings and values associated with blackface.[27] Then I examine the ways legal theorists have addressed intention, practice, and reception, especially in artistic freedom cases involving public officials who have performed in blackface, to present the complex ways intention and reception have been theorized in legal terms. These seemingly disparate points of analysis enable a more complexly informed discussion of the potential, and potential pitfalls, for Shakespearean productions in blackface. Ultimately, I contend that the conflicting desires for a return to Shakespeare's original intent and for an appropriation of the cultural and political semiotics of blackface may signal the problems with Shakespeare and Shakespeare's cultural capital rather than any inherent problems with the performance of blackface itself. At the end of the chapter I focus closely on the dual meaning of "original" as both originary and wholly new to demonstrate the tension created by Shakespeare's authority. As the epigraph for this chapter illustrates so neatly, there is a real tension between the rhetoric of authenticity, which seems to rely on a false and exclusive sense of the original, and originality, which wants to claim itself as "designedly plural" and, therefore, inclusive.[28]

THE DISTANCE BETWEEN INTENTION, PRACTICE, AND RECEPTION

Three contemporary examples of non-Shakespearean blackface performances illustrate how challenging it is to attempt to control the semiotic significance of a blackface performance. They demonstrate the failure of intention to guarantee specific responses from audiences. In 1981 the experimental New York City theatre troupe the Wooster Group put on *Route 1 & 9*, a production that melded scenes from Thornton Wilder's 1938 play *Our Town* with a reconstruction of Pigmeat Markham's blackfaced comedy routine. Dewey "Pigmeat" Markham, of course, was a black minstrel comic who blackened up well into the 1940s. He is most well known for his "heayah come da judge" routines. I offer two different accounts of the *Route 1 & 9* controversy to emphasize the unusual tensions that arise in determining the significance of mimetic intention in blackface performances (see Figure 5.1).

The first comes from Errol Hill and James Hatch's *A History of African American Theatre*. Hatch writes of the 1981 performance:

> Performed by four white actors in blackface, the piece generated a widely reported racial controversy. Because of the blackface segment, the New York State Council on the Arts cut Wooster's funding by 43 percent. . . . Comments by the director and one of the actresses provide a glimpse into how successfully the racist history of blackface had eluded both white women.[29]

According to Hatch's assessment, the production got away from the "white women" who organized the show. Because of their naïveté, his argument follows, the "racist history of blackface eluded" them, revealing the problematic nature of their intentions. Hatch is careful not to condemn blackface outright. Instead, he relies on an argument based on intentionality, thereby creating a space for the reader to imagine that he would welcome, perhaps even applaud, a blackface production that did take the "racist history of blackface" seriously. This subtext also implies that these "white women" unwittingly foiled this important opportunity. In other words, Hatch's analysis of their intentions impacts and determines his analysis of the production and its reception.

John Strausbaugh provides an entirely different account of the controversy surrounding the *Route 1 & 9* production. Here is Strausbaugh's assessment:

In 1981, even a very high-concept and well-intentioned use of blackface landed the experimental Wooster Group in trouble. . . . The idea was to comment on Wilder's lily-white portrait of a "typical" American town, not to make fun of Black people, but some critics and audience members missed the point entirely.[30]

For Strausbaugh, unlike Hatch, the intentions of the Wooster Group's organizers were pure: "not to make fun of Black people." The problem, according to Strausbaugh, rested squarely on the shoulders of the "critics and audience members [who] missed the point." For their diametrically opposed receptions and assessments of *Route 1 & 9*, Hatch and Strausbaugh nevertheless implicitly agree that intentionality is central to interpreting the semiotic meaning of a blackface production. Both return to *their* interpretations of the intentions of the creators of *Route 1 & 9*. But as must become clear from their opposing understandings of the Wooster Group's intentions, intentionality is always subject to interpretation in production. Even artists themselves revisit their own conceptions of their intentions after performing something in front of an audience.

One need only think of my second example, the scandal involving the comedian Dave Chappelle, to find a concrete example of this. As many will recall, in November 2004, Chappelle was taping a sketch for his television show in which he appeared in blackface when he suddenly left the set and subsequently fled the country without explanation.

In the first interview following his departure, Christopher Farley, a reporter for *Time* magazine, explains that Dave Chappelle:

thought the sketch was funny, the kind of thing his friends would laugh at. But at the taping, one spectator, a white man, laughed particularly loud and long. His laughter struck Chappelle as wrong, and he wondered if the new season of his show had gone from sending up stereotypes to merely reinforcing them. "When he laughed, it made me uncomfortable," says Chappelle. "As a matter of fact, that was the last thing I shot before I told myself I gotta take a fucking time out after this. Because my head almost exploded."[31]

Although Chappelle's intentions were to send up stereotypes, his comments seem to indicate that he feared two distinct but interrelated problems. First, he expresses a fear that he succumbed to a simplistic reinforcement of racial stereotypes, that he internalized and, therefore, reproduced racist portrayals of blacks. This fear is

FIGURE 5.2 Dave Chappelle as the Black Pixy/Minstrel. Film still from *Chappelle's Show*.

FIGURE 5.3 Dave Chappelle reacts with disgust to his inner Black Pixie/Minstrel. Film still from *Chappelle's Show*.

familiar and has been explored in many plays, novels, films, and, of course, literary and performance criticism. In fact, one might even label it the "Othello Syndrome" because *Othello* is one of the first Western texts to demonstrate the potential violent outcome of internalizing the racist constructions of blackness. Chappelle's second fear, however, is slightly more complicated and less familiar. He seems to fear that even if his intentions are pure—sending up stereotypes instead of reinforcing them—he will not be able to control the reception of the images he creates. He cannot control why white (or black) spectators laugh *or even* how "loud and long" they laugh.

As many journalists and academics have noted, Chappelle's story eerily brings to life my third example, Spike Lee's 2000 film *Bamboozled*, in which a black television writer attempts to write a modern day minstrel show satirizing the American desire for portrayals of unsuccessful blacks. In the film, the black writer, Pierre Delacroix (played by Damon Wayans), explains that his producer:

> wants a coon show so that's what I intend to give him. The show will be so negative, so offensive, and racist. Hence, I will prove my point. The point being that [he], the network, does not want to see Negroes on television unless they are buffoons.[32]

Unfortunately for Delacroix, "Mantan: The New Millennium Minstrel Show" proves a huge success with both white and black audiences.

As a film project that satirizes almost every figure within it, *Bamboozled* asks its audience to think about the exact nature of Delacroix's motives, his intentions. Although he verbalizes an intent to send up stereotypical portrayals of blacks, he also seems to have internalized some of the racist values of white America: he changes his name; he puts on an affected accent; he seems to disavow his family, and so forth. And yet, it is not simply Delacroix's mixed motives—his mixed intentions—that enable the success of the minstrel show. Rather, the film hauntingly portrays the shooting of the pilot episode in which Delacroix watches, expecting the audience to be outraged by the resurrection of these blackfaced minstrel portrayals. While the audience is at first shocked, they come to love it by the end of the episode, applauding wildly. The film powerfully asks the viewer to think about who/what controls the semiotic significance of blackface in historical, cultural, political, and practical terms.

When explaining the satirical flip of the film, however, Spike Lee eschews the discourses of both intention and reception. Instead, Lee says, "with a twist of fate, they ['the audience and American popular culture'] end up loving this racist, stereotypical show."[33] By employing the notion of "fate" in this instance, Lee renders

FIGURE 5.4 "Sleep'n Eat" (played by Tommy Davidson) and "Mantan" (played by Savion Glover) star in "Mantan: The New Millennium Minstrel Show." Film still from *Bamboozled*.

FIGURE 5.5 "Mantan: The New Millennium Minstrel Show" proves a huge success with both black and white audience members. Film still from *Bamboozled*.

political, cultural, and social engagement/action powerless because he ascribes the change to an uncontrollable cosmic force. Lee's rhetoric about fate signals his unwillingness to declare what the relationships between intention, practice, and reception are when blackface is employed.

As W. J. T. Mitchell argues, however,

> *Bamboozled* is a metapicture—a picture about pictures, a picture that conducts a self-conscious inquiry into the life of images. . . . [Spike Lee] talks sometimes as if he had achieved a standpoint outside the "madness" of images, the "distorted" images of film and television. And yet if there is one thing *Bamboozled* makes clear, it is just how difficult it is to find this critical standpoint, to achieve a "just estimation" of images that transcends distortion and madness.[34]

Mitchell argues that Lee's rhetoric about *Bamboozled* being "outside the 'madness' of images" ignores the way the film itself presents the impossibility of achieving that outsider status. Building on Mitchell's argument, I want to highlight the way Lee's rhetoric also eschews distinguishing between intention, practice, and reception. Many of the initial negative critical responses labeled *Bamboozled* "a mess" politically, rhetorically, and visually precisely because of Lee's reluctance to resolve the complex relationship between intention, practice, and reception.[35]

LEGAL THEORISTS ON BLACKFACE AND INTENT IONALITY

These recent examples of non-Shakespearean blackface, then, demonstrate the tensions between practice, intention, and reception. The assumed intention may not be clear to the audience or critic, as the Wooster Group's *Route 1 & 9* exemplifies; the intention may not even be clear to the artist him/herself, as the Chappelle case illustrates; and the intention may prove completely irrelevant when certain images—like blackface—have "lives" of their own, as *Bamboozled* reveals.[36] When calling for a return to blackface performances of *Othello*, critics sometimes invoke the history of minstrelsy and blackface in the United States, and they sometimes invoke the more recent history of minstrelsy that I discuss in the previous section, but they never invoke the legal history of blackface, artistic freedom, or public arts funding. Legal theorists, however, seem to pick up where W. J. T. Mitchell ends his analysis of *Bamboozled*: that is, they deliberately forgo discussions of intention when determining the semiotic significance of blackface performances. There are two different but related sets of legal cases that can inform this analysis: the first set involves the legality of dismissing public officials who have performed in blackface in public, and the second set involves the legality of regulating public arts funding for controversial pieces of art. An analysis of these legal cases and the legal theories that support them reveals how judges and legal theorists avoid analyses of intention. Although they often include discussions of the artists' intentions, legal theorists time and again explicitly weigh the importance and significance of reception over the relevance of intentionality.

There are three recent cases involving public officials who have dressed and/or performed in blackface when they were off duty. In the first case, *Berger v. Battaglia*, a Baltimore police officer sued the Baltimore Police Commissioner for ordering him to cease appearing in public wearing blackface. Bobby Berger became a police officer in Baltimore, Maryland in 1972. During much of his time as a police officer he performed off-duty as a singer, often appearing in blackface to sing Al Jolson songs (he specialized in "Mammy"). The police department had not received any complaints about his behavior until 1982 when he moved his routine to a bigger venue in a local Hilton Hotel. When members of the NAACP complained both at the hotel and through local media outlets, the police commissioner ordered Berger to cease his act "on pain of being found in violation of the department's rule prohibiting activity on the part of a member of the department that tends to reflect discredit upon himself or upon the department."[37] Berger sued the police commissioner, arguing that his First Amendment rights (i.e., freedom of speech) were being violated. The initial finding in 1983 by the district court ruled against Berger, but upon appeal, the United States Fourth Circuit reversed the district court's findings and ruled in favor of Berger. Later the Supreme Court refused to hear the case, thereby upholding the Circuit court's decision (1986).

The second case *In re: Ellender* involves a judicial district court judge from Louisiana, Timothy Ellender, who went to a Halloween party in 2003 wearing an orange prison jumpsuit and handcuffs, which he borrowed from the local sheriff of his parish, a black afro wig, and blackface. He was escorted by his new wife, who was dressed as a police officer. When pictures of the judge in blackface and prison jumpsuit appeared in the local and national press, a commission was formed to investigate whether his actions violated certain canons of the Code of Judicial Conduct in Louisiana. The Commission and later the Supreme Court of Louisiana found that Judge Ellender's actions did indeed violate certain codes of conduct, and they ordered that he be suspended from the bench without pay for one year. In addition, he was ordered to take a course at one of the local universities that would "allow him to gain insight into the attitude of other racial groups, particularly groups where interrelations are marked by antagonism, discrimination and conflict."[38]

The third case, *Locurto v. Guiliani* was decided in April 2006, and involves one New York City Police officer (Joseph Locurto) and two New York City Firemen

(Jonathan Walters and Robert Steiner) who created a float for the Broad Channel Labor Day parade. Broad Channel is a small, predominantly white island community in southeast Queens, New York. The float was called "Black to the Future: Broad Channel 2098," and depicted what the island community would look like if it were integrated in the future. All three men donned blackface, black afro wigs, and overalls with no t-shirts, or cut-off jeans and old-looking t-shirts. As court documents reveal, "The float itself featured two buckets of Kentucky Fried Chicken on the hood of the flatbed truck. One of the participants ate a watermelon and . . . yelled at the crowd, 'Crackers, we're moving in.'"[39] After the *New York Times* and other local and national media sources ran articles about the parade, the NYPD and FDNY created commissions to investigate the actions of their officers. Both commissions found that Locurto, Walters, and Steiner acted in a manner unbecoming to their positions and ordered their dismissals. Locurto and friends then filed a lawsuit against Mayor Rudolph Guiliani and other officials, claiming that their First Amendment rights had been violated. The plaintiffs won in the district court, and the city was ordered to reinstate them, but the Second Circuit Court of Appeals finally ruled against the plaintiffs, arguing that their dismissals were legal and appropriate.[40]

While it may seem as if I have taken us far from the debate about blackface performances of *Othello*, I am interested in these recent legal findings because they offer a fascinating discussion about the tension between intention, practice, and reception. All three cases include lengthy discussions of the public officials' intentions for donning blackface. In *Berger v. Battaglia*, Bobby Berger argued that he was merely interested in entertaining people with "music . . . he had been interested in since childhood, when his family and neighbors gathered together at this parents' house for weekly sing-alongs."[41] In *In re: Ellender*, the court papers state that Judge Ellender's "intent [was] to be humorous by implying that Mrs. Ellender, who was newly married to him and who was reportedly young and attractive, had her husband under her control."[42] And in *Locurto v. Guiliani*, the plaintiffs argued not only that they wanted to be funny, but also that they "intended to promote an integrationist message."[43]

And yet, in two of the three cases the judges dismissed the relevance of the public officials' intentions. In *In re: Ellender*, for example, the Supreme Court of Louisiana ruled that

We agree with the mitigating evidence presented that Judge Ellender did not intend to offer an affront to the African-American community. Nonetheless, his behavior exhibits his failure to appreciate the effects of his actions on the community as a whole.[44]

Thus, the Court acknowledges and even accepts Judge Ellender's statement of intent, but it weighs the communal reception of his actions more heavily, specifically citing the negative media attention his actions garnered. Likewise, in *Locurto v. Guiliani*, the Second Circuit Court of Appeals finds:

> Whatever the plaintiffs' [Locurto, Walters, and Steiner] intentions, the message their actions conveyed was, from the vantage of our nation's history, sadly unoriginal. . . . We . . . find that the defendants' [the NYPD and FDNY] interest in maintaining a relationship of trust between the police and fire departments and the communities they serve outweighed the plaintiffs' expressive interests in this case.[45]

Like the judges in *In re: Ellender*, this court finds that the negative media attention "generated" by the public officials' actions was an important factor in the court's ability to assess the effect on the community.[46] And this effect on the community—one might call it the community's reception of these actions—outweighs the plaintiffs' First Amendment claims. Furthermore, Bobby Berger seems to have fared better legally precisely because there was not the immediate and widespread media focus on his blackface routines. After all, he did perform in blackface for close to ten years before anyone complained. To put it another way: his intentions could be weighed more heavily precisely because a negative community reaction was not immediate *and* perceptible through media coverage.

While debates about the balancing mechanism used to weigh the plaintiffs' First Amendment rights against their ability to perform their public-service positions efficiently are fascinating in terms of jurisprudence, I am more interested in the way this balancing mechanism privileges discussions of reception over intention.[47] It seems that First Amendment legal theorists widely agree that the theory upholding the right to free speech and artistic expression is one that is governed by "audience-oriented" ideas. In the 1973 landmark case *Miller v. California*, the Supreme Court established a three-pronged system for determining whether a particular speech act is *not* protected by the First Amendment, and the system heavily privileges audience reception. Two of the prongs of *Miller*, for example, require the court to determine whether the "average person, applying contemporary community standards would find that work, taken as a whole, appeals to prurient interest" and "whether the work, taken as a whole, lacks serious literary, artistic, political, or scientific value."[48] The emphasis in this approach on the "average person" and "community standards" focuses the law in reception theory, or, as legal theorists have termed it, audience-oriented theory. In addition, the Supreme Court has employed a "marketplace of ideas" theory, arguing that "it is the purpose of the First Amendment to preserve an uninhibited marketplace of ideas in which the truth will ultimately prevail."[49] This theory emphasizes that the communicative nature of speech must be "effective" with regard to the audience, otherwise the audience will not buy it in both literal terms and philosophical ones.

Again these cases, and the legal theories that underpin them, specifically do not support intentionality. As Anne Salzman Kurzweg, writing in the *Harvard Civil Rights-Civil Liberties Law Review*, asks, "Should an art piece be 'saved' from censorship or an artist escape an obscenity conviction because of what the speaker intended to accomplish via his creative act?"[50] The answer, according to the present audience-oriented interpretation of the First Amendment, is a resounding no, and this is supported by the second set of cases that I briefly discuss. These cases examine the legality of regulating public funding for controversial pieces of art. As I reported earlier, the Wooster Group's funding was cut by forty-three percent by the New York State Council of the Arts after they produced *Route 1 & 9*. Although the Wooster Group did not pursue a legal means to restore their public funding, a similar case came to court in 1992 and was finally resolved by the Supreme Court in 1998.[51]

When Congress eliminated money from the NEA's budget after the controversy involving the Mapplethorpe and Serrano exhibits, they adopted the Williams/Coleman Amendment, a bipartisan compromise, that dictated that the Chairperson of the NEA, in establishing procedures to judge the artistic merit of grant applications, shall "take into consideration general standards of decency and respect for the diverse beliefs and values of the American public."[52] Despite the fact that artists like Karen Finley sued the NEA on the basis of discrimination, the Supreme Court ruled that the amendment was legal. The ruling in effect solidified the audience-oriented interpretation of the First Amendment. Unlike Judith Butler's fascinating examination of "linguistic vulnerability," here I am not addressing the untenable nature of censorship.[53] Rather, I am challenging the notion, supported by "speaker-oriented" theorists, that a critical investigation of intention in performance is more semiotically relevant than a critical investigation of reception (the audience-oriented model).

ORIGINS, ORIGINAL, ORIGINALITY

By challenging the focus on intentionality when theorizing the semiotic import of blackface, I do not mean to present a stable, predictable, or even static view of reception. Unlike legal theorists like Anne Salzman Kurzweg, Lawrence Solum, and Eliot Krieger, who advocate for a speaker-oriented interpretation of the First Amendment because it might avoid the "undesirable majoritarian results" of an audience-oriented one, I do not believe that reception is static when it is "collectivist."[54] Intention, practice, and reception cannot be disentangled: they inform and challenge each other, as I hope the examples I have provided throughout this chapter demonstrate. I also do not want to suggest that determining reception is a simplistic matter. Reception is not universal, and there are, of course, ranges of reception. That is precisely why the three legal cases involving public officials in blackface rely on media coverage to determine "the effects of [their] actions on the community as a whole."[55]

Likewise, reception is not static because it can also change over time. The initial critical reception of *Bamboozled*, for example, was horrendous. The film was panned in the popular media, and it did not fare well at the box office either. Since the special edition of the DVD was released, however, the critical reception has changed considerably: it is now regarded as an important text and is often included on college and university syllabi. The film's release on DVD enabled a different kind of viewing, one that was frame-by-frame repeatable, rewindable, and skippable—in other words, audience controlled. Where critics panned the film initially for being "contradictory" and "confused," they now engage in asking, "To what degree do viewers participate in the very processes they are positioned by the film to criticize."[56] And, "Could it be the case that our oppositional gaze and attendant practices depend upon the effigy's characteristic talent for absorbing blame, and thus, that they perpetuate our dependence upon scapegoating and its attendant cruelties?"[57] As these questions demonstrate, the discussion has moved dramatically away from a discussion of intention to an attempt to untangle the processes and meanings of reception. The collectivity of reception is neither static nor fictional. Rather, it is fluid and quite palpable through media coverage, published reviews, blogs, message boards, and so forth.[58]

Because of the flexibility and mutability of reception, appropriations of stereotypes and negative images are potentially possible. By *appropriation* I mean the attempt to control and alter the meaning of disempowering rhetoric (e.g., nigger, bitch, queer, etc.) by those who did not initially contribute to the creation of dominant society's rhetoric (e.g., people of color, women, homosexuals, etc.). As Judith Butler argues, one can appropriate images, labels, and even entire discourses, but there is no way to cleanse "language [or performance] of its traumatic residue, and no way to work through trauma *except* through the arduous effort it takes to direct the course of its repetition."[59] Taking charge of the repetition of a painful discourse and/or performance, one may be able to appropriate and instrumentalize it, to create the "oppositional gaze" for which bell hooks advocates.[60]

This certainly occurred for the Wooster Group when they performed Eugene O'Neill's *The Emperor Jones* in blackface to much acclaim in both 1998 and 2006.

Despite the fact that the group was widely criticized for its use of blackface in *Route 1 & 9* in 1981, critics hailed *The Emperor Jones* for highlighting "the performative nature of race."[61] Kate Valk, the white actress who performed in blackface, "makes it clear that Brutus Jones is a white man's idea of a Negro."[62] The audience remains "at all times powerfully aware that we are witnessing an actress fashioning, with superb precision, a simulacrum of a stereotype."[63] These positive reviews demonstrate that the Wooster Group was able to appropriate and make politically and artistically active this old racist performance trope: they successfully appropriated, instrumentalized, and altered the use of blackface in the reviewers' eyes.

Although it is difficult to pinpoint any one reason for the different receptions of *Route 1 & 9* and *The Emperor Jones*, it seems clear that both the timing and the material affected reception: a blackfaced performance of *The Emperor Jones* in the 2006 post-*Bamboozled* world enabled the appropriation of blackface more readily than did *Route 1 & 9* in the Reagan era. In other words, the combination of the historical, cultural, and political worlds along with the text itself necessarily affects the reception of blackface performances. It is interesting to note that while the reviewers quoted above take into account the audience's awareness of the performative nature of race, they implicitly privilege the "*relationality* of image and beholder," to borrow W. J. T. Mitchell's phrase.[64] This *relationality*, of course, does not occur in historical, cultural, and/or political vacuums; rather, the "*relationality* of image and beholder" is informed by these various factors. This, of course, returns us to Susan Bennett's notion of the "production-reception contract" that I described at the beginning of the chapter: they are mutually influential.

Does this type of understanding of the mechanisms behind reception, then, not open the door for an instrumentalized blackface performance of *Othello*? If this type of analysis—one that encompasses performance and legal approaches to, and theories of, blackface—complicates a simplistic understanding of the relationship between practice, intention, and reception; and if attention to the "*relationality* of image and beholder" challenges the notion that intentionality creates meaning; then perhaps a blackfaced performance of *Othello* is not only viable, but also desirable. This is certainly the position that Jenna Steigerwalt takes in her provocative essay about performing race on original-practices stages. She writes, "Questions of race become frightening territory for original-practices companies as they attempt to maintain the goodwill of their ticket-buyers and donors. However, original-practices companies were also founded on the spirit of exploration and discovery, and in the belief in Shakespeare's ability to speak to everyone, which places them precisely in the opportune position to encourage experimentation and genuine discourse."[65]

And yet, one must acknowledge that Shakespeare is *the author*. While Mitchell brilliantly discusses the difficulty of controlling the meaning of certain images— they have their own "lives," as he says—with Shakespeare the difficulty is in controlling the meaning of his authorship and authority. Despite the fact that the recent history of blackface performances demonstrates how complex the relationships between intention, practice, and reception are when there is an attempted appropriation of blackface, these recent productions did not have to deal with the strange power of Shakespeare's authorship *and* the myth of Shakespeare's intentions.

As many scholars have noted, and as I have attempted to demonstrate in earlier chapters of this book, Shakespeare is one of the few authors who is assumed to have written timeless and universal plays (as Steigerwalt notes, there is a "belief in Shakespeare's ability to speak to everyone").[66] The construction of Shakespeare (a man who wrote plays in the sixteenth and seventeenth centuries for white men who performed in blackface and cross dressed) as the universal Bard (the poet who speaks for all ages) exemplifies a cultural desire for historical unity, cohesion, and organization. This, of course, is just simply a fantasy. Thus, in the case of blackface performances of *Othello*, it is important to acknowledge the power of the "Shakespeare Factor." Unlike other great playwrights, whose plays continue to be produced and enjoyed, Shakespeare alone has been described as the father of all humanity—a cultural construction that challenges almost all critical approaches to his work.[67] If Mitchell alerts us to the "lives" and "loves" of objects, then Shakespeareans must alert us to the authorship and authority of Shakespeare.

The issue, then, becomes how one can assess the relationships between intention, practice, and reception when they come to blackface *and* Shakespeare. As I demonstrated at the beginning of this chapter, the scholars and practitioners who have called for modern blackfaced performances of Shakespeare have reached their practical positions through radically different theoretical stances. Nonetheless, many frame their arguments in terms of a return to early modern *original practices*, and the dual meaning of "original" is apt for their calls. They want blackface to be original in the sense that it is accurate to Shakespeare's practices *and* intentions: as Quarshie says, Othello was "a role written for a white actor";[68] and, as Bland says, a "blackfaced Othello" was "Shakespeare's original intent."[69] But they also want blackface to be original in the sense that it is wholly new, a twenty-first-century creation that helps the audience understand the constructed nature of blackness: as Vaughan says, the text "call[s] attention to the Moor as an impersonation";[70] and, as Richmond says, this impersonation of blackness "display[s] the tragic fact that racism may distort it's victims' own behavior."[71] In other words, they hope the original practice (in the sense that it is both true to the seventeenth century *and* wholly new) will help create an activated and oppositional gaze—one that is "designedly plural," to return to the epigraph for this chapter.

But what semiotic work is Shakespeare doing in this formulation? Why Shakespeare? It is jolting to hear Spike Lee state, "Of course, no one uses blackface anymore,"[72] because it is Shakespeareans who hope that the practice can be revived through the Bard, the ultimate undead dead of literary and cultural figures. As Steigerwalt identifies, original-practices companies are invested in the "spirit of exploration and discovery," believing always that they are exploring the past in order to discover a new future. Or, they believe that original practices are "designedly plural" because this notion enables an espousal of the union of the origin, the original, and unique originality. It is no wonder, then, that one of the actors who auditions to star in "Mantan: The New Millennium Minstrel Show" in *Bamboozled* recites lines from Shakespeare's *Hamlet*! In fact, Kim Hall's new critical edition of *Othello* includes an entire section on minstrelsy in which she reminds her reader that "T. D. Rice first 'jumped Jim Crow' in New York after an Edwin Booth/Thomas Hamblin *Othello*."[73]

Interestingly, the critics who have attempted to place the most pressure on the semiotics of race in Shakespearean performance often end their investigations with the equivocal statement that their interests might just be leaving Shakespeare behind. Celia Daileader, for example, speculating about whiteface and blackface performance potentials in *Antony and Cleopatra*, muses:

> What if an actress of color—like Whoopi Goldberg in her appearance at the Oscars—were to 'whiten up' for the Liz Taylor look and play the beat-the-messenger scenes with allusion to Vivien Leigh's Scarlett O'Hara? A white actor in blackface as the messenger could invoke Hattie McDaniel's eye-rolling Mammy. . . . Then again, that would have little to do with . . . Shakespeare's play.[74]

Daileader admits that her fantasy about the potential to flip the traditional semiotics of race in *Antony and Cleopatra* takes her far away from "Shakespeare's play," but it is unclear if she is willing to go into that unscripted territory.

Likewise, Sujata Iyengar wonders if the significance of cross-racial casting in single-sex productions amounts to a racial bedtrick. She concludes, "we see something that diverts us (in all its senses) because it is an unexpected link in a chain of anticipated substitutions, but that does not question those expectations themselves, or why we have them. For that, we might have to leave Shakespeare behind."[75] Like Daileader's thought experiment about *Antony and Cleopatra*, one must wonder how willing Iyengar is "to leave Shakespeare behind" in the pursuit of the answer as to why audience's have certain "expectations" about both race and gender. Is Iyengar willing to leave Shakespeare to pursue this angle?

While these speculations end on slightly ambivalent tones, I rather agree with Hugh Quarshie's final assessment. After fantasizing about a production of *Othello* that would emphasize the "political and military context" of early modern Venice, the "ruthless pre-Christian culture" of the Venetians, and the "manner and extent of Othello's reaction to betrayal," Quarshie quips, "But, you may say, that's another Othello, not Shakespeare's. That's rather the point, isn't it?"[76] Dealing with the fraught reception of blackface minstrelsy in contemporary American society, we might do well to leave Shakespeare behind. By saying this, I am not suggesting that anyone should give up teaching, writing, or producing Shakespeare's plays. I, for one, certainly do not plan to do anything of the sort.

Instead, I am arguing that we will have to dispense with the cultural force of Bardolatry before we can advance creating and enabling an oppositional gaze for blackface performances. The appropriation of blackface might occur, but it will not occur through Shakespeare because the enduring legacy of Bardolatry enables the conflation of intention with production and the erasure of reception ranges. Shakespeare (the man, the plays, and the performances) is too strong a force in the cultural imagination to be discussed without a type of fictive intention. When it comes to Shakespeare, reception is always written out of production because it is implicitly positively written into it. The force of Shakespeare's cultural capital is too strong to forego the fantasy of the Bard's intentions as race-neutral or even race-progressive. Moreover, an uncomplicated promotion of this fantasy will not enable the appropriative moves that many scholars and practitioners demand. For that we will have to leave Shakespeare behind. In the next several chapters I explore different venues in which Bardolatry is left behind in the service of flipping the script on Shakespeare, race, and performance. As I will demonstrate, the common tension surrounding original(ity) is foregone when Shakespeare's authority is uncoupled from the text and performance.

FIGURE 6.1 The cast of Will Power to Youth's original adaptation of *Romeo & Juliet* (2007). Will Power to Youth is the flagship arts education and job training program at The Shakespeare Center of Los Angeles. Photo by Michael Lamont.

This country cannot expect a generation raised on gangster films and sex studies to maintain its leadership in the world. Or even its unity as a nation. Shakespeare has shaped our language and our culture. His works provide a common frame of reference that helps unite us into a single community of discourse.
—AMERICAN COUNCIL OF TRUSTEES AND ALUMNI[1]

A vital if subtle connection exists between a discourse in which those who are to be educated are represented as morally and intellectually deficient and the attribution of moral and intellectual values to the literary works they are assigned to read.
—GAURI VISWANATHAN[2]

6

Reform

REDEFINING AUTHENTICITY IN SHAKESPEARE

REFORM PROGRAMS

I BEGIN THIS chapter on Shakespeare, reform, and the erasure of race with two oppositional statements. In one corner we have the conservative, although self-de-scribed as "independent," organization the American Council of Trustees and Alumni (ACTA), a group that advocates for "academic freedom, excellence, and accountability at America's colleges and universities" and the "strengthen[ing] of general education" requirements, including the requirement of Shakespeare courses.[3] With two publications that lament the decline in *required* Shakespeare courses in English departments, ACTA declares, "A degree in English without Shakespeare is like an M.D. without a course in anatomy. It is tantamount to fraud."[4] For ACTA, it is an actionable outrage that "at the University of Virginia, English majors can avoid reading *Othello* in favor of studying 'Critical Race Theory.'"[5] The logic behind ACTA's outrage is that the theories and texts that address contemporary racial issues are not only supplanting the Western (i.e., "universal") canon, but also are at odds with it: "While Shakespeare and other traditionally acclaimed authors . . . are no longer required, many institutions . . . require students to study 'non-canonical traditions,' 'under-represented cultures,' and 'ethnic or non-Western literature.'"[6]

In the other corner we have Gauri Viswanathan's history of the formation of English literary studies as a discipline. Contra ACTA, Viswanathan sees the development of the Western literary canon as an "imperial mission of educating and civilizing colonial subjects in the literature and thought of England, a mission that in the long run served to strengthen Western cultural hegemony in enormously complex ways."[7] Viswanathan goes on to locate Shakespeare in the center of England's government-sponsored imperial endeavor by noting that schools run by missionaries rarely included plays by Shakespeare because they "reflected a pagan rather than a Protestant morality and would therefore exert an unhealthy influence on the natives," while the "books prescribed in government schools" included "Shakespeare's *Hamlet, Othello,* and *Macbeth.*"[8] Although Viswanathan does not advocate "that today's students must close their English books without further ado because those works were instrumental in holding others in subjugation," she does argue that "sustained cross-referencing between the histories of England and its colonies" will "progressively illuminate" Western imperialism.[9]

These arguments are diametrically opposed, and neither seems to offer the hope of a middle ground. According to their rhetoric, one must either accept that Shakespeare offers the potential to have "unity as a nation," or, that national unity comes at the price of "subjugation." Where exactly does this leave reform programs that utilize Shakespeare—the programs geared towards prisoners, gang members, inner city youth, low income families, rural communities, *and* business executives? After all, these programs are highly successful and profitable: this is a booming business in both the nonprofit and for-profit markets. Must these programs espouse a neocolonial rhetoric that positions them as working "to expose students [and others] to the enlightening and inspiring power of literature as literature," to quote ACTA?[10] Or, can they reject the inherent violent subtext of the imperial rhetoric that claims the need to introduce "in whole or in part, *by implantation or engraftment,* the improved Literature and Science of Europe, embodying, as these do, all that is magnificent in discovery, ennobling in truth, and elevating in sentiment"?[11]

And where exactly does a discussion about race fit into this dilemma? As Ania Loomba saliently points out, a critical engagement with race tends to disappear in colonial, neocolonial, and postcolonial rhetoric. The colonial rhetoric that ACTA appropriates makes a discussion about race irrelevant. As Loomba argues, "In the colonies Shakespeare was taught as the simultaneous epitome of a *particular* (special and unique) 'Western' and 'English' culture, and of *universal* human values, an approach that is still widely recycled. Thus Shakespeare, race, and colonialism have been connected by the very approaches that claim to be 'above' or not interested in these issues."[12] Likewise, postcolonial scholarship is not consistently willing to link imperial endeavors with early constructions of race and ethnicity.[13] To rectify this trend in postcolonial scholarship and pedagogy, Loomba advocates that teachers unite critical dialogues about race and neoimperial endeavors in explicit ways.

The reform programs that employ Shakespeare (or, what I call "Shakespeare reform programs") are all conducted by thoughtful, caring, and generous teachers, actors, directors, and business people, and the results that they advertise are stunning: they seem to be successful in multiple ways. Nevertheless, these programs seem to walk a tightrope between the neocolonial rhetoric espoused by groups like ACTA and the advocacy rhetoric espoused by postcolonial scholars like Viswanathan. Shakespeare reform programs vary in their target participants (prisoners, urban youth, rural youth, businessmen, etc.), facilitators (amateur directors, professional actors, teachers, politicos, etc.), and duration (years, semesters, weeks, hours, etc.). They are united, however, in their belief that personal reform can be achieved through Shakespearean study and performance, including the specific skills of close reading, analysis, embodiment, and reading/memorization. My argument builds on work done by others who have examined the disparate types of Shakespeare reform programs and those who have approached these programs through a postcolonial lens.[14] For as Niels Herold argues, "if postcolonial Shakespeare is about the complementary mechanisms of cultural inculcation and distancing, of imitation and resistance, then . . . [institutional Shakespeare] is a subaltern culture that relates to the dominant as the fringe on the margins does to the center."[15] Shakespeare is the center, which all of these reform programs position themselves as both distanced from and approaching towards.

Where I believe my work will differ significantly from that which has come before is in its dogged attention to the evasion and erasure of critical dialogues about race in these programs. The tightrope between neocolonial and postcolonial ethics and aesthetics which these reform programs traverse seems manageable only when dialogues about race are removed. To maintain the tightrope metaphor, critical discourses, dialogues, and debates about race seem to create a weight that threatens to topple the balance of these high-wire reformers. It is not that race is completely elided. Rather, it is audible in certain rhetorical moments and then eerily erased in others, only to echo and reverberate on the lower levels like a ghost or specter. This, I believe, signifies the ever-complicated place that race holds in discussions of both Shakespeare and reform.

With regard to Shakespeare, as this entire book attempts to reveal, dialogues about race and the semiotics of race (to return to a notion discussed at length in chapter 4 and chapter 5) are often assumed to be at odds with an espousal of

Shakespeare's universality. With regard to reform, the ethos is very different; it seems akin to a more politically correct avoidance of discussions about racial and ethnic specificities. Highlighting the moments of avoidance, erasure, and elision in discussions by and about these reform programs, I demonstrate how difficult it is to paint these programs in a progressive light. Despite the fact that many of these programs were created by people who have progressive beliefs— like an unflagging conviction that people can reform and improve if they learn certain skill sets—most of the programs avoid critical discussions about race in service to the notion that race, the history of racial constructions, and the history of racial inequalities are irrelevant in the teleological move towards personal improvement. Building on the theoretical argument I develop in chapter 5, I focus on the logic and rhetoric of the organizers and proponents of these reform programs to demonstrate how their stated intentions challenge their progressive beliefs.

In addition, this chapter differs from other work on Shakespeare reform programs through its employment of arts education evaluative lenses. In an influential study conducted by the Harvard Graduate School of Education research group, Project Zero, the ways arts education programs define, achieve, and evaluate excellence, or what they call "the signs of quality," are identified and defined.[16] While not all of the reform programs I examine would self-identify as "arts education programs" (especially the business-oriented Movers & Shakespeares program), they all employ and produce performances of Shakespeare's plots, scenes, and/or actual plays. In addition, all of the reform programs emphasize the process of collaboration and debate about the text over the final product, thereby promoting several of the "broad purposes of arts education," such as fostering creative thinking; providing ways to understand the world; providing ways to engage with community, civic, and social issues; providing a venue for self-examination; and helping the development of individual identities.[17]

Although not all of the matrices employed in *The Qualities of Quality* will be appropriate for my examination of Shakespeare reform programs, the detailed discussion about the "different lenses of quality" will provide an informative and unique way to engage the ways these programs define their strategies and desired outcomes.[18] Ultimately, I argue that the rhetoric espoused by the organizers and proponents of Shakespeare reform programs renders a clearly progressive outcome difficult to achieve. Because these programs rely so heavily on the fantasy of Shakespeare's authority, authenticity, and textual stability (instead of the notion that Shakespeare is merely a catalyst or medium), the high-wire tension between neocolonialism and progressive advocacy is maintained.

SHAKESPEARE THE INCORPORATOR

Prison programs that work to reform inmates through the study and performance of Shakespearean texts have existed in the United States since the American Civil War.[19] According to Niels Herold, the practice may be even older in the United Kingdom if one acknowledges that the sailors aboard *The Dragon* in 1607, who famously performed *Hamlet* and *Richard II* when they were off the coast of Sierra Leone, were "impressed seamen": that is, incarcerated individuals who were forced to labor shipboard.[20] According to Amy Scott-Douglass, "While prison Shakespeare is not an entirely new phenomenon, the 1980s and 1990s were especially remarkable in that a significant number of prison Shakespeare programs were initiated by professors and theatre directors across the country."[21] In the United States, Shakespeare programs are now employed in prisons in California, Indiana, Kentucky, Massachusetts, Missouri, and Wisconsin, to name a few. In the United Kingdom, there are similar programs, like Shakespeare Comes to Broadmoor, and the London Shakespeare Workout Prison Project.

Although there are no national statistics on the success of these programs, Lawrence Brewster's oft-cited report notes that participants in the California Department of Corrections (CDC) Arts-in-Corrections (AIC) program "demonstrate improved behavior through fewer disciplinaries [even] when those inmates who were disciplinary free before entering the program are excluded from the sample."[22] In fact, a frequently cited statistic is that AIC participants "have 75% fewer disciplinary actions and a recidivism rate that is 27% lower than the general prison population."[23] Likewise, the Shakespeare Behind Bars program at the Luther Luckett Correctional Facility in Kentucky boasts that, in twelve years, "30 convict players have earned their release. One has committed suicide; the rest have achieved a zero recidivism rate," which is remarkably better than the national average of 60% recidivism and/or death in renewed criminal activity.[24] If these figures are representative, then Shakespeare prison programs are hugely successful.

There have been numerous popular and scholarly works devoted to describing and analyzing these programs, and one might argue that it is the reform venue that attracts attention because it is neither wholly progressively humanistic nor wholly regressively Foucauldian. That is, it is hard to claim with any degree of certainty if these programs are successful because they teach critical thinking, reading, and self-embodiment. As the London Shakespeare Workout Program proclaims, "For many offenders entitlement to [the language of Shakespeare] has been all but previously impossible. . . . [T]he glory and the power of Shakespeare's language . . . is something that the prison residents can suddenly find for themselves; something they can share, and most importantly, something which they can own."[25] This is, of course, the promise of liberal humanism: that access to an education can be transformative; that knowledge and the tools for critical thinking are powerful. On the other hand, it also appears as if these programs merely inculcate the prisoners with a sense that morality and redemption stem from white, Western authors and their white, Western texts. For example, a prisoner in the Luther Luckett Correctional Facility unabashedly claims that Shakespeare is god-like: "Shakespeare still lives even though he's dead. His spirit lives on."[26] Unlike the rhetoric and ethos of liberal humanism, this sounds less liberating and more controlling—a hierarchical superstructure that keeps the author/text as superior and the reader/performer as abject and wanting (as in Viswanathan's estimation cited in the epigraph).

It is precisely in this grey area between a progressive humanistic rhetoric and a regressive neocolonial rhetoric that racial constructs and conflicts reside, hovering between the progressive realm that renders race irrelevant and the regressive realm that renders race erased or white-washed. Yet the critical attention to these programs has not engaged in the strange racial dynamics in a clear and coherent fashion. As Amy Scott-Douglass notes, many of these programs adopt a "color-blind policy when it comes to casting," and the common "approach to racial conflict and racial slurs in the plays seems to be not to talk about them directly."[27] In turn, the writers who address these prison productions rarely turn a critical eye to the way race is erased in the service of reform. These writers will faithfully note the racial makeup of the casts, usually commenting on the racial integration of the casts. For example, Jack Hitt, in his now-famous story on National Public Radio's *This American Life* about a prison Shakespeare performance of *Hamlet*, notes the cast was "half black, half white."[28] Yet he does not remark on the significance of this makeup unless it is to suggest that these prisoners, who are often known for creating segregated lives in prison, are integrated in this one prison venue. In other words, writers like Hitt describe these scenarios as unique experiences within prison, implying that they are inherently progressive. All of the Shakespeare prison programs employ colorblind casting—in which any actor of any race can play any role—and this fact has lured critics into an awed position of reverence over critical engagement.

Amy Scott-Douglass is one of the few scholars who has attempted to encourage a dialogue about the issues of race in the texts and the implications for casting and performance. In *Shakespeare Inside*, she recounts a discussion with several of the black actors in the Shakespeare Behind Bars program in which "the men are reluctant to talk" about race.[29] One inmate begins by protesting that "It's not about race; it's about humanity," but then another flatly states that he has not "seen any black Shakespearean character . . . that has a certain level of integrity or honesty about him."[30] The conversation ends on an ambivalent note with the group agreeing that Aaron the Moor from *Titus Andronicus* is a problematic character—perhaps a product of Shakespeare's youth and inexperience—while they describe Othello as "capable of remorse," "gentle," and "compassion[ate]."[31] The concerns about Shakespeare's (in)ability to create a black character with "integrity or honesty" are lost in this narrative of Shakespeare's progress, development, and increased racial sensitivity.

Scott-Douglass, of course, is aware that "race, performances of race, and injustices of racism" affect every facet of prison life.[32] Yet she accepts the prison program's logic that "the lived experience of brotherhood and not the physical approximation of kinship" should guide the rationale behind casting.[33] Here is Scott-Douglass's fuller account of the logic behind the prisons' colorblind practice:

> What matters more than anything else, they will tell you, is who is the best actor for the part. This, of course, is the mantra of colorblind casting in commercial theatre, but the unspoken and subjective criteria for what makes an actor the "best" actor in commercial theatre is hard to measure. In prison theatre, the criteria are very clear. The best actor for the part is the one whose history is the most similar to the character he or she is playing.[34]

In some ways the prison casting policy provides a tremendous advantage over casting practices in commercial theatres because age, race, gender, and physical ability are deemed irrelevant when positioned next to the inmate's "history." Similarly, one participant in the San Quentin Prison program claimed that Shakespeare programs "give us a chance to regain our humanity. To peel back the layers of who we are as men, and to know maybe I am worth something."[35]

But what "history" and what self-identity are deemed worthy? Yes, it is the history of past crimes, relationships, and victimizations. Scott-Douglass provides the example of a black, male inmate who plays Macbeth opposite a white, male Lady Macbeth: "their own relationship had been stormy in the past, so they thought it would be good for them to play the Macbeths; secondly, they are both in for murder, so they can identify with the Macbeths and feel as though they have a lot to learn from playing them."[36] But is that the only history worthy of exploration? Is there nothing rehabilitative or redemptive about a detailed examination (the inmates devote close to a year's time of focused rehearsal and performance) of one's racial, ethnic, or cultural history? Does identifying one's history as something separate from one's racial, ethnic, and cultural history not amount to an erasure? If redemption comes through self-examination, what tools are provided to disentangle the complex notions and constructions of the self on both a personal level and a social one? There are no clear answers to the questions I pose, and, thus, an enduring lacuna surrounds race in the logic and rhetoric of performance-based inmate rehabilitation programs.

Although not all prison Shakespeare programs read or perform an entire play, the Shakespeare Behind Bars program prides itself on studying and performing the plays in the First Folio. Part of the pride comes from working through the difficulties of an entire *Shakespeare* play, in which Shakespeare's name synecdochally stands for great literature, old literature, and, therefore, difficult literature. One inmate admits he used to hate Shakespeare, "But that was because I didn't understand him. I was ignorant to the fact of what he actually was saying. Big G, my roommate, was always quoting Shakespeare. . . . He'd quote it, and then after he'd leave I'd look it up."[37] The program's emphasis on the inmates' ability to grapple with and perform an entire Shakespeare play is often noted by the inmates with pride: the logic follows that there are no shortcuts to the text when the inmates are dealing with the First Folio. The reading skills that Shakespeare Behind Bars promotes are similar to the ones promoted by Rafe Esquith's widely regarded Hobart Shakespeareans, whose motto actually is "There are no shortcuts." Like Shakespeare Behind Bars, Esquith's fifth-grade Hobart Shakespeareans study and then perform an entire Shakespeare play "unabridged."[38]

Started in 1986 by Rafe Esquith in the Hobart Elementary School in Los Angeles, California, the Hobart Shakespeareans are a group of students who volunteer to meet, read, rehearse, and then perform a Shakespearean play after school. Because the public school serves an economically challenged area, many of the children in Hobart are the children of immigrants and English is not their first language. In fact, Esquith describes his classroom as an English as a Second Language (ESL) classroom with half of the children from Spanish-speaking families and the other half from Korean-, Chinese-, Vietnamese-, and Thai-speaking families. An iconoclast who rejects the pressures from his school administration to teach district-assigned textbooks, Esquith always teaches the classics, including John Steinbeck's *Of Mice and Men*, Alex Haley's *The Autobiography of Malcolm X*, Harper Lee's *To Kill a Mockingbird*, Lewis Carroll's *Alice in Wonderland*, Mark Twain's *The Adventures of Huckleberry Finn*, and *Anne Frank: The Diary of a Young Girl*. Of course, Shakespeare also plays a large part in Esquith's curriculum.

As Esquith advises, it is important for teachers to create a curriculum that taps into their own interests and enthusiasm: "Read your favorite books with your students; they will respond to your enthusiasm for the material. Remember: the goal is to demonstrate the joy of reading; the material used is less important than the teacher's level of excitement."[39] Because Shakespeare has been one of Esquith's lifelong passions (e.g., his father used to read him passages from Shakespeare at night), he decided early in his career that Shakespeare would be a great language-learning tool. About his third year at Hobart, he writes, "After a few weeks, I have a plan to help them with English. I love Shakespeare. I am still a beginner in the classroom, but I have a passion. . . . I tell the parents that by learning English, their children can have better lives."[40]

While Esquith is careful to note that "Shakespeare in our class is part of a larger picture. When we work on baseball, music, geography, it's all really the same lesson," he is most well known for the Hobart Shakespeareans, the students who volunteer to work on a Shakespeare play after school for the entire year.[41] With a nationally aired documentary about the program, a wide-range of international media coverage, a long list of famous patrons including Sir Ian McKellan, Hal Holbrook, Michael York, and Sir Peter Hall, and even foreign touring companies that market Hobart Elementary School as one of their U.S. destinations, the Hobart Shakespeareans have become the public face of Esquith's pedagogical theory and practice.[42] Moreover, it is the fact that these nonnative English speakers are performing "an unabridged play by Shakespeare" in "flawless" English that generates this attention.[43] Like the successful figures cited by Shakespeare prison programs, Esquith's students outperform their classmates on standardized texts, and many go on to prestigious colleges and universities.

I want to examine Shakespeare's position in Esquith's productions because I think that position impacts the contradictory ways issues of race in the texts, classroom, performance, and education policy are figured in the program's rhetoric. Despite the fact that Esquith urges teachers to teach literature about which they are passionate, and despite the fact that he readily admits that his program will not work well in all classrooms for all teachers, his rhetoric about Shakespeare makes the author, the texts, and the language seem *essential* to success. When asked "why Shakespeare," Esquith backs away from the answer that it was *his* passion. Instead he says, "Shakespeare tackled universal themes that we can all relate to: for example, honor and love."[44] He describes the plays as universally relevant and provides an anecdote about a young female student who played Prince Hal: "When asked what she thought *Henry IV* was about, the young girl who played Hal said the play was about 'how you find honor in a dishonorable world.' What is more relevant to a girl living and growing up in LA?"[45] In this logic, the girl's appropriative desires are highlighted (Shakespeare is whatever she wants him/it to be), but Shakespeare's universalism is also maintained (Shakespeare is always relevant and essential to a good education).

When pressed about moments in the texts that might challenge a sense of universality—the moments of racism, sexism, and homophobia in so many of the

FIGURE 6.2 The Hobart Shakespeareans perform *Hamlet* in their elementary school classroom. Film still from *The Hobart Shakespeareans*.

plays—Esquith claims three contradictory notions. First, he says that he alerts the students to these moments because that is part of a close, critical reading: noting these moments is an essential component to reading comprehension. Second, he claims that the plays are products of the time period in which they were written, and that they record languages and sentiments with which we may not identify in the twenty-first century: "Shakespeare records language that was appropriate for his time period."[46] And finally, Esquith argues that that the plays are commenting on racism, sexism, and homophobia and not trafficking in them themselves: "I think about these moments in terms of Hamlet's advice to the players. The purpose of playing is to 'hold the mirror up to nature'"; and "Do you think Shakespeare could write? Do you feel uncomfortable at times reading the plays? Maybe you are supposed to feel that way."[47] The logic behind these statements is obviously contradictory and moves from an argument that all language is political and worthy of close examination, to historical knowledge requires political leniency, to universal texts are universally good.

Similarly, Esquith offers contradictory comments on the significance of the races and ethnicities of his students. When talking about his students, Esquith both acknowledges the importance of his students' racial, ethnic, and cultural heritages and emphasizes the need for them to function and thrive as *Americans*. On the one hand he stresses, "I don't mind if they speak Korean with their friends and families because knowledge of multiple languages is good."[48] On the other, he says, "I want these kids to be Americans" and "I want these kids to feel like they're Americans."[49] Like many school productions, Esquith promotes a race-and gender-blind approach to casting: any student of any race or gender can play a part. Part of the ethos behind this decision stems from the meritocracy Esquith establishes in his classroom in which "all of the students know the [entire] play by heart" as a function of working through the play for a year.[50] But part of the ethos behind the practice also stems from Esquith's notion that it is important to strip the students of what he calls their "egos" because he teaches them "that there is only one star in the production: Shakespeare himself."[51] The juxtaposition of the children's "egos" with the "star" of "Shakespeare himself" renders race in the precarious position of being both highly visible and in need of blending in.

Because of the contradictory nature of these statements, many conservative critics have lauded Esquith, even when he espouses his progressive beliefs. For example, Abigail and Stephen Thernstrom, whose book *No Excuses* argues that there are no social or systemic reasons for racial gaps in learning, highlight Esquith's approach as a model for conservatives. The Thernstroms write, "'High expectations' are a current educational buzzword, with much hand-wringing about just how high those expectations can be for black and Hispanic children in poverty. There is no hand-wringing in Esquith's class."[52] The Thernstroms celebrate Esquith's approach precisely because the exact position and significance of the children's races, ethnicities, and cultures is kept in a strange status of limbo: they are important to reveal what anyone/everyone can accomplish, and they are unimportant next to Shakespeare's "star." Thus, at the end of their chapter on "Hispanics" the Thernstroms point to "Rafe Esquith's class" as they argue that success for Hispanic students depends on schools introducing these students "to the history, culture, and institutions of their adopted country."[53] This rhetoric, of course, brings us back to the neocolonial rhetoric employed by ACTA in this chapter's first epigraph.

Naturally, Rafe Esquith states that this attention from the right has not been wholly welcomed. Although he lists Abigail Thernstrom in the acknowledgments for *There Are No Shortcuts* ("Abby Thernstrom's right balances my left. She keeps me tough."), he also says, "I feel very uncomfortable with right wing support. I cannot control who loves what I do. Remember that my father was called by the McCarthy HUAC folks (and he refused to name names). It depresses me that the right believes that good behavior is somehow a conservative value."[54] Nevertheless, the neoconservatives embrace Esquith's approach precisely because it is Shakespeare—British Shakespeare, Western Shakespeare, white Shakespeare,

classical Shakespeare, classically difficult Shakespeare—who brings his His-
panic- and Asian-American students into "the history, culture, and institutions" of
the melting pot of America. Both for Esquith's left and Thernstrom's right (and the
prison programs discussed earlier) self-actualization comes through the adoption of
Shakespeare's language and culture. While those on the political left can argue that
the students are appropriating Shakespeare for their own ends, those on the political right can argue that it is *Shakespeare* who is transforming the students. Both
"Make Shakespeare Your Own" and "Make Yourself Shakespeare" remain viable.

Thinking about these programs in terms of the "lenses of quality" described by
Steve Seidel in *The Qualities of Quality*, I would like to discuss the collaborative
component that Seidel highlights. He argues that "quality" in arts education programs "seems to be, at least in part, a product of dialogue and debate that is probing,
frequent, collaborative, and explicit."[55] The way Shakespeare is constructed in the
prison programs like Shakespeare Behind Bars and inner-city school programs like
the Hobart Shakespeareans renders this type of "dialogue and debate" difficult.
The inmates and students are encouraged to produce "unabridged" versions of the
plays because their full-fledged incorporation into Shakespeare and, by extension,
America is the goal. Like the Goth queen's claim when she marries the Roman
emperor in *Titus Andronicus* ("I am incorporate in Rome" [1.1.459]), however,
incorporation does not occur without violence: to be incorporate means to be a
member of the whole, but it also means to be ingested and digested by the body
politic. In these programs, Shakespeare symbolically stands in for the body politic
that seeks both to accept and to digest/melt away the racial, ethnic, cultural, and
social differences of those who may not at first glance appear to be part of the
whole: Make Yourself American through Will Power.

THE EXPOSURE IS ALL

Not all Shakespeare reform programs focus on incorporation, however. Nonetheless, these programs still walk the tightrope of espousing the value of Shakespeare
through the rhetoric of liberal humanism and espousing the value of Shakespeare
through the rhetoric of neocolonialism. As chairman for the National Endowment
for the Arts from 2003 to 2009, Dana Gioia launched one of the largest programs
in the agency's history: the "Shakespeare in American Communities" initiative
brings performance and educational materials related to Shakespeare to every
community in the United States. Explaining the impetus behind the NEA's paradigm shift, Gioia states: "Historically, the agency awarded grants in an isolated
and disconnected way to individual organizations around the U.S. These grants

had enormous positive impact, but they supported disconnected events, one-offs, as it were, that had little cumulative effect. We wanted to create a new paradigm for the Arts Endowment with programs that would have national rather than merely local impact."[56]

Shakespeare became the artistic focus for this paradigm shift because "his position as the central myth-maker of English-language theatre actually invites artists to take certain risks that they would not do in contemporary realistic theatre."[57] While the NEA does admit that Shakespeare "remains the most widely produced playwright in America," they nevertheless argue that "many of our youth have had few opportunities to experience high-quality presentations of Shakespeare. Until now."[58] Thus, in 2003, six theatre companies were selected to tour with performances and educational activities through all fifty states, "introducing young people to the power of live theater and the masterpieces of William Shakespeare."[59] In 2004 the program expanded to include military bases through a partnership with the Department of Defense (DoD), which provided $1 million to the NEA. In that year, eighteen military bases received full-length productions (primarily of *Macbeth*).[60]

In the summer of 2004, the NEA launched the next phase of the initiative through the expanded "Shakespeare for a New Generation" program, which provides $25,000 grants to approximately forty theatre companies a year to "support performance and related educational activities designed to deepen the appreciation and understanding of Shakespeare for participating students."[61] With an epigraphic quote on their promotional brochure from Tina Packer, the artistic director of Shakespeare & Co., the initiative seeks to position itself as one that unites arts and education seamlessly: "Engagement with great poetry in a dramatic setting is one of the most important learning opportunities we can provide young people in this country. . . . They not only improve language skills, but also awaken empathy for others, and thus help to define the aesthetic and ethical standards of a culture."[62]

Nevertheless, the NEA was not solely focused on these lofty goals. For example, in a separate report about the challenges that face nonprofit theater in the United States, the NEA claimed that "the percentage of the U.S. adult population attending non-musical theater has declined from 13.5 percent to 9.4 percent. As these trends worsened in the last six years, even the absolute size of the audience has declined by 16 percent."[63] Realizing that living, contemporary playwrights might object to "subsidizing the works of an Elizabethan British playwright," Gioia declared that "The task of nurturing a new generation of theatergoers is beyond the ability of any [contemporary] playwright, however brilliant."[64] Thus, the Shakespeare for a New Generation program's emphasis on

FIGURE 6.3 The National Endowment for the Arts' "Shakespeare in American Communities" logo. Featured in the film *Why Shakespeare?*

"build[ing] future audiences by educating and inspiring students to become informed theatergoers" is no small task because the NEA-sponsored performances are conceived as "the perfect gateway to a lifetime of enjoying the performing arts."[65] The "new generation," in other words, may also have been conceived as the "new market," an audience that in the future would revive the flagging non-musical theatre market.

The target audience for these NEA-sponsored Shakespeare performances was not simply "middle and high school students" or "young people" in general. Instead, it was specifically "under-served" schools and communities whose students "lack access to the performing arts due to geography, economic conditions, ethnic background, or disability. This may include schools in rural areas, inner cities, or on Native American reservations."[66] Gioia, in fact, consistently promotes the diverse audience to whom Shakespeare is being introduced, repeatedly referring to "small towns, inner-city neighborhoods, and military bases."[67] When asked specifically how the NEA defined "under-served communities," Gioia responds, "We never had a single definition. . . . We wanted to reach the places in the U.S. that didn't have easy access to the arts. . . . We put special emphasis on rural towns, inner-city neighborhoods, and economically depressed areas."[68] What exactly does it mean to conceive of the new generation/market as stemming from the "under-served"? While on the surface the rhetoric suggests

that the benefits for the under-served are educational—exposure to great art
and informed discussions about it—the logic to the subtext suggests that the
benefit is really to society at large. After all, it is the larger society that will benefit if these under-served populations become the model arts consumers. As
Gioia promotes, the initiative had multiple objectives: "The actors got paying
work. The theater companies got federal support. The communities had professional theater available. And students got to see theater for free."[69]

It is only fitting, then, that the NEA partnered up with the Department of Justice (DoJ) to support Shakespeare programs for "at-risk youth." In August 2009,
the Coordinating Council on Juvenile Justice and Delinquency Prevention, "an
independent body within the executive branch of the federal government," provided $125,000 to the NEA to support Shakespearean theatre productions that
target "at-risk youth."[70] Thus, within the Shakespeare for a New Generation initiative, the Office of Juvenile Justice and Delinquency Prevention (OJJDP) is providing extra grant money ($10,000–$20,000 in extra funding per theatre company)
for Shakespeare performances that are "targeted to youth involved with the juvenile justice system."[71] As Gioia explains, "I must confess that I mandated [the juvenile justice programs]. I believed that it was the NEA's mission to bring the arts to
all Americans. That included the incarcerated."[72] The new generation/market of
the under-served suddenly narrows to become the youth involved in the justice
system: "We eventually partnered to create Shakespeare programs for at-risk
youths, especially in areas of high gang activity as well as literacy reading programs in prisons."[73] The rhetoric about this population, however, does not figure it
as being comprised of future arts consumers, but rather as those whom Shakespeare can reform, in the manner of Shakespeare prison programs.

Race, however, is conspicuously absent from the NEA's rhetoric. Despite the
fact that the new generation is clearly being depicted as something that is not
suburban and white, the NEA mentions ethnicity, and specifically refers to Native
American populations, but eschews an engagement with explicit dialogues about
race. Like the population of inmates in adult correctional facilities, however, the
youth involved in the juvenile justice system are disproportionately people of color
from economically disadvantaged families: poor blacks and Hispanics. According
to the OJJDP, "The racial composition of the U.S. juvenile population ages 10–17 in
2007 was 78% white, 17% black, 5% Asian/Pacific Islander, and 1% American
Indian. . . . Of all juvenile arrests for violent crimes in 2007, 47% involved white
youth, 51% involved black youth, 1% involved Asian youth, and 1% involved American Indian youth."[74] These statistics are even more startling when one realizes that
the OJJDP includes "juveniles of Hispanic ethnicity . . . in the white racial category."[75] While it is clear that the phrase "at-risk youth" has multiple meanings,

including runaway youth, low-income youth, and youth in the juvenile justice system, it is also safe to assume that the phrase disproportionately refers to populations that come from disadvantaged financial, ethnic, *and* racial backgrounds.

Nonetheless, the solution is not to engage in the systemic issues that create these disadvantages, but rather to define American culture as uniquely informed by Shakespearean literature. In other words, like the claim by Abigail and Stephen Thernstrom that "some cultures are academically advantageous," the NEA/OJJDP program seeks to inculcate at-risk youth in the advantages of understanding Shakespeare's literature and, thereby, mainstream American culture.[76] The elision of a critical dialogue about the roles race and ethnicity play in cultural formation and identification renders them invisible. All that remains is the "culture" of Shakespeare, which is never specifically defined; all that we know is that it is "advantageous."

In addition, the NEA program implicitly assumes that the exposure is all. As Gioia explains, "I felt that the Shakespeare program met a huge, specific need. I saw arts education programs being taken away from schools across the country. As a working-class kid from LA, I knew how important those programs were to both students and teachers. . . . [The] students got to see theatre for free. For most of them, it was their first experience in professional spoken theatre. The program also helped support the efforts of overworked high school English teachers across the country."[77] While the NEA boasts that their free educational materials—which include a "Fun with Shakespeare" flyer, a recitation contest, a teacher's guide that provides lesson plans that fit into the NCTE English Language Arts Standards, a CD, and two videos—have reached more than 25 *million students*, the assumption seems to be that Shakespeare is not already being taught in schools: that students are not being exposed to Shakespeare. The deeper critical engagement about which Tina Packer speaks (helping to "define the aesthetic and ethical standards of a culture") does not seem to be a part of the process. While it is important to stress that the theatre companies that receive NEA funding do not have content or stylistic restrictions placed on them (they can stage which ever play they like in which ever style they like), they also do not have to create, facilitate, or engage in the critical dialogues about Shakespeare, race, and performance even when their target audiences are "at-risk youth." Once again it is difficult to disentangle a progressive intention/rhetoric from a neoconservative one. To highlight this fact I now turn to a program that was designed to fulfill conservative intentions.

Operating in a completely different realm, Ken and Carol Adelman's for-profit business consulting company, Movers & Shakespeares, also emphasizes exposure over deep, sustained, and critical engagement. Through Movers & Shakespeares the Adelmans typically offer full-day sessions focused on a key business topic such as leadership training, risk management, diversity training, ethics training, and change management. They create case studies from specific scenes in specific plays to address the larger business topic. Thus, the famous Crispin Crispian speech from *Henry V* is used to teach leadership training, while Petruchio from *The Taming of the Shrew* is used as a "case study of change management."[78] The Adelmans recognize the slightly bizarre notion that knowledge of Shakespeare is relevant, and indeed necessary, for modern business practices. In a book coauthored with Norman Augustine, the former Chairman and CEO of Lockheed Martin, Ken Adelman claims that it is "the Bard's profound insights into human nature that has made him so extraordinarily successful for four hundred years."[79] Thus, business and Shakespeare "mesh. For business involves people, and people—fundamentally—don't change."[80] As Marjorie Garber notes, "it is because of their credentials in government and business, not in English literature, that the Adelmans have clout in the world of the leadership institute. The real subject is leadership, and 'Shakespeare' is the image or comparison being used to convey every point."[81]

For example, when summarizing the lesson executives can take from Petruchio's behavior in *Taming of the Shrew*, Augustine and Adelman write, "Today's executives who hear Katherine-like protests against change must answer them. Speaking like Henry [V] or acting like Petruchio, who breaks cultural conventions during Bianca's wedding feast, can make the point that cultural mores and traditions are the antithesis of change."[82] Garber is correct to note that "nothing is more symptomatic of 'modern culture' than using Shakespeare characters and plots as the jumping-off points for discussions about business ethics and management decisions."[83] Nevertheless, this kind of appropriation "uses Shakespeare, but the use is not communicative. It does not go both ways."[84] Likewise, Niels Herold argues that Movers & Shakespeares "is a commercial appropriation . . . that dehistoricizes the Shakespeare 'product,' removing it from the historical conditions that made possible its artistic conception and commercial thriving."[85] The Adelmans' own rhetoric, of course, fuels these critiques because they have no qualms suggesting that they offer Shakespeare in "bite-sized pieces."[86] In fact, they advertise that they will provide summaries of the plays and only require that certain limited passages will be read during their workshops: no outside knowledge, reading, or thinking is required.

While critics like Garber and Herold have claimed that the Adelmans are trafficking in "Shakespeare," an idea and myth, instead of the actual plays themselves, I want to press the way that this trafficking works to render race culturally irrelevant. While Movers & Shakespeares does offer a "Diversity Workshop" that employs *The Merchant of Venice* as its case study, Ken Adelman admits that the workshop "came about because companies wanted it."[87] In fact, in their book

Shakespeare in Charge, which functioned as the blueprint for the creation of Movers & Shakespeares as a Shakespeare-based business consulting firm, Augustine and Adelman do not include anything on diversity training or management. Instead, *The Merchant of Venice* is their case study for their chapter on "Risk Management." They write, "Unlike most contemporary plays or other artistic creations, *The Merchant of Venice* extols business and shows respect for corporate executives and admiration for commerce in general. Within its story are sharp examples needed by every businessperson who has asked, 'When should I take a risk—and how can I best manage it?'"[88]

While Augustine and Adelman admit that the "treatment of the complex Shylock offers a startling and disturbing look into one of life's darkest corners," their case study eschews a critical approach to anti-Semitism by prioritizing the play's "brilliant understanding of the riskiness of business."[89] Thus, in their narrative, Portia becomes the model for executives who must manage risk because "she identifies all available options" and proceeds by "collecting facts and analyzing options."[90] Race, religion, and ethnicity do not seem to figure into Portia's risk management assessment, as Augustine and Adelman make clear. Although the Prince of Morocco hopes that Portia will "Mislike me not for my complexion" (2.1.1), Augustine and Adelman claim that the issue of race is "moot once he, fittingly, chooses the glitzy gold casket."[91] It is unclear why Augustine and Adelman call Morocco's choice fitting because they do not linger on race long enough to explain if it is the fitting element. His racial difference from Portia is noted by Augustine and Adelman, but it is only a passing reference and not an element that warrants deep thought, interrogation, or analysis.

Since business companies began to demand workshops on diversity training, however, Movers & Shakespeares created another case study of *Merchant*: one that examines the role of "the Other" in business and society. As Adelman declares, "*Merchant* seemed like a natural fit because the whole play is about 'the Other.' You have Shylock, the Jew, the Prince of Morocco, the black, and Portia, the woman confined not only by the will of her father but by the will of her *dead* father. Plus, you have a gay couple in Antonio and Bassanio."[92] For Adelman this fit is *natural* precisely because he reads the play as a commentary and condemnation of bigotry: "Although the play has been portrayed as an anti-Semitic play, it is really one that is about anti-Semitism in particular and society's dealing with 'the Other' or outsiders in general."[93] In this understanding, Shakespeare's play does not create or perpetuate racial stereotypes, but instead merely comments upon them. In this logic the plays are granted an objective and distanced vantage point, and Shakespeare becomes an enlightened and prescient thinker and writer; he not only understands human nature but also helps to model better behavior.

Adelman reports that, over the years, Movers & Shakespeares has conducted somewhere between twenty and twenty-five diversity workshops, and that the feedback from the companies served has been positive precisely because the training does not replicate a stereotypical approach to diversity training: namely, one that traffics in guilt. Adelman states, "our clients like it. At least they keep coming back for more. They like it because it's a type of diversity training that isn't focused on 'Aren't we all bad? Aren't we really racists, or homophiles or chauvinistic pigs?' We present a case study about diversity. We don't focus on making people feel guilty, but on how discrimination erodes the standards of a society and impacts the minority in a powerful way."[94] Careful to avoid an approach that inspires feelings of guilt, Movers & Shakespeares comforts its corporate clients through this case study approach. Instead of addressing issues of racial privilege, the workshop offers generalities about the erosion of social standards. Implicit in Adelman's rhetoric, moreover, is the notion that the target audiences for these workshops are *white, male* executives, who are leery of being made to feel "guilty," "bad," and "chauvinistic" when discussing issues of diversity. Likewise, his rhetoric implies that it is primarily "the minority" who is harmed by discrimination. While the society's "standards" may erode, it seems more important to avoid inspiring guilt than the potential threat this erosion may entail.

While the Adelmans consistently position Shakespeare as a timeless, universal, and universally relevant writer, *Shakespeare in Charge* offers a fascinating case study in the way Shakespeare's texts are sidelined in their business-focused appropriations. First, there are no notes about which edition(s) is being cited. Although this is not surprising because this type of appropriation is more about the application of Shakespearean ideals than the complicated history of textual editions, the absence of any notes about textual editions, of course, creates the fantasy of a stable Shakespearean text: universality is achieved through textual elision. Likewise, there are no act, scene, and line references when citations to the text are made in *Shakespeare in Charge*. In fact, line divisions are not even indicated, thereby frequently transposing verse citations into prose. For instance, Augustine and Adelman write, "Previously Antonio controls risk well by diversifying: 'My ventures are not in one bottom trusted, nor to one place. Nor is my whole estate upon the fortune of this present year.'"[95] This citation, of course, is in verse in *Merchant*: "My ventures are not in one bottom trusted, / Nor to one place; nor is my whole estate / Upon the fortune of this present year" (1.1.42–44). While their rhetoric creates a universally applicable Bard whose works can answer even the most modern and complicated problems of the twenty-first-century world, their actions consistently work to update his work. And, finally, one might be surprised how infrequently the text is quoted at all. While the plots are summarized in detail, one might counter that the plots are the least Shakespearean aspect of the plays, as Shakespeare freely borrowed, appropriated, and rewrote older poetic (e.g., from Ovid), theatrical (e.g., from Marlowe), and historical (e.g., from Holinshed) plots.

Thus, as other scholars have argued, the Adelmans seem to prize an exposure to Shakespeare over a deep engagement with his words, thoughts, and characterizations. Discussing their specific approach to their Diversity Training workshop, Ken Adelman explains that each "participant has a paperback version of the play in front of her."[96] Nevertheless, the specifics of the text seem to take a backseat to the Adelmans' positive interpretation of the play. Despite the fact that Movers & Shakespeares claims to offer a diversity workshop that will demonstrate "how discrimination erodes the standards of society," their approach makes an exposure to Shakespeare's plots more important than a critical engagement with his logic and rhetoric. And it is precisely this surface engagement that enables their elision of the disturbingly un-modern references to racial difference in many of the plays. Their espousal of Shakespeare's deep understanding of human nature comes at the price of a critical dialogue with the specificities of his plays.

While it may seem capricious to pair the NEA's Shakespeare in American Communities initiative with the Adelmans' Movers & Shakespeares program (one is a government granting agency for theatre companies, the other a for-profit consulting company; one financially supports full-length productions, the other offers "bite-size pieces" of Shakespearean text; one specifically targets under-served communities, the other targets privileged audiences), they are united in one significant way: both approach issues of diversity without explicitly inviting critical dialogues about race, privilege, and power structures. Despite their diametrically opposed missions and target audiences, both the Shakespeare in American Communities initiative and Movers & Shakespeares for-profit consulting firm traffic in a notion that the exposure is all. The complexities of race (historically, politically, and performatively) are tacitly acknowledged, but an exposure to Shakespeare is, nevertheless, the end result. And once again it is difficult to distinguish progressive Shakespeare from neoconservative Shakespeare in these programs: their logic and rhetoric end up resembling each other even when the intentions of the organizers are diametrically opposed.

REFORMING AUTHENTICITY

The sacrifice of critical engagement for mere exposure or aesthetic appreciation does not have to occur, however. It is not impossible to value Shakespeare, Shakespearean texts, and Shakespearean performance and critical dialogues/debates about constructions of race. Focusing on arts education programs that "provide a way for students to engage with community, civic, and social issues," Steve Seidel highlights Will Power to Youth, a program that "initiate[s] community dialogue about socially and culturally relevant local issues."[97] After the racially based civil unrest that rocked Los Angeles in 1992, "Shakespeare Festival/LA (SF/LA) was approached by civic leaders and philanthropic foundations to help address the needs of at-risk youth."[98] They developed an employment-based arts program that pays at-risk youth to study, adapt, and perform Shakespearean plays. According to WPY's *Impact Report*, "The Will Power to Youth process is a 200-hour, 7-week employment period that occurs during school break wherein young people are guided and supported by professional adult mentor-artists as they investigate, write, create, construct, and perform their own original adaptation of a Shakespeare play. In so doing, Youth Participants learn the importance of community, communication, collaboration, and cooperation."[99] The program consistently emphasizes the need to make Shakespeare's plays "relevant to, and inspired by, their personal lives."[100] As Steve Seidel writes, "By using the arts as a tool to examine and challenge unjust social dynamics, these student activists build a sense of individual and community identity while working to effect change."[101]

Featured in Lawrence Bridges's 2004 documentary, *Why Shakespeare?* a film that is included in the NEA's Shakespeare in American Communities educational packet, WPY seems to represent the vision of nontraditional Shakespeare—that is, nonwhite Shakespeare. While WPY's Artistic Director Ben Donenberg is white and middle-aged, the members of the company are all teenagers of color (primarily Hispanic). Featuring interviews with members of WPY, short recitations from professional actors, interviews with prominent poets, writers, and directors, and very short performance clips from Rafe Esquith's Hobart Shakespeareans, the documentary presents and privileges the voices of a much more diverse segment of the population than one might at first expect from a film about Shakespeare's relevance. While the documentary is in no way equitable in its representation (the largest featured group—41%—is white males), Hispanics, blacks, and Asians make up 41% of the interviewees. The answer to the eponymous question, "Why Shakespeare," seems to be voiced by an Asian male, who espouses a nonracialized American heritage that unites us all: "Well, Shakespeare is important because it is something that binds our heritage as Americans."[102] Likewise, Dana Gioia, who is also featured in the documentary, tells a story about being moved to tears by the Hobart Shakespeareans' performance of the St. Crispin Crispian speech from *Henry V* precisely because it was performed by "a little boy [who] had been raised in a non-English speaking home."[103] The value of Shakespeare, the film implies, is that it unites whites, blacks, Hispanics, and Asians, rich and poor as Americans.

Richard Burt critiques Will Power to Youth's program because it was taken up by George W. Bush's administration as a model for a successful, non-governmentally funded reform program. He reads the program as exemplifying the right's appropriation of the colorblind ethic: "One could easily read the Bush administration's use of Shakespeare as part of a concerted, far-reaching Republican right-wing multicultural agenda in which racism is disciplined in order to create a better-functioning workforce. That is, Shakespeare is not presented as part of white high culture but as open to all races and cultures."[104] Although he does not cite the documentary *Why Shakespeare?* one can imagine Burt's objection to it as a film that promotes "institutional Shakespeare . . . designed to integrate minorities and poor whites by warehousing them into service sector, low-income Mcjobs."[105] Burt finds it instructive that the right does not value only a "monolithic, traditional Shakespeare" and, instead, promotes "a mix of traditional and modernized Shakespeares."[106] About WPY, he claims that "neither authentic Shakespeare nor racial authenticity matters much."[107]

While I agree with Burt's assessment that the George W. Bush administration, and in particular First Lady Laura Bush, supported the efforts of WPY precisely because "Shakespeare is supposed to function as a prophylactic against kids joining gangs and going to jail . . . [and] as a backup to redeem kids who turn to crime," I disagree with his arguments about authenticity.[108] While the right may have wanted (and perhaps continues to want) to promote the program on the grounds that even the most abject—racially, culturally, and economically—are made into highly functioning citizens, WPY's focus on critical engagement with the text, the performance group, and their specific community emphasizes the crucial role active engagement ideally should play in citizenship. Unlike the prison programs that focus on incorporation, or programs like those run by the NEA or the Adelmans that focus on exposure, WPY focuses on a deep engagement that allows for complexities and contradictions both in the Shakespearean text and on personal and communal levels. As Chris Anthony, the Director of Youth & Education and Associate Artistic Director at the Shakespeare Center of Los Angeles (formerly the Shakespeare Festival/LA), says, "When I open the gift of Shakespeare, I find life. I find life in all of its complexity and contradiction, in all of its beauty and dismal banality."[109] Hers is not an uninformed, blind promotion of Shakespeare's universality. In fact, Donenberg, Anthony, and the WPY program in general seem to resist the notion that Shakespeare is always relevant. Their "Youth Participants" have to work to make Shakespeare relevant; they have to work to make him their own.

Thus, Burt's critique of WPY's lack of authenticity misses the mark significantly. It is precisely because the program values appropriation, adaptation, and revision that the at-risk youth who participate in WPY are enabled to bring their own voices, narratives, and civic concerns to bear on equal footing with Shakespeare and Shakespeare's texts. This is not dumbed-down Shakespeare; it is a critical engagement that encourages dialogue, debate, and critique. In fact, the focus of WPY is often on the group dynamics and on creating effective communication and problem-solving techniques within the performance group. As one of the participants in WPY explains, "Just becoming involved with different types of people and their beliefs [was important]. I had just been closed minded 'cause I grew up with that type of background: they've always thought a certain thing, and it's always been that sort of thing. But this has helped me to think of different ways."[110] I find it instructive that this young woman describes the benefit of her involvement in WPY in personal terms instead of terms about Shakespeare's universality; Shakespeare's name does not even come up in her assessment of WPY (see Figure 6.1).

In fact, it is the program's focus on fostering respect and trust that Steve Seidel identifies as "authentic." Writing about his group's observations of a WPY rehearsal, Seidel explains that the participants "were patient with each other, supportive, responsive to their director, disciplined, frustrated at moments, but committed to their work. . . . The *authenticity* found in much high quality arts teaching and learning provides a powerful environment for forming communities. But respect for and trust in the capacities of young people is the bedrock of these experiences."[111] While Burt defines "authenticity" in terms of veracity to the Shakespearean text and veracity to one's race and ethnicity, which he assumes to be muted in these nonauthentic performances, Seidel defines "authenticity" in terms of an environment that encourages and enables communication, cooperation, and collaboration. Although race and ethnicity are not explicitly mentioned by Seidel in his assessment of WPY, his attention to the program's aim "to initiate community dialogue about socially and culturally relevant local issues" challenges Burt's notion that the performances render the races of the participants inauthentically.[112]

The position of Shakespeare within WPY is both essential and extraneous. As the group's name makes clear, William Shakespeare is imagined to have, and is invested with, a great deal of power, and his power is envisioned as being shared with the at-risk participants who perform in adaptations of his plays. Even Seidel's book traffics in the rhetoric of empowerment through struggle: "Reading Shakespeare's plays is a challenge for just about everyone. Learning them well enough to perform them without a script is exponentially more challenging. For the teen actors participating in Will Power to Youth in Los Angeles, this is their job."[113] The logic behind this rhetoric is, of course, familiar by now: Shakespeare = difficult = good for you. Yet, Shakespeare's plots really serve only as a frame on which communication, cooperation, and collaboration are hung. The focus, then, is not on the frame, but on the garments on top.

Likewise, participants in WPY do not often reference Shakespeare when discussing their dreams, goals, and aspirations. As Victor Doroteo says in the documentary *Why Shakespeare?* "I am actually looking at [my] future right now. For me, right now, it is actually to be a famous musician. I want to get a band started, and actually go all the way to the end."[114] Thinking back to Chris Anthony's statement about her understanding of Shakespeare—that his plays represent the complexities, contradictions, beauties, and banalities of life—one understands how WPY enables Doroteo to articulate his non-Shakespearean goals. The plays do not end up being prescriptively good, universally applicable, or timelessly appropriate; instead, they become expansive and imperfect, allowing one to move far away from them—to become a musician and "go all the way." In other words, the WPY productions traffic in Shakespeare's name and Shakespeare's plots in the service of creating processes and performances that are authentic to the community's, the group's, and the individual's needs, in all of their beauties and banalities. What is more authentic than that?

REFORMING SHAKESPEARE, THE UNSTABLE

In assessing how quality arts education programs determine what content should be taught, Steve Seidel and the researchers at Harvard's Project Zero identify a common debate about the Western canon. Seidel writes, "many arts educators today argue that the curriculum must be diversified to include forms of art beyond the western canon, and that the curriculum must expose students to contemporary arts, non-western art, and folk and indigenous art forms."[115] Citing Philip Taylor's research, Seidel writes, "Taylor argues that a curriculum rooted in the Anglo-European tradition is narrow and 'leads to a blindness of contemporary issues.'"[116] Noting that "there is more consensus than disagreement" on this topic, Seidel concludes, "an arts education program that focuses solely on classical forms of art is seen by some as problematic today."[117] Nevertheless, WPY is featured by Seidel as one of the nineteen quality arts education programs in the country precisely because they do not reproduce Shakespeare's plays in their "classical forms," or what Burt would call the "authentic" Shakespeare. Instead, the program creates an unstable Shakespearean text that not only warrants, but also invites, revision and adaptation. Authenticity and authority, then, do not reside in the text or the fantasy of the author, but in the individuals who must work long and hard to communicate, cooperate, and collaborate.

As Margaret Jane Kidnie compellingly argues in *Shakespeare and the Problem of Adaptation*, the notions of a Shakespearean text, performance, play, and adaptation are constantly in states of flux. As a result, "there is no ideal iteration of any Shakespearean play towards which one can or should strive, either textually or theatrically. . . . Precisely what constitutes authentic Shakespeare is a question that can never fully be resolved since there is no a priori category that texts and stagings are productions *of*."[118] Kidnie's point, then, is that "it is precisely through such processes of debate that users continue to define their particular ideological, institutional, or political investment in the work."[119] All of the reform programs discussed in this chapter teach the process of Shakespearean performance as one that is fundamentally ameliorative. As I mention at the beginning of the chapter, however, the logic and rhetoric of these programs seem to tiptoe between a form of liberal humanism that espouses the benefits of learning for all, and a form of neocolonialism that espouses the benefits of learning specific texts; one focuses on individuals, the other on texts. As Kidnie argues, this tension is especially acute for Shakespearean performances and Shakespearean texts precisely because of the instability of the text itself: there are so many editions, let alone performance scripts, that it is difficult to identify the authoritative one.

While the confusion has reached a type of fever pitch in the twenty-first century with multiple, competing sources for authoritative texts and scripts (especially with the ubiquity of the internet), many reform programs traffic in an espousal of textual stability and authority. In the Shakespeare Behind Bars program in the Luther Luckett Correctional Complex, for example, the prisoners pride themselves on their performances of plays in the First Folio. Likewise, the Hobart Shakespeareans are lauded for performing "unabridged" texts. Although focusing on exposure over specific textual authenticity, the NEA's Shakespeare in American Communities initiative and the Adelmans' Movers & Shakespeares consulting company also traffic in the stability of Shakespeare—the stability of an identity. In the creation and promotion of this authority and stability, however, issues of race, power, and structural inequality are either rendered secondary or irrelevant.

Will Power to Youth, on the other hand, wrestles authority, authenticity, and stability from the text and the author to invest them in the at-risk participants, who are paid to engage with Shakespeare. Thus, dialogues, discussions, and debates about the significances and insignificances of race in their lives, communities, and performances come to the fore. They are empowered to make Shakespeare's texts relevant to their lives so authorship and authenticity always resides in their (collective) hands. Reform programs that utilize Shakespeare, thus, should look to reform Shakespeare. WPY offers the best example of the value of instability.

FIGURE 7.1 "Everyone dies?! It's so stupid!" Video still from a 2007 YouTube performance of *Othello*.

Cyberspace and race are both constructed cultural phenomena, not products of "nature"; they are made up of ongoing processes of definition, performance, enactment, and identity creation.
—Beth E. Kolko, Lisa Nakamura, and Gilbert Rodman[1]

It is a widely accepted notion that media interactivity is power.
—LISA NAKAMURA[2]

7

Archives

CLASSROOM-INSPIRED PERFORMANCE VIDEOS

ON YOUTUBE[3]

IT IS NOW a common pedagogical practice in secondary schools, colleges, and universities to incorporate performance into the Shakespearean classroom. As Samuel Crowl explains, "The past twenty-five years have seen a revolution in performance approaches to teaching Shakespeare. Many professors . . . have turned their classrooms into rehearsal spaces where students spend more time on their feet speaking the text to one another than at their desks taking notes on imagery, characterization, theme, or historical context."[4] While the incorporation of performance in the classroom no longer seems surprising, what has come as a bit of a surprise is the willingness of our twenty-first-century students to upload their performance projects to the Internet: their willingness to beam these readings, recitations, and full-blown performances through cyberspace for anyone to watch and comment upon. Live performances are often discussed as being ephemeral, but archives have been created specifically to preserve and record their existence. Yet traditionally, no widely available archive has been established to record and preserve classroom-inspired performances. These exist as the ephemerals of ephemerals—until now, that is, with the popularity of the classroom-inspired YouTube video.

Although there are many Internet sites that enable video file sharing, YouTube has quickly become the most popular. Founded in February 2005, officially launched in November 2005, and purchased by Google in October 2006, YouTube advertises itself as "empowering [people] to become the broadcasters of tomorrow," and the company's official tagline is "Broadcast Yourself."[5] Having grown up with the notion that broadcasting one's life online is *de rigueur*, our students frequently upload materials produced in our classrooms: lecture notes, exam questions, entire essays, and filmed performance assignments. Casually typing "Shakespeare" into the YouTube search engine, one will encounter over 25,000 uploaded video clips related to Shakespeare: a strange combination of Do-It-Yourself (DIY) videos, pirated film and television clips, music videos, and mashups (mixing different media sources together, like the visuals from a film and the sound from a popular song). The current "Generation M"—Generation Media, eight to eighteen year olds who have grown up with, and on, the Internet[6]—has created what is now a large and complex archive for classroom-inspired Shakespeare performances.

YouTube offers a unique space to analyze the ways this generation negotiates performances of Shakespeare and performances of race, as they incorporate popular culture into classroom formations. YouTube's interactive platform thus provides Shakespeareans access to the production and reception of a new performance genre—the classroom-inspired performance video. Analyzing these videos and the responses to them (including the dynamic online exchanges between producers and users), Shakespeareans have a window into production and reception that highlights some uncomfortable aspects of the texts that are often glossed over in the classroom, specifically the dynamics of race and gender in Shakespearean performance. While Internet sources are often treated as too unstable and fleeting for serious consideration, YouTube offers nothing short of the largest contemporary performance archive for both production and reception. The key feature of YouTube is not passive viewing, but response and dialogue—that is, social interactivity. Participants are encouraged to respond to postings in textual and visual comments, providing a dialogic trail of reception responses. This chapter uses a close reading of three YouTube videos to demonstrate the unique interpretative opportunities this platform reveals, as well as the research and pedagogical implications exposed by these opportunities.

More specifically, in this chapter I analyze the ways Asian-American students conceptualize, contest, and perform American blackness within their amateur Shakespearean performances.[7] In the clips discussed, *Othello* is unmoored historically, linguistically, and narratively. Like many online student performance videos, these videos update the language, setting, and even the plot of *Othello*. In addition, these videos challenge traditional racialized performances of Othello with casts comprised solely of Asian-American students. Therefore, Othello's difference from the rest of the characters is visually unmarked (unlike performance videos that feature a black Othello or employ blackface). But the clips are disturbingly rooted in a familiar performance strategy; they update Othello's narrative by framing it in a fantasy of contemporary, black-American culture. The number of rap or "gangsta" adaptations of *Othello* on YouTube is immense, perhaps attributable to the popularity of showing and employing the Reduced Shakespeare Company's Othello-rap as a classroom resource.[8]

Asian-American students make a useful case study of Generation M work on self-broadcast platforms because "they inhabit a range of positions in relation to the Internet," Shakespeare, and American popular culture.[9] First, Asian Americans are among the least visibly represented groups in contemporary Shakespearean performance. There are very few Asian-American actors employed in Shakespearean theatre companies in the United States, and even fewer represented in contemporary American film adaptations.

Second, while Asian Americans are often stereotyped as digitally gifted, a type of "model minority" when it comes to cybertechnology, they often inhabit a precarious position in relation to the production of popular American culture. As Lisa Nakamura argues, "Asian Americans are far less visible as producers of a distinctive and commodified 'youth culture' than are African Americans."[10] While urban African-American youth are assumed to be the producers of what is cool— like hip hop, urban attire, and contemporary slang—Asian Americans are often positioned as the consumers of the commodified versions of this popular youth culture, despite the fact that they frequently have greater access to both cybertechnology and the sophisticated tools for interactivity.

And third, because, as Francesca Royster argues, "*Othello* is often retold as a story of the black experience in white culture," Shakespeare's Moor is frequently performed through a fantasy of black, urban, gangsta culture.[11] If Asian Americans are not assumed to be culturally related to Shakespeare—the "naturalized American hero," to borrow Kim Sturgess's phrase—they are also not assumed to be culturally related to his *othered* characters.[12] So it is revealing to watch how these students attempt to access Shakespeare through popular American culture *and* popular American culture through Shakespeare. A group often stereotyped as the consumers instead of producers of trendy "youth culture," Asian-American students create fascinatingly rich cyberproductions: important pieces that reveal their tenuous positions both inside and outside of popular American cultural production. Antagonisms within urban Asian-black relations have resulted in bouts of violence, and the production and consumption of cultural identities have frequently provided the spark for these antagonisms. Of course, the full scope of the complex relationships between Asian Americans and black Americans is beyond the purview of this chapter, but classroom-inspired performances of *Othello* frequently provide unique instances to analyze these relations.[13] These videos tell us something about the desire for, and problems with, "identity tourism" online:

"performances online [that use] race and gender as amusing prostheses to be donned and shed without 'real life' consequences."[14] These videos, however, also reveal the limits of the Shakespearean text as a vehicle to address contemporary cultural and racial formations.

A BRIEF NOTE ON METHODOLOGY

Because I do not have an account with YouTube, I have not uploaded any videos, saved any videos as "Favorites," nor added "Commentary" via "Video Responses" or "Text Comments."[15] In addition, I have not contacted any of the people whose videos or comments I cite. In the parlance of Internet research methodology, I have been *lurking* on YouTube: that is, watching the video postings and reading the commentaries, but not contributing anything myself. In addition, I have been *harvesting* both the videos and commentaries: that is, collecting and saving the ones I find most interesting for research and publication purposes.

Although I attempt to follow guidelines for conducting ethical online research, as many scholars have noted, this area is extremely murky because it is relatively new.[16] The debates about online research are still ongoing: does Internet research constitute human subjects research? Is cyberspace a private or public space? Are online communications private or public? Does reading, citing, and analyzing postings on Internet sites, like YouTube, entail an "intervention or interaction" with the individuals who create them, and, thus, require oversight by an institutional review board (IRB)?[17] Even if an IRB determines that one's research does not require oversight, one still must ensure that one's approach to online communications is ethical.

Heidi McKee and James E. Porter's recent work has helped to inform the ethical and methodological decisions I made for this chapter. Adapting Malin Svenings-son's grid for mapping research data, McKee and Porter advocate for an approach that distinguishes nonsensitive information from sensitive information and private information from public information in order to determine the ethical dimensions for informed consent.[18] As the YouTube videos and commentaries I am analyzing stem from school projects that were not only graded by teachers but also shared with classmates both offline and online, and as these videos and commentaries are not about private, personal, and/or sensitive information (they are performances of Shakespearean scenes), I see them residing safely in the nonsensitive/public quadrant of the grid. Moreover, they fall within the half of the grid in which informed consent is not ethically necessary.

That said, I am sensitive to the fact that I am working with the public and non-sensitive postings of young adults (many of whom are legally deemed *minors*). The

debates about whether online communications are private or public are exasper-
ated when one asks whether minors have the capability to understand the public
nature of the Internet. In independent studies, Susannah Stern and Magdalena
Bober conducted research with young adults, and they both determined that adolescents with personal Web pages understood that their postings were public.[19]
And yet, both Stern and Bober warn against treating their findings too liberally.
They both advocate protecting the identities of the young adults cited in research
so as to ensure that no harm can come to them as a result of one's research. Bober
intones, "The identities of participants should, therefore, always be protected by
rendering quotes anonymous or by using pseudonyms, especially when the
research touches upon sensitive issues."[20]

Thus, this chapter employs a hybrid mode that blends close reading techniques
from the humanities with ethically guided research algorithms from the social sciences. Because I view classroom-inspired performance videos on YouTube as an
archive of production and reception, I am attentive to both visual and textual
postings from a traditional humanist's perspective. Read in this mode, these texts
reveal a great deal about contemporary understandings and uses of Shakespeare,
race, and performance. Ethical guidelines from the social sciences advise protecting the identities of minors in one's research.[21] Thus, aside from indicating the
platform and date source videos and commentaries were posted to YouTube, I do
not cite the specific URLs or usernames. (This is an important measure because
many participants include their full names within the video and/or comments,
despite the fact that YouTube discourages doing so.[22])

This is a significant methodological departure for a Shakespeare scholar. We are
used to providing full citations for all media: texts, editions, performances, criticism, and so forth. Our work is often assessed by another's ability to verify such
citations and to explore the text in question for him/herself. In this context, however, providing hyperlinks to these videos to make them available for illustration
would exponentially expand the reach of the online text beyond what the initial
user-producer intended/imagined.[23] Of course, diligent readers will be able to find
these videos on their own (my graduate students found them within minutes). Yet
this chapter follows standard social science practice in not serving as the source
for direct hyperlinks. Hyperlinking is a mode of distribution and disclosure as well
as citation. For the videos analyzed, as social scientists remind us, the key consideration in disclosure is whether or not presenting a given link might in any way do
harm to the students' status or reputation, now or in the future. Given the charged
topics of this close reading (the racial formations the students perform) and given
the age of the participants, unless I can answer no to that question (I cannot) the
default is nondisclosure.

Having said all of this, I want to emphasize that research that incorporates Internet sources is still in its infancy. At the moment of writing this chapter (August 2008), there are no critical essays or books that address how to cite YouTube postings. Consensus on the ethical, methodological, and theoretical issues involved in Internet research is desperately needed, especially as a large segment of the user-producers of interactive sites like YouTube are minors. No doubt this kind of work is coming, but we as Shakespeareans and educators should think about our positions within this debate as well. After all, our students are the minors and young adults who are posting these videos onto YouTube, MySpace, Facebook, and so forth.

IDENTITY ON THE INTERNET

Despite the fact that early advocates of the Internet praised its potential to transform identity (Sherry Turkle famously extolled its ability to create "a more fluid sense of self"),[24] more recently scholars have leveled that some identities may be more "fluid" than others because "individuals can experience more or less inter-activity and representational power depending on what they are doing on the Internet."[25] In other words, the Internet as a medium may create opportunities to challenge unitary and fixed notions of identity, but it does not do so for everyone at every moment equally. As Lisa Nakamura enumerates, there is a complex web that affects identity formation on the Internet:

> The multilayered visual culture of the Internet is anything but a space of uto-pian post-humanism where differences between genders, races, and nation-alities are leveled out; on the contrary, it is an intensely active, productive space of visual signification where these differences are intensified, modu-lated, reiterated, and challenged by former objects of interactivity. . . . Object and subject are not mutually exclusive roles: it is not possible to definitively decide who is being *interacted* and who is being *interactive* except in specific circumstances.[26]

The medium creates an environment that enables individuals to play an active role in their identity formation—both on a personal level and a public one—but at different moments those same individuals may be the object (instead of the active subject) of someone else's online interaction.

Of course, the tension between who is the being interactive and who is being interacted upon, to borrow Nakamura's terms, occurs both textually and visually as the Internet has developed to incorporate multiple media. Cyber-passing—the act of presenting oneself as a different race, gender, and/or sexuality online—provides an interesting example of the ways objects and subjects of interactivity are unstable. Early Internet critics, like Jerry Kang, celebrated the potential of cyber-passing because "the racial signal I broadcast becomes the product of voluntary choice and intentional experimentation. This might prompt me to look at race differently, as less fixed."[27] Kang focused on the individual who chooses to enact the cyber-passing because that is a "voluntary choice" that could potentially destabilize fixed notions of racial identity.

When Kang wrote his influential essay for the *Harvard Law Review*, however, the Internet was still predominantly text based: so cyber-passing would have been an act through, and of, words alone. Early interactive Web sites were all text-based. Thus, MUDs (multiple-user dimensions) and MOOs (multiple-object oriented) were sites that enabled user interaction, but they did not have a visual component. While it becomes clear that cyber-passing is viewed as less utopic when the Internet encompasses visual culture, it also becomes clear that cyber-passing does not work in the same way for everyone.[28] There are those who actively choose to enact another race, gender, and/or sexuality, and there are those whose races, genders, and/or sexualities are deemed desirable or undesirable. Often this is dictated by another significant difference: there are those who are afforded the luxury of being interactive—those who have the tools, skills, and resources to be interactive online—and those who are interacted upon—those who have not been afforded the tools, skills, and resources to master interactivity.

Despite the fact that the young adults who make up Generation M are often discussed in the mainstream media as being the post-race generation,[29] linguistic research of online chat rooms proves that race remains a salient point of discussion for members of Generation M. Analyzing thirty-eight half-hour transcripts of online chat rooms whose participants reported themselves to be between the ages of thirteen and seventeen, Brendesha Tynes found that "high school and college students often mention their own race and request the race of their conversational partners."[30] In fact, race and ethnicity were *frequently* mentioned: "37 out of 38 half-hour transcripts had at least one racial or ethnic utterance," and the "mean number of racial utterances in each transcript, that is, within a half-hour of chat, was 8."[31] Furthermore, the research conducted by Tynes complicated the conclusions of "offline research" which argued that race is a "less salient" category for white adolescents: "in our data, this was much less the case," with white adolescents using both implicit and explicit racial discourses.[32] Thus, not only is Generation M actively engaged in employing and keeping "salient" racial discourses, but also this occurs more online than it does offline. Far from embodying the utopic space that Sherry Turkle imagined, the Internet may actually push racial discourses to the fore more than offline interactions do.

TITUS ANDRONICUS AS AN *AMERICAN* GANGSTER/GANGSTA

Although it might seem counterintuitive to use performances of Shakespeare to analyze contemporary perceptions, performances, constructions, and appropriations of race, his ubiquity in the American educational canon, and the central positioning of *Othello* within that canon in twentieth- and twenty-first-century classrooms, creates a unique opportunity to delve into Generation M's digestion of both the canon *and* constructions of race. It is important to assess how much agency, how much freedom to be truly interactive, students of color have when processing the racial politics inside, and outside of, Shakespeare. I specifically did not want to focus on adolescent blacks performing in *Othello* not only because I address black American responses to Shakespeare in other chapters, but also because Shakespeare has been so thoroughly "naturalized" as American that Shakespeare's Moors are often assumed to be no different from African Americans. My college students often treat and discuss Shakespeare's Moors as the cultural ancestors to African Americans. In fact, when searching for the proper word to describe Othello, my students frequently call him an "African American." Therefore, I explore how Asian-American adolescents navigate these murky waters. What follows are analyses of three DIY YouTube video performances of Shakespeare by Asian-American students. Two focus specifically on *Othello* for the reasons I enumerate above. I begin, however, with a 2006 YouTube video performance of *Titus Andronicus* because it so neatly exemplifies the myriad issues at play in performances of Shakespeare, constructions of race, and interactions with cultural production.

The 2006 YouTube video of *Titus Andronicus* is performed by five Asian-American high school students, who, at the end of the video, make it explicit that this video stems from an assignment in their "Shakespeare '06" class.[33] In the comments posted to the video, someone states, "I really hope this was for some kind of class project and not what you guys do for fun," and one of the participants responds, "Yes, this was a class project that we did one night . . . haha good times . . . gooood times."[34] The video is representative of many of the DIY school assignments posted to YouTube in that the students update the language of the play, while leaving the plot intact. This video is slightly different from the vast majority of high school assignments posted to YouTube, however, in that it shows a condensed version of the entire play instead of focusing on one or two specific scenes in isolation. While I will return to the pedagogical implications of these decisions at the end of this chapter, here I focus on the ways the students navigate performing race in the video.

Running for a total of thirteen minutes, the video condenses act one to one minute, act two to three minutes, acts three and four to three and one-half minutes, and act five to four minutes. With three boys and two girls in the group, the students play multiple roles and identify their roles with white poster-board name tags that hang around their necks. So, for example, the student who plays Aaron also plays Lavinia. Because of their limited numbers (and time), the students reduce many of the roles drastically. Aaron's role is significantly shortened, without any attempt to include his big speeches in acts two, three, or five. In fact, one of the comments added to the video page praises the video's overall quality but questions the excision of these speeches: "Wow, this was amazing. My roommate and I were just watching this and you guys really summed it up pretty well. We were hoping for the 'I have done thy mother' line from Aaron, and his speech about killing 10,000 more. But this was still really cool. I loved it."[35] The center of this video performance, however, is clearly Titus Andronicus. The student who plays Titus appears in almost every scene, and it is his speeches that are maintained and updated the most scrupulously. While there are two comments posted that criticize the video—one explicitly states, "The language is insipid, child-like"[36]—most of the posted comments praise the students' understanding of the play and their ability to infuse it with humor—"haha this is really good—you've summarized the play really well and made it funny at the same time."[37]

If "interactivity is power," to return to the adage used as one of the epigraphs for this chapter, then it is clear the five students who uploaded this production of *Titus Andronicus* to YouTube are technologically empowered. Although I cannot speak authoritatively as to whether all five of the students are equally conversant with interactive media, it is clear that at least one has film production skills. Not only is the video conceived and directed well (the use of multiple camera angles, for example, helps mask the fact that there are scenes in which one student is playing two roles), but also it is edited well (the white-washed fade away during the cutting of Lavinia's hands is eerily effective). In addition, the video contains diverse musical overlays: from music montages (Radiohead blares over Lavinia's rape scene), to music for emphasis behind the dialogue, to very brief musical interludes between scenes. The students also added textual emphases at various points: from introductory notes about "The Bard at his Bloody Best," to subtitles when the dialogue is muddled, to extratextual commentary (when Tamora is introduced, the screen reads, "Roman Emperor takes Evil Goth Lady as bride.").

The video is immersed in the cultural markers of white, middle-class America: that is, cultural markers that are often assumed to be neutral or just American, but which are, in fact, racially marked as white. The music included, I think, provides the clearest cultural landscape for this video: hear in your mind Radiohead, Smashing Pumpkins, Broken Social Scene, and Coldplay (there is one other band featured, but I will get to that in a moment). This play list could be featured on the satirist Christian Lander's blog "Stuff White People Like."[38] In fact, Lander wrote a short piece for *Vanity Fair* entitled, "Stuff White People Like: Coldplay," and he jokes that "By understanding a white person's feelings toward the band, you can evaluate, recognize, and eventually exploit the type of white person you are dealing with." According to Lander the types of white people are "basic, standard, and advanced."[39] The music is slightly edgy, slightly indie, but with absolutely no blues, Latin, or ethnic roots—that is, no clear influences by non-Western, non-white music. The music is so prevalent in the video—filling a total of six of the thirteen minutes—that it offers an aural landscape that draws attention to the ways these students are negotiating race.

This aural landscape matches the students' decision to have Titus as the focus of their performance. Unlike many of my students who revel in Aaron's character and speeches, Aaron is barely present in this performance. Instead of allowing the student who plays Aaron to update his first speech in act two, the actor is provided with an onscreen textual blurb that reads simply, "Aaron the Moor: Tamora's Dirty Lover." Likewise, instead of an updated version of Aaron's speech to Lucius in act five, an onscreen textual blurb appears declaring, "Aaron spills the beans on every evil deed done." While the Goths and the Romans are not performed as being visually different from each other (in other words, the students do not try to emphasize the ethnic and racial differences between them performatively: they all wear the same casual American outfits of jeans, t-shirts, and hoodies[40]), the student who plays Aaron does wear a black-and-white image of Laurence Fishburne's face. Of course, Laurence Fishburne's connection with black Shakespearean characters is well established through his portrayal of Othello in the 1995 film version.[41] The fact that these students create a mask with Laurence Fishburne's face instead of that of Harry J. Lennix, the black American actor who played Aaron in Julie Taymor's 2000 film *Titus*, may indicate that they are not familiar with the film.[42] On the other hand, it may indicate that the students are reading Aaron as Othello: in other words, as the standard imagined trope for Shakespearean blackness. Clearly, they want to separate Aaron from the rest of the cast visually, but in doing so, they rely on the notion that this visual mask says more about Aaron's characterization than his long speeches convey. In a moment of comic levity, they even have Aaron's baby outfitted in a Laurence Fishburne mask in miniature.

Thus, implicitly the students separate Aaron's blackness from the Roman and Gothic whiteness *and* from their own racial identities, while the Roman and Gothic whiteness is not separated from their own racial identities. Performatively, this normalizes their own racial identities because "Roman" and "Gothic" are not visually or linguistically differentiated from the young Asian-American students who perform the roles. This is not to say that their Asian-ness is rendered invisible. On

FIGURE 7.2 Laurence Fishburne as Aaron the Moor's baby. Video still from a 2006 YouTube performance of *Titus Andronicus*.

the contrary, the students' Asian identities become the symbols—the faces and voices—for the universal condition, and, I think, this is an empowering move. Yet it comes at a price: the complete alienation and distancing of blackness. While some may argue that the students are merely following the lead of the play itself— clearly, *Titus Andronicus* renders Aaron "Other" both visually and linguistically[43]— they do not challenge the racial politics of the play itself. Rather, their performances are empowered because they keep black as Other (even if Fishburne is interpreted as a friendly Other).

At one moment, however, the performance implicitly invites the audience to interrogate the play's racial politics *and* the politics of contemporary American cultural production. Unlike Julie Taymor's 2000 film *Titus*, which alludes to Anthony Hopkins's turn as Hannibal Lecter in *Silence of the Lambs* when Titus appears to feed the "pasties" to Tamora, these students link Titus's desire for revenge with black-gangsta culture. The student who plays Titus walks into the kitchen in slow motion. He is wearing an apron, but he struts towards the camera, slightly listing to one side while staring intently into the camera. The music dubbed to overlay this action is the Geto Boys 1992 gangsta-rap anthem, "Damn it Feels Good to be a Gangsta." Known for initiating the popularity of the southern-style hip hop that blends soulful melodies with explicit lyrics about gangsta culture, the Geto Boys celebrate the authenticity of the "real gangsta-ass nigga."[44] Of course, the authenticity of racial and cultural identity is always unstable, and the desire to appropriate and perform another racial and cultural identity has endured through centuries of debates about identity politics, as critics like Judith Butler, Susan Gubar, E. Patrick Johnson, and Eric Lott have explored.[45] What is fascinating about this moment in the performance of *Titus Andronicus*, however, is the way all of these issues suddenly bubble to the surface, destabilizing the students' racial constructions and popular American cultural production.

Visually, the students appear to be borrowing from, or alluding to, the iconic slow motion, tough guy, white gangster (*not* black gangsta) walk that Quentin Tarantino made famous at the beginning of his 1992 film *Reservoir Dogs*.[46] The student's Titus is as purposeful and menacing in his strut as Tarantino's white gangsters are (played by Harvey Keitel, Tim Roth, and others). But the employment of the Geto Boys music makes any racial separation between white gangster and black gangsta impossible. As many will remember, this Geto Boys song was employed in the 1999 cult comedy *Office Space*, in which a white executive exercises and exorcises his rage by blasting "Damn it Feels Good to be a Gangsta" during his commute to work.[47] In fact, "Damn it Feels Good to be a Gangsta" explicitly uncouples black from gangsta culture (and even black from "nigga") with lyrics like, "Now gangsta-ass niggas come in all shapes and colors," and an ending verse that is supposedly voiced by the then-President George H. W. Bush:

Damn it feels good to be a gangsta
Getting voted into the White House
Everything looking good to the people of the world
But the Mafia family is my boss

. . .

To all you Republicans that helped me win
I sincerely like to thank you
Cuz now I got the world swingin' from my nuts
And damn it feels good to be a gangsta[48]

These lyrics point to an element of gangster/gangsta cultures that has been satirized in the popular media like *Jackie Brown*, *The Sopranos*, and *Vibe* magazine.[49] Despite the fact that the notion of "authenticity" is important in gangster/gangsta cultures, they are highly imitative of each other. Both the Mafia gangsters and black gangstas pride themselves on being original, rooted in a specific culture, and performing culturally rooted practices. Yet they emulate each other, while simultaneously disavowing the need to do so.

Although the *Titus Andronicus* performance video does not include these lyrics, the pairing of the song, the walk, and the plot (cooking two children into pies for their mother to eat) helps to destabilize simplistic understandings of race and cultural production. After all, this is a video that contains an Asian-American teenager, who is playing a Roman character written by an Elizabethan Englishman. Through his performance, this teenager is channeling a white director's vision of white gangster culture—a director who is a self-described devotee of black culture—while adding the music of a black, southern, gangsta-rap band whose lyrics link "real gangsta-ass niggas" with white Republican presidents. This moment effectively destabilizes the notion that any one race produces, owns, and/or controls culture: culture becomes a performance that can, and will, be appropriated by different people at different times.

Shakespeare's position in these Asian-American students' construction (or deconstruction) of culture is central because the play is *Titus Andronicus*. Unlike *Othello*, which I turn to shortly, this play has not yet been effectively appropriated into the American cultural imagination as *American*. And unlike the character Othello, Aaron is neither widely known nor a character who is frequently linked with the plight of black Americans. For these Asian-American students, then, their updated version of *Titus Andronicus* exhibits both slight pangs of anxiety and great celebrations of freedom with regard to the constructions and performances of race. The pangs of anxiety are revealed through their employment of the Laurence Fishburne mask and, thus, their avoidance of blackface. What seems to lie behind this performance choice is the notion that blackness is Other *and* that performing blackness as Other is a politically and socially charged issue. Yet the great celebrations of freedom come from their deconstructions of gangster/gangsta cultures: the ways they signal both cultures as American, which necessarily includes them, as Asian Americans, as well.

GANGSTA *OTHELLO*: COMPLICATING IDENTITY TOURISM ONLINE

On YouTube, *Othello* is regularly a vehicle for students to access, explore, and appropriate black cultural performance. The next YouTube posting I examine typifies this phenomenon. Labeled as a "gangster" adaptation, it signals the ways presumed racial and ethnic cultural distinctions may be blurred and deconstructed in Shakespearean performance.[50] This 2007 video neatly exemplifies the rich interpretive elements that are available to those willing to analyze the reception of classroom-inspired Shakespeare videos. A posted comment describes the adaptation as

"Chinese folks trying to be black la cosa nostra," making explicit the ways the boundaries bleed between gangster and gangsta.[51] Running approximately seven minutes, the video updates the end of act four, scene one of *Othello*, tracing Lodovico's arrival in Cyprus and Othello's destructive turn towards jealousy.[52] The setting of the play, however, has been transported so that Cyprus becomes "Grove Street" (although the students consistently pronounce it "Groove Street") and Venice becomes "Compton." To accompany the South Central Los Angeles-inflected flare of the setting, the language of the play is completely rewritten and subtitled throughout. For example, when Lodovico arrives in Groove Street, he greets Othello and Iago with, "What is up my home dizzles for shizzles," and Othello replies, "No much G, just chillin." Moreover, four of the six students in the video are clearly nonnative English speakers, and the emphasis on the gangsta rhetoric and dialect is particularly jarring because of their lack of fluency in English in general.

Tricia Rose captures what many scholars view as the impetus behind mainstream appropriations of black culture: "white teenage rap fans are listening to black culture, fascinated by its differences, drawn in by mainstream social constructions of black culture as a forbidden narrative, as a symbol of rebellion."[53] For critics like Rose, the diminution of African-American hip-hop culture to a generic "symbol of rebellion" is part and parcel of America's history of denying black authorship. Likewise, Susan A. Phillips argues that "the privilege to flirt inconsequentially with gang culture is an undeniable aspect of their ['middle-class youth's'] socially unmarked racial and class categories."[54] Several of the comments posted to the video support these arguments against appropriation. One post complains that the performance in fake black slang is "degrading [to] the black race."[55] And another objects, "that was the dumbest shit ever . . . u aint gangstas . . . damn son . . . yo fuck you n ur gay ass crew . . . D.O.C. fo life. if I evea see yo face ima get my crew to beat on you . . . you don't wanna fuck wiff us crips yo . . . so shut ur dumb ass up . . . fag."[56] Clearly, then, there was some online discussion about the politics of "identity tourism," again, as a performance that renders race a prosthetic that can be worn or performed with the presumption that no "real life" consequences will ensue.

Yet the students in this video—young, recent immigrants, who are newly speaking English—do not seem to be afforded the "privilege" of "identity tourism" in exactly the ways described above. The students do not seem to be operating from positions of "privilege": they are interpreted as cultural outsiders, as many of the posted comments make clear; they are the cultural outsiders. As one person posts, the video is "Probably some English practice thingy, like a language school project or some English practice learning slang."[57] Over and over again the posts stress that the students' Asian identities are decidedly marked, visible, and non-neutral, as opposed to Phillips's assumption that cultural appropriations signify the "unmarked" nature of the "racial and class" status of the participants: the students are "Asian," "Chinese," "Viets," and "Fobs" (at least 15 posts include this acronym for newly immigrated people: "Fresh Off the Boat"). Their need to "learn to speak English" is also stressed frequently.

I will begin with my own interpretation of the video—as a classroom-inspired performance that demonstrates the need to break out of the limitations of the Shakespearean script—only to show how anomalous my scholarly reading is against the posted online comments discussed below. Like many DIY YouTube Shakespeares, this *Othello* is comprised of part of a scene and not the entire play. More particularly, this video depicts the very end of act four, scene one, focusing on the equivalent of seventy lines of the playtext (4.1.205–279). Yet the video does not announce itself as filming only part of one scene; instead, it announces itself simply as *Othello*. While it is clear that it is an updated version of *Othello*—it is called "gangster" after all—it is not clear that this is not an updated version of the entire play. This ambiguity provides the potential to reimagine Shakespeare's role in performances of cultural and racial identities. First of all, it is difficult to tell what distinctions, if any, are maintained between Othello, the Venetians, and the Cypriots. The student who plays Othello, for example, is neither more nor less gangsta than the other characters in the video. All six of the students speak the same stilted slang, and no visual markers—costumes, props, makeup—have been employed to separate the characters. Thus, while this video traffics in troubling racial stereotypes, it does not traffic in ones constructed by Shakespeare. This is an all-gangsta world, and, therefore, Othello is not isolated by his racial and cultural differences.

Second, Desdemona does not die in this version of *Othello*. Othello beats her mercilessly in front of Iago and Lodovico but she survives and runs away. Without referencing the final deaths in Shakespeare's act five, this YouTube *Othello* does not provide the near pornographic murder that occurs in Desdemona's bed. Absent a familiarity with Shakespeare's version of the play, one could imagine that Desdemona lives a happy life away from Groove Street and Compton. She expresses no desire to return to Groove Street or Compton in this rendition, nor is she fated or destined to return. She is not fatally punished for her cross-cultural love affair because no boundaries are actually crossed.

This *Othello* exercise concludes, however, with its most significant revision. Despite its close re-writing of the ending of act four, scene one, the video's ending offers something wholly original. After Lodovico expresses dismay at having seen Othello beat Desdemona, the Venetians are set upon by two "Groove Street Hoodrats," who proceed to taunt, rob, and chase them out of Groove Street. If Groove Street stands in for Cyprus, then this video gives voice to a population that is nearly silenced in Shakespeare's original: the Cypriots who are in need of protection from the Turks, but who must pay the high price of Venetian colonization for that protection. By contrast, this YouTube *Othello* allows the representatives of the silenced, the invisible, and the colonized to talk back, giving them a highly visible autonomous existence. As they take back Groove Street, the "hoodrats" symbolize the potential power of the nonnative speakers in this video—likely given a school assignment to demonstrate their ability to understand a canonical text of Western civilization by translating it into modern slang. The students, like the "hoodrats," have the opportunity to demand to be recognized on their own "turf." The questions the "hoodrats" ask are appropriate questions for the students to ask of their teachers and viewers: "Yo guys what are you guys doin on our turf yo? . . . Yeah man, what do you guys think you are man?" Whose "turf" is Shakespeare and Shakespearean performance? Whose "turf" is gangsta culture? And what "turf" are we willing to recognize as belonging to the recent immigrants in our classrooms?

This said, my interpretation of the classroom-inspired video is at complete odds with those posted to the video. Based on the posted comments, I am alone in recognizing the ways the video pushes the boundaries of racial and cultural production. More disturbingly, many posts use the occasion of this video to unleash racist, anti-immigrant, sexist, and homophobic screeds: "Jesus fuck . . . that was absolutely fucken horrible. Get back on your ship and go back to China." "Wack u all losers go do ur math or something." "I want to lick her pussy." "I bet they have some crazy orgies." "I just want to stick my dick in her mouth." "What a bunch of fags." "Nice nice show how nigers are gay." "This is so gay . . . watching it has actually made me gay and now i must kill myself. Thanks."[58] If online "identity tourism" marks a degree of the power of privilege, it is fully harnessed here by the *unseen viewers* who know how to search, watch, and comment upon the videos without having to suffer any "real life" consequences for their blatant and unmasked racism, sexism, and homophobia. In a diagram, Michael Wesch describes the privileged power position of the unseen viewer in YouTube as follows: "anonymity + physical distance + rare & ephemeral dialogue = hatred as public performance."[59]

And yet, something in these responses goes beyond the general "hatred as public performance" that Wesch describes. In fact, there is something downright Shakespearean about the comments, as if the respondents are channeling Iago's racism and sexism. Despite (or perhaps because of) the fact that the video resists and rewrites the disturbing elements of Desdemona's death, the numerous sexualized responses to the female student's portrayal of Desdemona seem to attempt to reinscribe them: to strip this Desdemona of her life outside of *Othello*; to put the female student-actress into a subjugated role; and by labeling them as "gay," to police and humiliate the male student-actors' inability or unwillingness to subjugate Desdemona.

The respondents also make it clear that they want race to remain contentious both inside and outside of the text. One viewer, for instance, declares that the video is "even worse then with white actors," making it clear that the Shakespearean plot is *not* read as racially un-marked.[60] Furthermore, it is the blending of Shakespeare (which seems to be explicitly read as "white" in the commentator's mind), black gangsta culture, and the newly immigrated Asian players that viewers' find humorous. The video has received over 200 posted comments (and over 47,000 overall viewings). Of these, the vast majority employ acronyms for humor: "ROFL," "LOL," and "Haha" ("rollin on the floor laughing," "laugh out loud," and laughter, respectively). No posts comment on plot revisions. Instead, the responses explicitly and implicitly work to recreate and reinstate the power of Iago's rhetorical position as that of "The Man," the one who controls the positions and actions of both women and minorities. In my reading, this classroom-inspired performance video seems to indicate that the students may not fit into Shakespeare comfortably—and that they stand ready to articulate that resistance. The posted responses to this video, however, indicate that many anonymous respondents want to make sure that the actors' discomfort continues.

LOCATING THE LIMITS OF *OTHELLO* THROUGH *WONG FEI HUNG*

The final YouTube video I analyze exemplifies the fascinating production revisions made in classroom-inspired YouTube Shakespeares when they directly challenge the logic of a play and the unpredictability of online engagements.[61] Like the other two videos discussed above, this 2007 YouTube video is described as fulfilling a class project. And like the students in the two other videos, these six Asian-American students understand and update the Moor by crossing the performative borders between gangster and gangsta culture. For the most part, they dress in the white shirts, black suits, and thin black ties that Quentin Tarantino made famous as the modern uniform for white and black gangsters in *Reservoir Dogs* and *Pulp Fiction*.[62] They substitute lollypops for the ubiquitous cigarettes that Tarantino includes in his gangster wardrobe, but hold them dangling between their index and middle fingers to emphasize the sign for which they stand. The gangsta flair is evident from the opening frame when Eminem and 50 Cent's 2006 collaboration "You Don't Know" is dubbed over the character introductions.

Who run it?
You know, you actin' like you don't know
We run it
You know, but you actin' like you don't know[63]

The song makes it clear that gangsta culture, while often associated with black, urban youth, is, in fact, nondiscriminatory. This blending of different cultural signifiers is the solution to a "modern day depiction of what happened in *Othello*," as the video's written prologue indicates.[64] Unlike the *Titus Andronicus* video, which has a white, indie rock aural landscape, the music in this video is eclectic, ranging from hip hop and rap (Eminem, 50 Cent, T.I.), to Catholic hymns (Andrea Bocelli), to techno club music (East Clubbers), to pop (Christina Aguilera), to a Chinese movie anthem (the theme to *Once Upon a Time in China*).

This YouTube *Othello* updates the language and the setting of the play, focusing closely on act two, scene three in which Iago deliberately gets Cassio drunk. Running for a total of twelve minutes, it self-consciously and explicitly addresses the tensions between Shakespeare's play and modern issues. For example, the plot summary provided as a textual prologue reads in part: "there were these two guys supposedly, a guy and a girl, who loved each other very much. but the twist is the guy is black, and the girl is white! which, was like, MAJOR taboo waay back then. . . . *SPOILERS* everyone dies, so yea . . . kinda depressing. but that's life! and Shakespeare is teaching us all about it!" Since the students advertise their video as a "parody," the juxtaposition of the colloquial language, spelling, and punctuation with the summary of Shakespeare's plot is humorously jarring.

What also comes across, however, is that Shakespeare's plot of forbidden interracial love seems so foreign and dated as to be implausible. It was a "MAJOR taboo waay back then," but it may not be to these students, the rhetoric implies. The video keeps coming back to the absurdity that "everyone dies": it is stated in the prologue and voiced as the first line of spoken dialogue when the student who plays Roderigo reads the Folger edition of *Othello* and blurts out, "Everyone dies?! It's so stupid." The same thought is intimated at the end of the video when the students playing Cassio and Iago debate how to recover one's "rep" and "street cred." Cassio wonders, "Iago, what am I going to do?" In a metadramatic moment the student playing Iago replies, "What is Cassio going to do?" "I don't know. Check the book" (see Figure 7.1). Their expressions of shock and dismay that the play ends tragically implicitly challenge the assumption that Shakespeare, Shakespeare's plays, and Shakespeare's plots are for all times and all people. Hence the prologue's sardonic remark, "that's life! and Shakespeare is teaching us all about it!" The implication: they do not buy that Shakespeare is teaching them what they need or want to know.

Although the students update the scene in a stereotypical fashion (gangster/ gangsta), their production reaches beyond these cultural models. In fact, the students seem to have chosen this scene (2.3) as a way to break out of the tragedy of the play. Filming in a nicely appointed basement with a built-in fireplace and bar, the students construct this scene as more fun-loving than tragic. For example, the songs that Iago sings to ignite the night of drinking are imagined as blending into Cassio's drunken fantasies. Using a simple lip-synching technique, the student who plays Iago "sings" the club song, "It's a Dream," with three students serving as his back-up singer-dancers, bopping up and down to the fast techno beat. "Singing" along to the female vocalist's vapid lyrics ("I remember the time of my life. / In the southern light I saw the dream in the sky"), this Iago tilts his head from side to side, looking extremely sweet and innocent.[65] This is no tragic villain. The levels of cultural overlay impart the parodic effect for which the students are clearly aiming, deconstructing any sense that the tragic ending of *Othello* is inevitable.

While the updates to the plot provide a type of historical challenge to the notion of Shakespeare's universality, the students' version of the fight scene between Cassio and Montano expressly challenges the racial aspects of the cultural landscape of *Othello*. Moving the scene outside into a snow-covered backyard, the fight is conducted with swords. The players make it clear that this is no homage to traditional Renaissance stage fights when one shouts an introduction in Chinese and the theme song to the 1991 Chinese film *Once Upon a Time in China* (*Wong Fei Hung*) begins. With slow motion photography and an over-dubbed heart beat, the Chinese lyrics to the theme song play almost to completion. This staging invites us to consider the relevance of a Chinese cultural and racial identity to these students and their understanding of *Othello*.

Once Upon a Time in China is a decidedly anti-Western film. Set in late nineteenth-century China, the film depicts the fight waged against English, French, and American forces by the legendary martial arts hero Wong Fei Hung (1847–1924). Deeply invested in inspiring pride in the cultural practices handed down by the "ancestors," such as the practice of the martial arts, the film depicts the colonial endeavors by Western countries as not only repressive and violent, but also culturally dangerous.[66] Wong Fei Hung, played by Jet Li in the film, pointedly asks, "If the government regards martial arts training as illegal, the skills passed down by our ancestors will be lost forever. And if we are attacked by thieves, how are we to defend ourselves?" The "thieves" to which Wong Fei Hung alludes are, of course, the foreign countries who, the film suggests, plunder the material and cultural goods from China while simultaneously enforcing an adherence to their own Western ideals. Those who object to the cultural imperialism are referred to as "Chinese devils" by the Western traders.

The cultural conflict depicted in *Once Upon a Time in China* is emblematized in the relationship between Wong Fei Hung and Aunt Yee. When Aunt Yee returns to China from a stay in America, where she has been completely Westernized, Wong Fei Hung assumes the role of her protector. While she wonders why he is stuck in the old ways (he does not update his fashion with Western suits, for example), he wonders how she could forsake their cultural identity. The fight with the foreign powers, thus, becomes a fight to win back the Chinese women, who, the film suggests, are too easily swayed by cultural imperialism. Ultimately, Wong Fei Hung prevails by defeating guns and cannons with traditional Chinese martial arts, and, of course, he wins back the women, who are almost sold into slavery in America.

The theme song to *Once Upon a Time in China* serves as a leitmotif for Chinese cultural and racial pride, reprised in all of the major battles with the foreign traders. Included in an adaptation of *Othello*, this leitmotif interjects a significant symbol for Chinese pride, challenging the limited range of cultural and racial constructions depicted in the play. *Othello*, of course, does not seem to admit the possibility of cultural and racial pride for Othello, let alone for the Chinese. Thus, despite the fact that the students do not explore the racial and cultural tensions between Othello and the Venetians and/or Cypriots in this adaptation (aside from the seemingly ubiquitous performance of the borders between white gangster and black gangsta cultures), they attend to the connections between seemingly disparate histories of colonialism and imperialism: the expansionist zeal of the Renaissance (the cultural landscape within the play *Othello*), the first British Empire (the cultural landscape when *Othello* was written), and the age of imperialism (the cultural landscape of *Once Upon a Time in China*). *Once Upon a Time in China*, after all, does not end tragically for Wong Fei Hung, as it does for Othello. He is not divided against himself (culturally or racially), and he does not have to sacrifice himself for cultural unity. Instead, Wong Fei Hung becomes one of "our [China's] legendary heroes," as the film trailer promotes.

The students' persistent questions about the need for a tragic ending to *Othello*, coupled with their use of this distinctive leitmotif, implicitly deconstructs notions of Shakespeare's universal applicability. The video identifies the students' cultural and racial identities as noticeably absent from the play, and it frames the play's actual presentation of cultural and racial tensions as woefully inadequate. The problem the students proclaim is that *Othello* is not broad enough to encompass their own relationships with cultural and racial identity. If all the play offers them is that "everyone dies, so yea . . . kinda depressing," then that is not how it has to be. Shakespeare's script is not the only script for cultural and racial conflicts. This stunning YouTube video has garnered no posted responses and thus no history of reception. The number of viewings (shy of 600 in three years) has remained relatively static, without the representative spikes and online dialogue associated with hyperlinking elsewhere.

IMPLICATIONS FOR RESEARCH AND PEDAGOGY

Close readings of these three YouTube videos suggest some implications for Shakespearean research and pedagogy within this new archive of classroom-inspired performances. In terms of research, YouTube provides a new platform to record and assess the production and reception of Shakespearean performances that also presents methodological and ethical challenges. Because this archive is unlike established and institutionalized ones, Shakespeareans need to think through our opportunities and obligations as we mine its potential meanings and uses. The videos discussed in this chapter, for instance, highlight aspects of Shakespeare production and reception we rarely address directly. The preponderance of sexist, racist, and homophobic responses to the second video palpably demonstrates the ways anonymity (afforded by the YouTube platform) can unleash disturbing aspects of the play that are often suppressed or addressed in euphemistic terms (e.g., the uncontainable power of Iago's logic and rhetoric). Yet, paradoxically, anonymity can allow us to confront these textual effects directly, in essays such as this one and in the classroom, without directly attacking those who re-circulate it.

Beyond its ethical sensitivity to the age of the producer-users whose videos are discussed here, this chapter sidesteps the larger methodological question of the value of participatory research for Shakespeare studies: that is, research that directly engages the creators, participants, and respondents to these performance videos. While I have chosen not to do participatory research for this project, this decision has been challenging because it frequently necessitated sacrificing specificity. The chapter uses the generic term "Asian American" because I could not determine which specific ethnicity each participant identifies with; it uses the broad category "classroom-inspired performances" because I was not certain whether these videos stemmed from actual school assignments or extra-curricular recreational projects. Nor could I be certain exactly how the respondents came to comment on the videos: as friends, classmates, or random YouTube participants? These issues, I think, lead one to ask what aspects of social science research methods we as Shakespeareans are willing to adopt/adapt if we accept the You-Tube platform as a type of performance archive.

In a different register, we need to think more systematically about how to interpret a video's worthiness for scholarly attention. Is significance a matter of quantity? Do the number of responses generated (or the number of hyperlinks created) to the second video make it more worthy of study than the final video discussed, which generated no posted comments or hyperlinks? Or, is meaning and significance determined by quality, which could be a factor of either a video's uniqueness or representativeness?

In terms of the archives' potential uses, how do we mine an archive so deeply unstable as YouTube? Producers of YouTube videos can remove them at any point; and YouTube itself can alter videos by removing soundtracks, visuals, and any material it deems unacceptable. For instance, the *Titus Andronicus* video that I analyze now only exists on YouTube without any sound because the producers included copyrighted songs. When I first encountered the video, YouTube was not policing videos for pirated music so I watched and heard the "original" production. That "original," however, no longer exists on YouTube. How can we use, research, and write about materials that may not be accessible to others in the future? What role should durability and accessibility play in our research, and has this question changed from its earlier incarnations as we mined the often-inaccessible world of rare books and manuscripts?

In terms of Shakespearean pedagogy, if we accept that performance-based pedagogy has value then we must interrogate the meanings and uses of the work our students produce. If performance facilitates a deeper and more complex understanding of the Shakespearean text, what happens when a performance complicates the identity politics within the classroom? All three videos, for example, implicitly acknowledge the Asian and Asian-American students' racial and cultural distance from the text by performing Moorishness as gangster/gangsta. These videos all have wonderfully productive moments of fissure: like the linking of Titus with the blurred racial border between gangster/gangsta cultures; like the re-writing of *Othello* with the silent Cypriots revolting; like the explicit declaration that *Othello*'s tragic ending is "stupid." While the ways these students' challenge Shakespeare's universality and timelessness is refreshing—and in that sense the videos are original and entertaining—their performances of blackness are often regressive, limiting, and un-original. Racial constructions within the Shakespearean text are complex, but the complexity of racial constructions has only grown exponentially in the 400-year interim. How much time are we willing to devote to topics outside of Shakespeare's historical-cultural moment simply because they are inspired by the performance itself?

The ethical obligations of performance-based pedagogues mirror those of scholars. Many of our students choose to upload their performances to video-sharing Web sites like YouTube (whether or not it was part of their official school assignment), enabling long public afterlives for their work. The importance of Internet interactivity, as I have shown, is the opportunity for dialogues and debates across the borders of nation, race, ethnicity, sexuality, age, class, physical ability, educational background, etc—often for long periods of time. What is, or should be, the teacher's relationship with a performance assignment once it has a life in the archive of YouTube? Certainly we should equip our students to understand the complex nature of interactivity (e.g., reception cannot be contained, especially in an online platform like YouTube that enables anonymity). We might seek to harness the interactivity of YouTube by inviting our students to create textual and/or video responses to other videos. As more student performances of Shakespeare are uploaded to YouTube, our classroom assignments could involve metacritical and intermedial responses to other videos, thereby modeling critical viewing skills and responsible public discourse online.

Does our relationship with and responsibility to the classroom-inspired Shakespeare video end with the semester? What happens when our student's video becomes the material for someone's research? Or when our role as the assigner of performance-based work becomes the material for someone's research? As more scholars engage in participatory research involving the YouTube performance archive, these questions will recur with increasing frequency.

Situated at the nexus of performance studies, race studies, and Shakespearean research and pedagogy, the classroom-inspired performance video should be viewed as a genre in and of itself, archived, accessed, and analyzed on YouTube and similar platforms. As I hope this chapter demonstrates, this genre entails ethical, methodological, theoretical, and pedagogical challenges. In turn, these challenges necessitate new hybrid modes of engagement with Shakespearean performance, production, and reception. Oh, brave new world, indeed.

FIGURE 8.1 John Ortiz (Othello) and Philip Seymour Hoffman (Iago) in The Public Theater's 2009 production of *Othello* (directed by Peter Sellars). Photo by Armin Bardel.

Shakespeare's music, on the other hand, is not distinct from his narratives or from the actors' behavior; we need to both see and hear his characters' intentions. Which means, unavoidably, that Othello *must* be black.

—HILTON ALS[1]

Shakespeare can also serve as a beard for transgressive desires about race or female independence.

—FRANCES TEAGUE[2]

8

Conclusion

PASSING RACE AND PASSING SHAKESPEARE

IN PETER SELLARS'S *OTHELLO*

I WOULD LIKE to conclude this book with another pass through the meaning of the title: *Passing Strange*. In chapter 7, I examine Asian-American students who upload their performances of *Othello* onto YouTube, and I discuss their performances of American blackness as strange moorings and unmoorings of Shakespeare's play. I employ the verb unmoor because it is a nautical term that means to release a ship from its anchors (moorings), and this is an apt construction for what occurs performatively in these YouTube videos: they are released from many racial anchors. Of course, the pun on Moor as a Muslim in this metaphorical framework was also irresistible.

Nevertheless, I could have framed chapter 7 in terms of passing—in terms of Asian-American students passing for Shakespearean Moors through their appropriations of stereotypical black American cultural performances. So in these final pages I return to the notion of passing more directly to ask what it might mean to pass race and pass Shakespeare. While most of these final pages will be devoted to Peter Sellars's 2009 stage production of *Othello* starring John Ortiz as Othello and Philip Seymour Hoffman as Iago (see Figure 8.1), I begin with another parsing of passing.

The phrase "passing race" that I employ in the title to this concluding chapter is meant to register on several contradictory levels. On the one hand, it can mean to fake race with the implicit assumption that race is essential and stable—racial passing. On the other, "passing race" can mean to do or perform it correctly—to pass a test. Or, on a different register "passing race" can mean to skim over race, which might signify its inconsequential nature—to pass it by quickly. Or, it can mean to do away with race or to skip it completely—to pass it over.

Of course, the phrase "passing Shakespeare," then, has the same multivalent and contradictory meanings. In this phrase, Shakespeare is performed either authentically or inauthentically; he is rendered as either inconsequential or, worse, inessential. There are frequent debates about the nature of performing race in the popular and academic presses, and there are frequent debates about performing Shakespeare. When they are obviously paired—and, as I hope this book has demonstrated, they are always paired in contemporary American constructions, although many have just been too wary or negligent to address that dyspeptic elephant—notions of passing, in all of its significations, come to the fore, and debates often ensue.

Peter Sellars's 2009 stage production of *Othello* (coproduced by the Public Theater and the LAByrinth Theater Company, both in New York) sparked just such a controversy precisely because debates about passing and performance came to the surface through the production's nontraditional casting. Although nontraditionally cast classical productions are usually assumed to feature actors of color (which I discuss at length in chapter 4), *Othello* presents a unique performance history that moves from blackface to black-actor dominated (which I discuss at length in chapter 5). Sellars's production, however, destabilized the traditional narratives about Shakespeare, race, and performance that this play has invited and inspired precisely because his Othello was not black and the rest of the cast was not universally white. In other words, he presented the play in a type of racial Technicolor that challenged his audiences and critics.

In *Passing Strange*, I intentionally tried not to privilege *Othello* not only because so much good scholarship has already been written about the play and its constructions and performances of race but also because there are so many other rich textual and performance sources that frequently slip under the radar because they are popular and ephemeral (like the YouTube videos discussed in chapter 7). Nevertheless, *Othello* is a uniquely pressured text with a uniquely pressured performance and cultural history. As the Nigerian novelist Ben Okri writes, "Othello haunts the English stage" because of the unfinished nature of the play's significance in history.

What matters is that because of Shakespeare's genius Othello haunts the English stage. He won't go away. He is always there on the stage, a reminder of his unexplained presence in the white consciousness, and a symbol of the fact that black people and white are bound on the terrible bed of history. Doomed to his relentless cycle, he will not vanish from our dreams. And yet I dream of ways of liberating him from that bondage.[3]

By casting a Latino actor as Othello, Sellars challenged audiences and reviewers to rethink how race and racism function in our twenty-first-century world. To borrow Okri's words, Sellars invited the audience to liberate the play "from that bondage" and to leap "out of Shakespeare's terror."[4] While Sellars was explicit in his desire to change the cultural narrative we Americans have about *Othello* and race, he seemed stunned by the resistance to these changes from audiences and the critical community. In my estimation, notions of passing played a large role in the negative reactions the production (and Sellars himself) inspired.

Speaking with Laurence Fishburne about the challenges that face a black actor playing Othello, the classically trained black actor Harry J. Lennix said, "If you're a *black man* . . . and have any pride it's an extraordinarily problematical character to play."[5] As I explored in chapter 5, some black actors, like Hugh Quarshie, are refusing to play the role because it is a construction of a "white consciousness" (again, to borrow from Okri). Traditionally, Othello has been the only black character in a sea of white Venetians, who, when pushed, resort to racist epithets about the bestiality of blackness: "Even now, now, very now, an old black ram / Is tupping your white ewe" (1.1.88–89). Accordingly, Othello's gullibility, jealousy, rage, and destructive acts reflect his racial insecurity and loneliness: "Haply, for I am black, / And have not those soft parts of conversation / That chamberers have; or for I am declined / Into the vale of years" (3.3.267–270). More recently, theatre companies have experimented with casting black actors as Iago and Emilia to explore how racism can also fuel the actions of blacks (and people of color in general).[6] Nevertheless, these productions have not been plentiful, and the dominant production mode still privileges the uniqueness of Othello, *the* Moor of Venice (i.e., the only one).

This narrative of racial insecurity based on racial solitude (or near solitude), of course, is outdated in our multicultural, multiracial, and multilingual America because there are very few places in which a black man exists in isolation. The most isolated parts of our twenty-first-century American world are much more integrated than even the most vibrant trading centers in Renaissance Europe. So is it possible to make *Othello* say something of contemporary relevance to a twenty-first-century audience? Or must it exist as a museum piece of a bygone history and culture, and of bygone cultural constructions?

This is precisely the challenge Peter Sellars took up in his 2009 production of *Othello* (performed at New York University's Skirball Center). With eight members in the multiracial cast (three Latino actors, including John Ortiz as Othello, three black actors, and two white actors, including Philip Seymour Hoffman as Iago), Sellars's production interrogated how race and racism continue to function in a more integrated society. As the production notes make clear, there is nothing postracial in this world: the characters and audience members are not supposed to be blind to the races and ethnicities represented onstage or in the production. The racial, ethnic, and power dynamics may have changed (an Obama-like figure functions as the Duke/President), but racism and racial insecurities persist even when everyone is racialized (white, brown, and black). In other words, race and racism do not have to be boiled down to a simplistic dyad of black and white; they endure together even as we elect leaders of color for our integrated societies.

In other words, the questions that propelled Sellars's examination of *Othello* were not ones that stemmed from the Renaissance. While Ben Okri gives voice to the feeling that contemporary audiences feel trapped and "bound on the terrible bed of history" that Shakespeare created,[7] Sellars wanted to acknowledge that audiences bring new interpretations to old texts: the text is the same, but our visions are not. Thus, he approached the text and the production of that text from the lens of a twenty-first-century post-Obama worldview. As Sellars writes:

> The Obama era has thrust the world into a new search for language to describe race and relationships. Does this new language reflect a power shift or a shift in perception? Are those related? And the pushback to the age of Obama, the open disgrace of the [Sonia] Sotomayor confirmation hearings, in which a series of ignorant, intemperate, aging white men treated a distinguished legal scholar like their maid, and she was forced, in public, for purposes of entering the power structure, to accept it—where do we find ourselves now? What does it mean to all of us as we watch this woman of dignity publicly repudiate the phrase "a wise Latina," and everything it might stand for, including her own being?[8]

As must be clear from this statement, Sellars's questions were based on a very specific and contemporary historical moment: the 2009 racial and political American landscape. Past lenses through which *Othello* was explored and performed do not provide the framework for his approach, and he expected that they would not form the framework for his audience either.

Sellars intentionally did not seek to update the text of *Othello*, opting to keep Shakespeare's language largely intact (save a radical editing of the first and fifth acts), because he wanted to explore what happens when one pairs Shakespeare's language with new historical and cultural environments: "[T]he play itself doesn't change, but we who are reading it and interpreting it bring to it new realities and new possibilities."[9] Barry Edelstein, the Director of The Public Theater's Shakespeare Initiative, explains exactly how Sellars encouraged his cast to approach the text. While many who work in mainstream productions of Shakespeare repeat the mantra that "Shakespeare's characters say what they mean and mean what they say," Sellars urged his actors to search for "subtext, insinuation, half-truth, misdirection, and hidden meaning" in every line.[10]

Therefore, in this production Iago has a clear motive to "hate the Moor" because Othello *is* having an affair with Emilia (1.3.368). Likewise, Edelstein explains that Sellars eschewed taking "refuge in irony": there were no winks or nudges towards the audience. Instead, the actors had to grapple with expressing the truth of each line (even if that line is interpreted as having immense subtext).[11] And, finally, Edelstein explains that while Sellars (like most modern stage directors) believes that lines must be cut in order to create a manageable production, he refused to cut "the text that seems most problematic."[12] "[T]he assumptions that make a passage seem dispensable are to him what theater exists to question in the first place," Edelstein writes. "Does a given line seem incomprehensible? Then we must ask what about our language has changed in 400 years that makes the line hard for us to understand."[13]

Again, the focus for Sellars's production was always on the moment in which it was created, highlighting the twenty-first century lenses that the actors and audience members bring to *Othello*. Truly disavowing a belief that the original and originary can ever be recovered, Sellars created and celebrated the notion that performance is adaptation.[14] And one of the central lenses for Sellars's production was a focus on the dynamics of race in an era in which black men are in positions of authority and Latinas become Supreme Court justices. The racial dynamics will not be the same as those constructed in the Renaissance, but that does not mean that those dynamics are completely harmonious. Sellars's Duke is black (played by Gaius Charles), Othello is Latino (John Ortiz), his lieutenant Cassio is black (LeRoy McClain), his ensign Iago is white (Philip Seymour Hoffman), the Governor of Cyprus is a black woman (Saidah Arrika Ekulona), Roderigo is Latino (Julian Acosta), and the accompanying wives, Desdemona and Emilia, are white and Latina respectively (Jessica Chastain and Liza Colón-Zayas).

The reviews of the production, however, rarely engaged with the explicit lenses through which Sellars wanted *Othello* to be viewed. The challenge for audience members and reviewers alike seemed to stem from the conflicting notions of passing that they brought to the production. The published reviews reveal that critics were uncertain exactly how Sellars was passing through race and Shakespeare. For example, many reviews revealed how difficult it is to discuss the semiotic meanings of race in any given production (as discussed at length in chapter 4). In many multi-racially cast productions, contemporary reviewers grapple with whether or not to notice race in their reviews. Is the audience supposed to be blind to the racial differences represented onstage? Or are the differences intentional and meaningful within the production? Many reviewers, in fact, have opted not to discuss race in their performance reviews.[15]

Instead, reviewers often focus on the actors' mastery (or lack thereof) of Shakespearean verse as a type of code that reveals the racial makeup of the acting company.[16] Melissa Rose Bernardo, for instance, writes that the white "Hoffman has the most ease with Shakespeare's language in this modern-dress production," and the implied subtext is that the actors of color in the company have less "ease" with the Elizabethan verse (I can almost hear the reviewer saying, "I hear black and brown people").[17] Likewise, John Simon includes this not-so-veiled code about the multiracial cast: "Sellars has reduced the cast to seven actors, mostly from LAByrinth . . . none of whom has the faintest inkling of how to speak verse and most of whom do not even manage anything passing for stage English."[18] Despite the fact that Simon talks about pronunciation, his reader gets a clear racial picture from his linguistic assessment of the actors' lack of fluency in "stage English."

Simon gets even bolder in connecting his linguistic assessment (although he would clearly term it an aesthetic one) with a clearly racialized one later in this same review. For instance, he goes on to add that Emilia is played by the "short overweight Liza Colón-Zayas with a pronounced Latino inflection," and that Saidah Arrika Ekulona's Bianca Montano sounds "exactly like the African madam she played in [Lynn Nottage's] *Ruined*."[19] Simon cannot see her Shakespearean role because he hears her blackness. This production does not sound or look like what he images Shakespeare should be. And he even pronounces that the production "offends Shakespeare," thereby attempting to restore authority to the dead author. Simon's use of the word "passing" (the actors cannot "manage anything *passing* for stage English"), however, indicates the exact problem that he has with the production. The actors cannot pass for white characters in his eyes, ears, or mind; they cannot pass for white actors; and, therefore, they cannot pass aesthetically for Shakespearean.

Other reviewers, however, viewed the production in terms of an entirely different type of passing: a passing over race, a willingness to rewrite/restage the play without race as its central component. For many reviewers this was lamentable, and they expressed feelings of disappointment and regret for the loss of the certainty that *Othello* is a play about race: a race play. Writing for the *Associated Press*, Michael Kuchwara condemned the "high-concept" production. "And he's given the production a post-racial sheen," Kuchwara notes with derision, "celebrating diversity rather than having the Moor stand out because of his blackness."[20] For Kuchwara, then, only Othello's blackness could render this play as one about race: without his blackness the play is "post-racial."

Likewise, Scott Brown writes for the *New York Magazine*, "It is 'postracial' in that Othello is no longer a black man in a white world, but a light-skinned, racially indeterminate man in a casually multiracial Venice."[21] Again, the production is interpreted as passing over race because it is multiracial instead of racially dyadic (one black man in white Venice and Cyprus). And, finally, in the *New York Post* Elisabeth Vincentelli cries that Sellars's production is filled with modern clichés including "politically correct racial elements that feel opportunistic (we're in the age of Obama in case you missed it) and random (Othello is played by Latino John Ortiz)."[22] In this critic's judgment, the production could not be addressing race because having more than two races and ethnicities onstage must mean that it is a production that celebrates political correctness. While some critics voiced praise for postraciality, they too frame the production as one that passes over race. "It is the sexual politics that are at the forefront of this Othello," Simon Saltzman celebrates in his *CurtainUp* review.[23] For these critics, then, the security of their understanding of the semiotics of race in *Othello* was disrupted by a belief that more than two races and ethnicities onstage renders race meaningless and, therefore, passed over.

Other critics, however, critiqued Sellars's *Othello* for passing over important cultural, racial, and performance histories that they believe can only be conveyed when Othello is performed by a *black man*. Hilton Als's review in *The New Yorker*, which I cite in part as the first epigraph for this chapter, offers the most thoughtful example of this type of review. His review begins with a discussion about classical texts that require "readers of color to police the pages, instead of immersing themselves in the solitary beauty of reading" because "nigger" is so frequently and casually used by the Hemingways, Cathers, Faulkners, and Bellows of the Western canon.[24] Then he declares that it is "sad to think that readers of color may even avoid *Othello*, one of Shakespeare's greatest plays" because they have seen blackface performances, like the famous 1965 film version starring Laurence Olivier.[25] And then, Als launches into a miniature history lesson about conceptions of Moors in the Renaissance and the subsequent performances of blackness in the period.

Als explains that *Othello* has traditionally provided one of the few classical plays that invites and enables discussions about race in performance. It is a play that addresses race directly, but critics since the early eighteenth century have debated the best ways to dramatize the play's terms. Samuel Taylor Coleridge, for example, famously quipped in one of his 1818 lectures on Shakespeare that "it would be something monstrous to conceive this beautiful Venetian girl falling in love with a veritable negro."[26] Accordingly, there was a long line of actors in the nineteenth century who decided that Othello was far more "tawny" than black. It was only in the late twentieth century that Othello became a role dominated by black actors.

This type of history echoes through the beginning of Als's review. Thus, summarizing the plot of the play, Als declares: "Violence, sex, acting out, internalizing the judgment of others: Othello becomes, in Cyprus's rocky terrain, Bigger Thomas's elder. And, like Bigger, he is essentially an existentialist figure, at once empty and full."[27] For Als, the payoff of this seventeenth-century text only comes when Othello is rendered historically, culturally, and racially full as a black man. He is rendered empty—that is, without the significance of that rich history—when his blackness is not essential. Without a black Othello, Als questions if the audience is really forced to "confront [its] own prejudices?" He pointedly asks, "Has Sellars unintentionally given in to the racism that sometimes infects the white-oriented theatrical avant-garde?"[28] These questions reveal, I think, Als's implicit belief that without a black Othello (remember, he declares that "Othello must be *black*") the production passes over history and allows Othello to exist as free-floating symbol, thereby, passing over what makes this "one of Shakespeare's greatest plays."

Of course, my response to all of the criticism of the production is that racism, insecurity, and betrayal do not cease to be dramatic issues when presented within a multiracial and multiethnic world. They simply become more complex, fraught, and difficult to disentangle. Clearly this is exemplified by the reviewers' inability to linguistically control and assess the semiotic meaning of race in the production. The reviewers consistently resort to expressions of longing for the bygone days of black and white, while Sellars challenges them to see the twenty-first century in a glorious racial and ethnic Technicolor.

As a disclaimer, I should state that I was tangentially involved in Sellars's 2009 *Othello* production because Sellars said my published work influenced his concept for the production. Thus, I saw the production twice, participated in two preshow events scheduled by the LAByrinth and Public theatre companies, and spoke at length with Sellars about his vision. While I was predisposed to like the production because of my tangential involvement with it, I have to admit that I felt challenged by it at times. This was not an *Othello* that was easily recognizable. It was paced slowly so that every word could be heard and understood: the show ran nearly four hours. The emotional arcs were surprising because all irony was removed, especially from Iago's asides. And the cast was small so that some parts were collapsed together: Bianca and Montano became one female character. These aspects made the show different, surprising, and at times irritatingly new, but the issues around race were refreshing and bold in my estimation.

While my reception of the racial politics of the production lined up seamlessly with Sellars's expressed intention, I appear to have been in the minority based on the published reviews of the show. Because of this disparity, I have wondered if my acceptance of the show's multiracial portrayal as one that is decidedly not postracial stems solely from my own vision. I have had to interrogate how colored my own vision is, and how colored it should be. Was the show truly challenging claims that we are living in a postracial world, or am I simply predisposed to read, interpret, and see race as semiotically meaningful in Shakespearean productions?

While I have written about the problematic nature of the semiotics of race in performance, I had never conceived of the issues as being related to notions of passing. Until seeing the show, I had not fully theorized the ways that notions of passing, authenticity, and textual/performance stability/instability come to the fore in nontraditional productions. I had not anticipated that notions of passing— again, I am willing to keep all of the multivalent definitions in play—are plagued by notions of the original and the originary. Whether or not one views passing as a radical act or one that reinforces conservatively constructed categories, one must acknowledge that all notions of passing privilege origins, originals, and originary moments. The difference comes with whether one believes that these categories and moments can be completely rewritten, ignored, faked, or adhered to.

While Sellars expected his audience to come with a deep immersion in the historical and political present (a 2009 Obama-era America), he did not anticipate that they would come with deeply entrenched memories of, and commitments to, older performance histories. I felt a slight burden of responsibility for this short-sightedness. Sellars's 2009 production of *Othello* wanted the audience to interpret the play in terms of a new racial, ethnic, and political framework, but the critics made it clear that they were haunted by older ones. Of course, part of my short-sightedness stems from the fact that the discourses of Shakespearean performance theory do not intersect with race studies in as deliberate and sustained a manner as they need to do to advance the dialogue.

At this moment I want to demonstrate the distances in theoretical and rhetorical approaches to Shakespeare and race that need to be traversed and bridged before we can create this deliberate and sustained dialogue between Shakespeare studies and race studies. In her book, *Shakespeare and the American Popular Stage*, Frances Teague celebrates and revels in the potential power of risk taking that is afforded the appropriators of Shakespeare (specifically in musical adaptations of Shakespeare). She writes, "Shakespeare can also serve as a beard for transgressive desires about race or female independence."[29] Of course, she appropriates the notion of a "beard" from queer rhetoric, in which a gay man hides his sexual identity behind a "beard" of a heterosexual relationship. This position is "transgressive" in

Teague's figuration because it is a disguise that has been freely chosen. Thus, when she asks, "What occurs when Shakespeare is a beard," her answer is "unconventionality," an ability "to take risks," and racial and sexual transgression.[30]

I want to place Frances Teague's celebration of transgression alongside Ben Okri's anxiety about racial passing because the statements exemplify how difficult it is to put these two writers and thinkers into dialogue. To return to Okri one last time, he writes, "Othello haunts the English stage. He won't go away. He is always there on the stage, a reminder of his unexplained presence in the white consciousness. . . ."[31] Teague, and I think Sellars, wants to invest the production with a degree of authority and autonomy that has the ability to reshape historical and cultural dialogues: the production is a beard because authority rests in the decision to wear the beard. On the other hand, Okri, and many other black actors and scholars, invest the cultural history with a degree of authority that resists appropriative moves: the production passes because authority rests in long-past racial constructions that are disempowering for many.

Teague and Okri reach radically different conclusions because they construct Shakespeare and race in such radically different logics and rhetoric. It is my hope, however, that *Passing Strange* has begun to untangle these differences so that a dialogue can actually ensue. It is not that Als and Teague, or Harold Bloom and Queen Latifah (as discussed in chapter 2), or Dinesh D'Souza and Maya Angelou (as discussed in chapter 3), or Robert Brustein and August Wilson (as discussed in chapter 4), or The Globe Theatre and Hugh Quarshie (as discussed in chapter 5), or the American Council of Trustees and Alumni and Gauri Viswanathan (as discussed in chapter 6) will ever agree. They may not be able to, and consensus is not necessarily my goal. Rather, I have striven to demonstrate the challenges that prevent more sustained and informed dialogues about Shakespeare and race in contemporary America.

As I indicated in chapter 1, however, the revelation and analysis of the challenges that prevent this dialogue are not the only goals for this book either. As a self-professed scholar-activist, a race woman, I have written *Passing Strange* as an act of intervention and activism. Towards advancing that goal, I conclude with some specific notes for each of my target audiences. (Here is my polemical side!)

Secondary School Teachers: You are the individuals who can make the largest difference in the future of race in America because you are teaching and guiding our children through the crucial years of their psychological development (including their racialized identity development). If you are an English teacher and you are responsible for teaching Shakespeare, please use the opportunity to facilitate discussions about race and performance. Although there is a lot of ground to cover when teaching Shakespeare—comprehension of the plots, language, and the

historical contexts in which the plays were written—do not be tempted to segregate or silo discussions about Shakespeare from discussions about race (historically or contemporaneously). Provide some performance history with regard to
race, and then enable and empower your students to debate how Shakespeare
should be performed with (or without) regard to the racial makeup of your particular classroom. Teach the power of interactivity by demonstrating constructive
ways to view, analyze, and comment upon Shakespearean performances on the
Internet, and encourage your students to incorporate an awareness of racial per-
formativity into their engagements. Despite the fact that "Generation M" is commonly labeled as the postrace generation, race is still a salient category for them,
and they need more concrete tools to facilitate their discussions and analyses of
this category. Shakespeare can and should be one of the lenses through which
these tools are disseminated.

Theatre Practitioners: In the realm of actor training, discussions about Shakespeare, race, performance history, and performance trends must be articulated in
a more systematic fashion. Despite the fact that many actor training programs
have incorporated important segments on multicultural theatre, almost none
have incorporated segments on multicultural classical theatre. As most American
classical theatre companies are no longer monoracial (i.e., all white), then all actors
of all races need to be trained in ways to address the semiotics of race in performance. In turn, theatre companies need to foster sustained and organized discussions both internally and externally (i.e., in their communities) to articulate what
their visions and goals are for the semiotics of race in their individual theatre company. If companies are sincere about their desires to diversify their audiences in
terms of both age and race (an important way to protect and increase revenue
streams), then they must move beyond the unspoken assumption that race, color,
and ethnicity do not matter onstage. Companies and their communities should
decide together if and how they should matter and when. These dialogues do not
have to result in one answer or one practical method. Instead they should create a
space in which the historical, cultural, theoretical, and practical issues of race unite
the company with their community; in fact, the result could be multiple practical
methods and dialogues about them in the future.

Community Activists: Many arts-based education/reform programs have discovered the power of Shakespeare in performance. Prison programs, inner-city
school programs, programs for at-risk youth, and business consulting programs
have all employed Shakespeare in performance to achieve their goals: nonrecidi-
vism, access to higher education, enlightened leadership, and so forth. The results
of these programs are stunning, and they reveal a hunger in the American population to engage in acts of sustained close reading, analysis, and performance.

Nevertheless, these tactics and goals do not have to be achieved through the erasure of discussions about race. If arts-based education/reform programs provide ways to rewrite and redistribute authority by presenting Shakespeare's texts as unstable (i.e., in need of stability and finality through interpretation and performance), then Shakespeare's authority does not have to trump the unique and specific cultural and racial dynamics of the group involved. A shift in authority through the promotion of textual instability does not have to entail a trashing of Shakespeare. Instead, authority is shared betwixt and between the author, the text, the performance, and the performers, creating a space for racialized histories, identities, and conflicts to enter the larger project of education and reform.

Shakespeare Scholars: Race, like gender, has had a faddish focus in Shakespeare studies. There are moments when the field seems to be expansive and inclusive, encouraging work that focuses on race, and at other times I feel like I am speaking to a very small audience of peers. If the field were to support the inclusion of race studies more systematically and consistently, then our ranks may diversify more rapidly and thoroughly. I find it incredibly depressing that I can name most of the Shakespeareans of color despite the fact that our professional organizations are relatively large. On the most simplistic level, this means that we need to encourage our undergraduates and graduates who are interested in both Shakespeare studies and race studies to pursue a career in academia. While not all of these students are people of color, many of them are. On a different level, it also means that we should encourage our students who are interested in Shakespeare studies and social activism. These students, I think, are less cultivated and encouraged to pursue an academic career because they have what might be deemed *practical* skills (e.g., working with the incarcerated or at-risk youth). Thus, these students often opt for jobs in the nonprofit sector instead of pursuing a doctorate. If they were truly invited into our ranks, however, our conversations and debates might change radically. While I recognize that not everyone in the field would welcome this move towards activism, I do think it would help to integrate our racial makeup considerably.

In chapter 1, I provided two anecdotes to demonstrate the typical debates about Shakespeare and race. In one anecdote a black, illiterate, recovering drug addict was described as being *freed by* Shakespeare to discover the road to literacy and recovery. In another, a black Shakespeare scholar was described as being *freed from* Shakespeare to focus on issues of race and racial activism. While I still view these anecdotes as framing the extremes of the American constructions of both Shakespeare and race, they also provide the logical and rhetorical distance we must bridge in order to create a dialogue. In *Passing Strange* I have tried to demonstrate, examine, and analyze less extreme examples of this distance, while always seeking ways to advance the conversation. My ultimate hope is that I have created new spaces and vocabularies for teachers, students, actors, artistic directors, theatre critics, reform activists, scholars, and others to debate what constructions of Shakespeare and race we want to put forward in the twenty-first century. I doubt we will agree, but our mutual understanding of the multiple and varied constructions should help to create new and vibrant conversations and performances that are not limited to the *freed by* and *freed from* binary of the twentieth century.

NOTES

CHAPTER 1

1. Mooney, *Black is the New White*, 15–16.
2. Singh, "Afterword," 238.
3. Akala, "Shakespeare."
4. For more extensive work on the use of "scare quotes" and "quotation marks" with Shakespeare see Garber, *Quotation Marks*; and Harries, *Scare Quotes from Shakespeare*.
5. Two canonical texts on the constructions and definitions of race in the United States are Jordan, *White Over Black*; and Omi and Winant, *Racial Formation in the United States*.
6. "Passing," Oxford English Dictionary.
7. Brontë, *Shirley*, 346.
8. Stevenson, *The Black Arrow*, 145.
9. Hardy, *Tess of the D'Urbervilles*, 82–83.
10. Conrad, *Heart of Darkness*, 51.
11. Ibid.
12. Schlossberg, "Introduction," 1.
13. Stew, *Passing Strange*.
14. Sontag, "A Musical Star Plucked from the Underground."
15. Quoted in Oldham, "Stew Interviewed by Madeleine Oldham."
16. Stew, *Passing Strange*, 25.
17. Schlossberg, "Introduction," 4.
18. For an excellent work on constructions of the past see Bennett, *Performing Nostalgia*.
19. To give you an idea of just how unoriginal my appropriation of Shakespeare's phrase is as a title for a book, here are the most popular works of fiction and nonfiction:

Aird, *Passing Strange* (a novel); MacLeod, *Passing Strange* (a novel); Sale, *Passing Strange* (a novel); Citro, *Passing Strange* (an historical book); Sandweiss, *Passing Strange* (an historical book); and Tuan, *Passing Strange and Wonderful* (a theoretical book).

20. Jones, *Othello's Countrymen*; Barthelemy, *Black Face, Maligned Race*; Loomba, *Gender, Race, Renaissance Drama*; and Hall, *Things of Darkness*.
21. Two texts that address the Astor Place Riots in depth are Levine, *Highbrow/Lowbrow*; and Cliff, *The Shakespeare Riots*.
22. See, for example, Bristol, *Shakespeare's America, America's Shakespeare*; Sturgess, *Shakespeare and the American Nation*; and Teague, *Shakespeare on the American Popular Stage*.
23. See, for example, Massai, *World-Wide Shakespeares*; Orkin, *Local Shakespeares*; and Dionne and Kapadia, *Native Shakespeares*.
24. Cartelli, *Repositioning Shakespeare*.
25. Erickson, *Citing Shakespeare*.
26. Royster, *Becoming Cleopatra*.
27. See, for example, Henry Louis Gates, Jr.'s now-canonical book that provides a theory for African-American literary criticism: Gates, *The Signifying Monkey*.
28. Two seminal postcolonial works that were published during, and contributed to, the culture wars are Said, *Orientalism*; and Viswanathan, *Masks of Conquest*.
29. For an excellent overview and analysis of the culture wars see Guillory, *Cultural Capital*.
30. Kaplan, "Introduction," xxv.
31. Ibid.
32. Ibid.
33. See, for example, Margaret Jane Kidnie's excellent new book, *Shakespeare and the Problem of Adaptation*.
34. See, for example, the amazing performance histories in Stern, T., *Making Shakespeare*; and Palfrey and Stern, *Shakespeare in Parts*.
35. John H. Bracey, Jr. quoted in Tidwell and Tracy, ed., *After Winter*, 413. See chapter 3 for more on this statement.
36. Drake and Cayton, *Black Metropolis*. Carby discusses their "account for the emergence of this idea" in her book *Race Men*, 4.
37. Neal, "Does Denzel Always Have to Represent?"
38. Quoted in Clarke and Tifft, "A Race Man Argues for a Broader Curriculum."
39. Carby, *Race Men*, 5. She writes, "What we have inherited from them and from others is a rarely questioned notion of masculinity as it is connected to ideas of race and nation."

CHAPTER 2

1. Simonson, *The Stage is Set*, 99.
2. See the Web sites MegaEssays.com and HelpMe.com for these examples.
3. Bristol, *Shakespeare's America, America's Shakespeare*, 5.
4. Ibid., 1, 5.
5. Quoted in Levine, *Highbrow/Lowbrow*, 31.

6. Auld, "Revelatory Brilliance."

7. Quoted in Shattuck, "One or Two Things He Knows about Teenagers."

8. Quoted in Sorenson, "To the Point."

9. Pearson, *Up From the Mission*, 341.

10. *Henry V*, dir. Kenneth Branagh.

11. *Scotland, PA*, dir. Billy Morrissette.

12. *Hamlet 2*, dir. Andrew Fleming.

13. *Suture*, dir. Scott McGehee and David Siegel. All dialogue comes from the DVD version of the film.

14. Freud, *The Interpretation of Dreams*.

15. Garber, *Shakespeare's Ghost Writers*, 169.

16. Greenblatt, *Hamlet in Purgatory*.

17. Omi and Winant, *Racial Formation in the United States*, 2.

18. Ibid., 1.

19. Ibid., 156.

20. Ibid.

21. Wilson, *The Ground on Which I Stand*, 29, 31.

22. Quoted in DiGaetani, "August Wilson," 280.

23. Burns, "Suturing Over Racial Difference," 74.

24. Thompson, "Practicing a Theory/Theorizing a Practice," 1.

25. The Wilson-Brustein debate was published in four issues of *American Theatre* 13, nos. 7–10 (September–December 1996). *American Theatre* allowed Wilson and Brustein to respond to each other throughout these issues.

26. Several critics have written about this disruption, including Massachelein, "Double Reading/Reading Double"; and Drake, "Review."

27. Miller, "Suture (elements of the logic of the signifier)."

28. Oudart, "Cinema and Suture," 36.

29. Silverman, "(On Suture)," 138.

30. Quoted in Romney, "How Did We Get Here," 33.

31. Quoted in Grundmann, "Identity Politics at Face Value," 25.

32. Quoted in Romney, "How Did We Get Here," 34.

33. Quoted in Grundmann, "Identity Politics at Face Value," 26.

34. Grundmann, "Identity Politics at Face Value," 24.

35. Giroux, "White Noise," 65, 67.

36. Du Bois, *The Souls of Black Folk*, 45.

37. Quoted in DiGaetani, "August Wilson," 280.

38. Du Bois, *The Souls of Black Folk*, 45.

39. Omi and Winant, "Once More, with Feeling," 1570.

40. Ibid.

41. Omi and Winant, *Racial Formation in the United States*, 158.

42. *Bringing Down the House*, dir. Adam Shankman. All dialogue and commentary come from the DVD version of the film.

43. Bloom, *Shakespeare*, 31, 4.

44. Ibid., 8.

45. Ibid., 313, 662, 721. For more on how Bloom's *Shakespeare* fits into popular treatments of Shakespeare in the late twentieth century see Thompson, "Rewriting the 'Real.'"

46. These are all actual titles of books that begin *Shakespeare and. . . .*

47. Ajax, *Shakespeare or Bacon?*; and Martin, *Shakespeare or Bacon?*

48. Jonson, "To the memory of my beloved, The Author Mr. William Shakespeare," lines 43 and 17.

49. Adam Shankman, the director of *Bringing Down the House*, got his start in Hollywood by choreographing and then directing music videos.

50. Simonson, *The Stage is Set*, 99.

51. Jones, *Othello's Countrymen*; Barthelemy, *Black Face, Maligned Race*; Loomba, *Gender, Race, Renaissance Drama*; Hall, *Things of Darkness*; and MacDonald, *Women and Race in Early Modern Texts*.

CHAPTER 3

1. Quoted in *After Winter*, 413.

2. D'Souza, *The End of Racism*, 337–386, 477–524.

3. Ibid., 477.

4. Smith, B., "Lenny Henry on his Leeds *Othello* Debut."

5. Hale, "Theatre Review."

6. Quoted in Ahad, "Shakespeare Role is Murder for Lenny."

7. This quotation is taken from the description of "Lenny and Will" listed on the BBC Radio 4 Web site: http://www.bbc.co.uk/radio4/arts/pip/46ff6/ (accessed June 8, 2009).

8. Reynolds, "Voices from Beyond the Radio 4 Compound."

9. This quote is taken from the description of "Lenny and Will: Act Two" listed on the BBC Radio 4 Web site: http://www.bbc.co.uk/radio4/factual/pip/sj2pl/ (accessed June 8, 2009).

10. Soyinka, "Shakespeare and the Living Poet," 1.

11. Ibid., 4.

12. Gates and McKay, *The Norton Anthology of African American Literature*. I remember these statements from when I was a graduate student at Harvard, and Gates was kind enough to confirm them via a personal email. Gates, Personal Correspondence.

13. Angelou, "Journey to the Heartland."

14. Ibid.

15. Ibid.

16. Cheney, *Humanities in America*, 14. For analyses of Cheney's appropriation of Angelou's statement see Chedgzoy, *Shakespeare's Queer Children*, 100–106; Erickson, *Rewriting Shakespeare, Rewriting Ourselves*, 111–123; and Garber, "Shakespeare as Fetish," 248–250.

17. Cheney, *Humanities in America*, 14.

18. Garber, "Shakespeare as Fetish," 249.

19. Cheney, *Humanities in America*, 32.

20. There was a discussion about a claim that Shakespeare, among other historical figures, was black on the white supremacist Web site "Stormfront": http://www.stormfront.org/forum/showthread.php/louis-theroux-meets-black-supremists-370794.html (accessed June 8, 2009).

21. See the Web site, "UK Commentators Blogspot": http://ukcommentators.blogspot.com/2007/02/self-hating-white-liberals-again.html (accessed June 8, 2009).

22. Gilroy, *Against Race*, 327–356.
23. Landry and MacLean, Introduction to "Subaltern Studies," 203.
24. Spivak, "Subaltern Studies," 206.
25. Ibid.
26. Ibid., 220, 232.
27. Ibid., 214.
28. Spivak, "In a Word," 4.
29. Quoted in Danius and Jonsson, "An Interview with Gayatri Chakravorty Spivak," 34.
30. Ibid., 43, 42.
31. Ibid., 43.
32. See, for example, Gilroy's chapter, "'Third Stone from the Sun': Planetary Humanism and Strategic Universalism," in *Against Race*, 327–356.
33. Quoted in Danius and Jonsson, "An Interview with Gayatri Chakravorty Spivak," 43–44.
34. Carpio, *Laughing Fit to Kill*.
35. Dhondy, *Black Swan*, 44.
36. Ibid., 45.
37. Ibid., 139, 164.
38. Of course, one must wonder what marvels could have been produced between Farrukh Dhondy and Jeffrey Masten, the literary critic who specializes in collaboration, authorship, and sexuality. See, for example, Masten, *Textual Intercourse*.
39. Dhondy, *Black Swan*, 41.
40. Ibid., 196.
41. Ibid., 148.
42. Ibid., 147.
43. Ibid., 143.
44. Ibid., 27.
45. Ibid., 213.
46. Ibid., 186.
47. "Review of *Black Swan*," *Publisher's Weekly*, 79.
48. Lockwood, "Review of *Black Swan*," 248.
49. "Review of *Black Swan*," *Kirkus Review*, 932.
50. Rees, "Skin Colour in British Children's Books," 92.
51. Dhondy, *Black Swan*, 200.
52. Ibid., 198.
53. Ibid., 217.
54. Ibid., 193.
55. Greene, *Greenes Groats-worth of Witte*, 3321–3322.
56. Dhondy, *Black Swan*, 124.
57. Eliot, "Seneca in Elizabethan Translation," 15.
58. Bate, "Introduction."
59. For thorough analyses of the proverb see Prager, "'If I Be Devil'"; Newman, K., "And wash the Ethiop White"; and Hall, *Things of Darkness*, 66–69.
60. On early modern notions of kin, kind, and kinship, see Adelman, J., *Blood Relations*; and Ephraim, "Jepthah's Kin."

61. Vaughan, A. and Vaughan, V., "Before *Othello*," 35.
62. BlackPlanet.com (accessed July 20, 2008).
63. Greenblatt, *Renaissance Self-Fashioning*, 253, 252.
64. Bartels, *Speaking of the Moor*, 194.
65. Ibid., 5.
66. Dhondy, *Black Swan*, 32.
67. Ibid., 8.
68. Again, Gates confirmed my memories from graduate school: Gates, Personal Correspondence.
69. Garber, "Shakespeare as Fetish," 250.
70. Ibid.
71. Henderson, "Introduction," 12.
72. Ibid.
73. Ibid.
74. Carpenter, "'The Forms of Things Unknown.'"
75. Henderson, "Introduction," 61.
76. Erickson, *Citing Shakespeare*, 3.
77. Ibid., 167.
78. Ibid., 169.
79. Garber, "Shakespeare as Fetish," 249.

CHAPTER 4

1. Brustein, *Letters to a Young Actor*, 130.
2. Green, *The Revisionist Stage*, 34.
3. Burt, "Civic ShakesPR," 165.
4. Green, *The Revisionist Stage*, 27.
5. Ellis, *Multicultural Theatre*, 4.
6. See, for example, Ellis, *Multicultural Theatre*; Ellis, *Multicultural Theatre II*; and Slaight and Sharrar, *Multicultural Scenes from Young Actors*.
7. Brustein, *Letters to a Young Actor*, 82, 83.
8. Ibid., 83.
9. Wilson, *The Ground on Which I Stand*, 33.
10. Ibid., 29–30.
11. Elm Shakespeare Company (New Haven, CT), http://www.elmshakespeare.org (accessed July 21, 2009).
12. Shakespeare on the Square (San Jose, CA), http://www.arclightrep.org (accessed July 21, 2009).
13. Florida Shakespeare Theatre (Coral Gables, FL), http://www.afn.org/~theatre (accessed July 21, 2009).
14. Parolin, "'What revels are in hand?'" 199–200.
15. August Wilson's keynote address at the 11th Biennial Theatre Communications Group National Conference at Princeton University was delivered on June 26, 1996 and was printed that same year. Brustein responded to Wilson's remarks (and Wilson countered) in four issues of *American Theatre* 13, nos. 7–10 (1996). Then in 1997

Theater magazine printed "Beyond the Wilson-Brustein Debate," a special edition consisting of seven pieces. Wilson and Brustein also met for a public debate at the Town Hall in New York on January 27, 1997.

16. Brook, *There Are No Secrets*, 102.

17. Ibid., 103.

18. Southern California Shakespeare Festival (Pomona, CA), http://www.class.csupomona.edu/th/scsf (accessed July 22, 2009).

19. East L.A. Classic Theatre (Los Angeles, CA), http://www.eastlaclassic.org (accessed July 22, 2009).

20. Levine, *Highbrow/Lowbrow*.

21. Green, *The Revisionist Stage*, 31.

22. Ibid.

23. For an overview of Welles's *Macbeth* see France, *Orson Welles on Shakespeare*. For an overview of *Macbeth*'s position within African-American cultural production see Newstok and Thompson, *Weyward Macbeth*.

24. Green, *The Revisionist Stage*, 33. Emphasis is my own.

25. Londré and Watermeier, *The History of North American Theatre*, 377.

26. Green, *The Revisionist Stage*, 76.

27. Brustein, *Letters to a Young Actor*, 124.

28. Brustein, "Reworking the Classics."

29. These definitions are paraphrased from Davis and Newman, *Beyond Tradition*.

30. Quoted in Hill, *Shakespeare in Sable*, 162–163.

31. Ibid., 163.

32. Lee, D., "The African American Shakespeare Company," 18.

33. For an analysis of the "magical negro" in contemporary popular culture see Gonzalez, S., "Director Spike Lee Slams 'Same Old' Stereotypes in Today's Films"; and Hicks, "Hoodoo Economics."

34. Young, "The Rough Side of the Mountain," 176.

35. For excellent essays that address audience confusion in nontraditionally cast productions see Anderson, "When Race Matters"; Iyengar, "Colorblind Casting in Single-Sex Shakespeare"; and Pao, "Ocular Revisions."

36. Newman, H., "Holding Back."

37. See Berry, "Shakespeare and Integrated Casting" for an example of this usage.

38. For an early theatre review that employs "interracial casting," see Hornby, "Interracial Casting."

39. Berry, "Shakespeare and Integrated Casting," 35.

40. Fichandler, "Casting for a Different Truth."

41. Schechner, "Race Free, Gender Free, Body-Type Free, Age Free Casting," 6, 10.

42. Ney, "Force of Will," 27.

43. Ibid., 27, 26.

44. See, for example, the other artistic directors' statements in Ney, "Force of Will."

45. Berson, "A Critical Look at Oregon Shakespeare Festival's Summer-Fall Lineup."

46. Rauch, "From the Artistic Director," 5.

47. Quoted in Parolin, "'What revels are in hand?'" 207.

48. Thompson, "To Notice or Not To Notice," 6.

49. Uno, *Monologues for Actors of Color*, viii–ix.

50. See, for example, Russell, *Acting*; and Hodge, *Twentieth Century Actor Training*.
51. Quoted in Edwards, *Advice to a Young Black Actor*, 33.
52. Hodge, "Introduction," 8.
53. Schiffman, "Minority Actors Discuss University Training Programs."
54. Aronson, "Changing Demographics," 96.
55. See, for example, Edwards, *Monologues on Black Life*; Edwards, *More Monologues on Black Life*; and Edwards, *50 African American Audition Monologues*.
56. Espinosa and Ocampo-Guzman, "Identity Politics and the Training of Latino Actors," 153, 151.
57. Wiles, "Beyond Race and Gender," 135.
58. Ibid., 131–132.
59. Reese, "Keeping It Real Without Selling Out," 163.
60. Schiffman, "Minority Actors Discuss University Training Programs."
61. Kaliswa Brewster quoted in Schiffman, "Minority Actors Discuss University Training Programs."
62. Two examples are the Oregon Shakespeare Festival's FAIR program and the Shakespeare Theatre's classical training workshop for minority actors.
63. Walker-Kuhne, *Invitation to the Party*, 68.
64. Kaliswa Brewster quoted in Schiffman, "Minority Actors Discuss University Training Programs."
65. Quoted in Rothstein, "Theater; Shakespeare on the Potomac."
66. See Schiffman, "Minority Actors Discuss University Training Programs."
67. Farrell, "Changing Culture and Practices Inside Organizations," 40.
68. Monette, *This Rough Magic*, 310. Partially quoted in Parolin, "'What revels are in hand?'" 201.
69. Ibid., 310–311. Quoted in Parolin, "'What revels are in hand?'" 202.
70. Shakespeare in Action (Toronto), http://shakespeareinaction.org (accessed July 28, 2009).
71. Walltown Children's Theatre (Durham, NC), http://www.shakespeareinamerican-communities.org/theatre/walltown.shtml (accessed June 9, 2009).
72. African-American Shakespeare Company (San Francisco, CA), http://www.african-americanshakes.org (accessed July 28, 2009).
73. Green, *The Revisionist Stage*, 180.
74. "Cultural Connections at OSF" from the 2009 OSF Playbill.
75. Walker-Kuhne, *Invitation to the Party*, 10.
76. Ibid., 63.
77. Ibid., 7.
78. Ibid., 11.
79. Ibid., 7.
80. Ibid., 12.
81. Oregon Shakespeare Festival Board Meeting Minutes, March 13, 2009, http://www.osfashland.org/_dwn/about/minutes/Board_Minutes_031309.pdf (accessed July 30, 2009).
82. Farrell, "Changing Culture and Practices Inside Organizations," 51.
83. Ibid., 52.
84. Walker-Kuhne, *Invitation to the Party*, 26.

85. Green, *The Revisionist Stage*, 4.

86. For a discussion of the RSC's 2007 productions of *The Winter's Tale* and *Pericles* as related to the director Dominic Cooke's approach to race see Thompson, "To Notice or Not to Notice."

87. LaBute, "Casting for the Stage should be Color-Blind."

88. Smith, A., *Letters to a Young Artist*, 157–158.

89. Tatum, *"Why Are All the Black Kids Sitting Together in the Cafeteria?"* 36.

CHAPTER 5

1. Rawson, "Stage Preview." I have italicized the words that Rawson cites from Rylance for clarity and readability.

2. An earlier and slightly shorter version of this chapter originally appeared in *Shakespeare Bulletin*. Thompson, "The Blackfaced Bard: Returning to Shakespeare or Leaving Him?" *Shakespeare Bulletin* 27, no. 3 (2009): 437–456. I am grateful to the editors and publishers of *Shakespeare Bulletin* for granting permission to print a revised version of the essay in this book.

3. Callaghan, *Shakespeare Without Women*, 75–96.

4. Quoted in Rawson, "Stage Preview."

5. Ibid.

6. Carroll, "Prologue," xvi–xvii.

7. Marks, "'Othello/Me,'" 117.

8. Bland, "How I Would Direct *Othello*," 31, 38.

9. Quarshie, *Second Thoughts about* Othello, 5.

10. Richmond, "The Audience's Role in *Othello*," 94–95.

11. Ibid., 96.

12. Vaughan, V., *Performing Blackness on English Stages*, 97.

13. Ibid., 98, 102. Vaughan, of course, borrows this phrase from others. Eric Lott and Ian Smith, writing about two different historical moments, both discuss the popularity of blackface performances as stemming from the collapse of vastly different viewing strategies: the mimetic belief in, desire for, and assumption about the reality of performance and the knowledge that the performance (enabled through the use of specific prosthetics) is unreal. Lott, *Love and Theft*; Smith, I. "White Skin, Black Masks."

14. Vaughan, V., *Performing Blackness on English Stages*, 94–95.

15. Ibid., 174.

16. Bland, "How I Would Direct *Othello*," 31.

17. Quarshie, *Second Thoughts about* Othello, 5.

18. Richmond, "The Audience's Role in *Othello*," 96.

19. Vaughan, V., *Performing Blackness on English Stages*, 94.

20. Davis, M., *The Poetry of Philosophy*, 3.

21. Jones, *Othello's Countrymen*; Tokson, *The Popular Image of the Black Man in English Drama*; Barthelemy, *Black Face, Maligned Race*.

22. Habib, *Black Lives in the English Archives*.

23. Callaghan, *Shakespeare Without Women*, 77.

24. Ibid.

25. Bennett, *Theatre Audiences*, 166–203.
26. Thompson, "Practicing a Theory/Theorizing a Practice," 13.
27. Of course, I borrow this phrase and notion from bell hooks. Hooks, "The Oppositional Gaze," 115–132.
28. Rawson, "Stage Preview."
29. Hill and Hatch, *A History of African American Theatre*, 445.
30. Strausbaugh, *Black Like You*, 38.
31. Farley, "Dave Speaks."
32. *Bamboozled*, dir. Spike Lee.
33. Lee, S., "The Making of *Bamboozled*."
34. Mitchell, *What Do Pictures Want?*, 301.
35. White, "Post-Art Minstrelsy," 12.
36. When I refer to images having "lives," I am, of course, borrowing this phrase and notion from Mitchell, whose book, *What Do Pictures Want?* is subtitled, *The Lives and Loves of Images*.
37. Quoted in *Berger v. Battaglia*.
38. Quoted in *In re: Ellender*.
39. Quoted in *Locurto v. Guiliani*.
40. Although I have not been able to find documentation that Locurto et al. are pursuing this case further, it seems logical that they will attempt to have the case retried before the Supreme Court.
41. Quoted in *Berger v. Battaglia*.
42. Quoted in *In re: Ellender*.
43. Quoted in *Locurto v. Guiliani*.
44. Quoted in *In re: Ellender*.
45. Quoted in *Locurto v. Guiliani*.
46. Ibid.
47. The Pickering "Balancing Test" was established with *Pickering v. Board of Education*, which involved the First Amendment claims of a public school teacher who was dismissed by the Board of Education of Will County, Illinois, after a local newspaper published a letter she wrote criticizing the Board's funding choices and purported lack of transparency. The court held that the scope of the public employee's First Amendment rights must be determined by balancing "the interests of the [employee], as a citizen, in commenting upon matters of public concern and the interest of the State, as an employer, in promoting the efficiency of the public services it performs through its employees." Quoted in *Pickering v. Board of Education*.
48. Quoted in *Miller v. California*.
49. Quoted in *Red Lion Broadcasting Company v. FCC*.
50. Kurzweg, "Live Art and the Audience."
51. See *National Endowment for the Arts v. Finley*.
52. Quoted in the Williams/Coleman Amendment.
53. Butler, *Excitable Speech*, 38.
54. Kurzweg, "Live Art and the Audience."
55. Quoted in *In re: Ellender*.
56. Lucia, "Introduction to Race, Media, and Money," 11.

57. Nyong'o, "Racial Kitsch and Black Performance," 374.

58. There is fascinating new work about how to gauge reception through Internet Web sites that include message boards. See Smith, C., "Nobody, Which Means Anybody."

59. Butler, *Excitable Speech*, 38. Emphasis mine.

60. Hooks, "The Oppositional Gaze," 115–132.

61. Harries, "On a Far-Away Island."

62. Als, "The Empress Jones."

63. Isherwood, "An Emperor Who Tops What O'Neill Imagined."

64. Mitchell, *What Do Pictures Want?*, 49.

65. Steigerwalt, "Performing Race on the Original-Practices Stage," 434.

66. Ibid.

67. Harold Bloom, for example, is explicit in his desire to silence critical approaches to Shakespeare; instead, he advocates for aesthetic approaches only. See Bloom, *Shakespeare*.

68. Quarshie, *Second Thoughts about* Othello, 5.

69. Bland, "How I Would Direct *Othello*," 31.

70. Vaughan, V., *Performing Blackness on English Stages*, 94.

71. Richmond, "The Audience's Role in *Othello*," 96.

72. Lee, S., "The Making of *Bamboozled*."

73. Hall, *Othello, The Moor of Venice*, 356.

74. Daileader, "The Cleopatra Complex," 218.

75. Iyengar, "Colorblind Casting in Single-Sex Shakespeare," 65.

76. Quarshie, *Second Thoughts about* Othello, 23.

CHAPTER 6

1. American Council of Trustees and Alumni (ACTA), *The Shakespeare File*, 10.

2. Viswanathan, *Masks of Conquest*, 4.

3. See ACTA's "Mission and History" statement on their Web site: http://www.goacta.org/about/mission-and-history.cfm (accessed November 1, 2009).

4. ACTA, *The Vanishing Shakespeare*, 11.

5. Ibid., 8.

6. Ibid., 7.

7. Viswanathan, *Masks of Conquest*, 2.

8. Ibid., 88, 54.

9. Ibid., 169.

10. ACTA, *The Vanishing Shakespeare*, 11.

11. Quoted in Viswanathan, *Masks of Conquest*, 40–41. Emphasis mine.

12. Loomba, "Teaching Shakespeare and Race in the New Empire," 160–161.

13. It is instructive to realize that Viswanathan's *Masks of Conquest* includes neither "race" nor "ethnicity" as thematic fields of reference in the index.

14. For the former see Burt, "Civic ShakesPR," and for the latter see Herold, "Movers and Losers."

15. Herold, "Movers and Losers," 153.

16. Seidel, et al., *The Qualities of Quality*, 5.

17. Ibid., 18–27.

18. Ibid., 79.

19. Scott-Douglass, *Shakespeare Inside*, 4.

20. Herold, "Shakespeare and the Performance of Rehabilitation." The history of the performances aboard *The Dragon*, however, is murky. For an excellent account of this, see Akhimie, "Strange Episodes."

21. Scott-Douglass, *Shakespeare Inside*, 4.

22. Brewster, "Abstract" for *An Evaluation of the Arts-in-Corrections Program of the California Department of Corrections*, 2.

23. Quoted in Battista, "Shakespeare Journeys Inside San Quentin Prison."

24. Herold, "Movers and Losers," 168, n. 33.

25. London Shakespeare Workout, *Mission Statement*, http://www.londonshakespeare.org.uk/Mission/prisonmission2.htm (accessed November 1, 2009).

26. Quoted in Scott-Douglass, *Shakespeare Inside*, 16.

27. Scott-Douglass, *Shakespeare Inside*, 55, 57.

28. Hitt, "Act V."

29. Scott-Douglass, *Shakespeare Inside*, 58.

30. Ibid., 58, 60.

31. Ibid., 62.

32. Scott-Douglass, "Shades of Shakespeare," 199.

33. Ibid., 200.

34. Ibid.

35. Quoted in Battista, "Shakespeare Journeys Inside San Quentin Prison."

36. Scott-Douglass, "Shades of Shakespeare," 200.

37. Quoted in Scott-Douglass, *Shakespeare Inside*, 17–18.

38. Esquith, *Teach Like Your Hair's On Fire*, 208.

39. Esquith, *There are No Shortcuts*, 39.

40. Ibid., 111.

41. Esquith, Phone Interview.

42. *The Hobart Shakespeareans*, dir. Mel Stuart.

43. Esquith, *Teach Like Your Hair's On Fire*, 208.

44. Esquith, Phone Interview.

45. Ibid.

46. Ibid.

47. Ibid. The final statement is Esquith quoting Hal Holbrook.

48. Esquith, Phone Interview.

49. Quoted from *The Hobart Shakespeareans*, dir. Mel Stuart.

50. Esquith, *Teach Like Your Hair's On Fire*, 217.

51. Ibid.

52. Thernstrom, *No Excuses*, 58.

53. Ibid., 119.

54. Esquith, *There Are No Shortcuts*, 210; Esquith, Phone Interview.

55. Seidel, et al., *The Qualities of Quality*, 73.

56. Gioia, Phone Interview.

57. Ibid.

58. NEA, *Shakespeare in American Communities*, 4.

59. NEA, "National Endowment for the Arts Announces 2008–2009 Shakespeare for a New Generation Grants."

60. Thirteen of the eighteen bases received the Alabama Shakespeare Festival's production of *Macbeth*. NEA, *Shakespeare in American Communities*, 5.

61. Ibid.

62. Packer quoted in an epigraph to NEA, *Shakespeare in American Committees*.

63. NEA, *All America's a Stage*, 1.

64. Gioia, "The Method in our Madness," 35.

65. NEA, *Shakespeare in American Communities*, 6.

66. NEA, "Shakespeare in American Communities: Shakespeare for a New Generation 2008–2009 Request for Proposals."

67. Gioia quoted in NEA, *Shakespeare in American Communities*, 1.

68. Gioia, Phone Interview.

69. Ibid.

70. NEA, "National Endowment for the Arts Announces 2009–2010 Shakespeare for a New Generation Grants."

71. Ibid.

72. Gioia, Phone Interview.

73. Ibid.

74. OJJDP, "Juvenile Arrests Disproportionately Involved Minorities," 9.

75. Ibid.

76. Thernstrom, *No Excuses*, 119.

77. Gioia, Phone Interview.

78. See the Movers & Shakespeares Web site, http://www.moversandshakespeares. com/index.php (accessed November 1, 2009).

79. Augustine and Adelman, *Shakespeare in Charge*, xi.

80. Ibid., xii.

81. Garber, *Shakespeare and Modern Culture*, 195–196.

82. Augustine and Adelman, *Shakespeare in Charge*, 67–68.

83. Garber, *Shakespeare and Modern Culture*, 197.

84. Ibid., 198.

85. Herold, "Movers and Losers," 156.

86. Adelman quoted in "Carol and Ken Adelman."

87. Adelman, K., Phone Interview.

88. Augustine and Adelman, *Shakespeare in Charge*, 130.

89. Ibid., 130–131.

90. Ibid., 134.

91. Ibid., 135.

92. Adelman, K., Phone Interview.

93. Ibid.

94. Ibid.

95. Augustine and Adelman, *Shakespeare in Charge*, 133.

96. Adelman, K., Phone Interview.

97. Seidel, et al., *The Qualities of Quality*, 24.

98. See the Will Power to Youth Web site, http://www.shakespearefestivalla.org/education/faq.php (accessed November 1, 2009).

99. Will Power to Youth, *Impact Report*, 3.

100. See the Will Power to Youth Web site, http://www.shakespearefestivalla.org/education/will_power_to_youth.php, (accessed November 1, 2009).

101. Seidel, et al., *The Qualities of Quality*, 24–25.

102. Quoted in *Why Shakespeare?*, dir. Lawrence Bridges.

103. Ibid.

104. Burt, "Civic ShakesPR," 158.

105. Ibid., 159.

106. Ibid., 160.

107. Ibid.

108. Ibid., 159.

109. Quoted in *Why Shakespeare?*, dir. Lawrence Bridges.

110. Kareem Monroy quoted in *Why Shakespeare?*, dir. Lawrence Bridges.

111. Seidel, et al., *The Qualities of Quality*, 38. Emphasis mine.

112. Ibid., 24.

113. Ibid., 38.

114. Quoted in *Why Shakespeare?*, dir. Lawrence Bridges.

115. Seidel, et al., *The Qualities of Quality*, 55.

116. Ibid. Citing Taylor, *Researching Drama and Arts Education*.

117. Seidel, et al., *The Qualities of Quality*, 55.

118. Kidnie, *Shakespeare and the Problem of Adaptation*, 9.

119. Ibid.

CHAPTER 7

1. Kolko, Nakamura, and Rodman, "Race in Cyberspace," 10.

2. Nakamura, *Digitizing Race*, 176.

3. An earlier and slightly shorter version of this chapter originally appeared in *Shakespeare Quarterly*. Thompson, "Unmooring the Moor: Researching and Teaching on YouTube," *Shakespeare Quarterly* 61, no.3 (2010): 337–356. I am grateful to the editors and publishers of *Shakespeare Quarterly* for granting permission to print a revised version of the essay in this book.

4. Crowl, "'Ocular Proof,'" 162.

5. For YouTube's rhetoric about its own creation see http://www.youtube.com/t/about (accessed July 1, 2008).

6. See Roberts, Foehr, and Rideout's collective study for the Kaiser Family Foundation, *Generation M.*

7. Throughout this chapter I employ the moniker "Asian American" because without conducting participatory research, which would require IRB approval and parental consent, the students' ethnicities cannot be established with absolute certainty.

8. *Reduced Shakespeare Company*, dir. Paul Kafno.

9. Nakamura, *Digitizing Race*, 171.

10. Ibid., 184.

11. Royster, "Rememorializing Othello," 53.

12. Sturgess, *Shakespeare and the American Nation*, 33.

13. See Prashad, *Everybody Was Kung Fu Fighting*.

14. Nakamura, *Cybertypes*, 13–14.

15. These terms and phrases are YouTube's.

16. For an overview of the ethical issues facing those doing Internet research see: Basset and O'Riordan, "Ethics of Internet Research"; Bruckman, *Ethical Guidelines for Research Online*; Buchanan, *Readings in Virtual Research Ethics*; Ess and Association of Internet Researchers (AoIR), *Ethical Decision-Making and Internet Research*; McKee and DeVoss, *Digital Writing Research*.

17. This language comes from the Office for Human Research Protections (OHRP), "Human Subjects Regulations Decision Charts."

18. McKee and Porter, "The Ethics of Digital Writing Research," 732.

19. Stern, S., "Studying Adolescents Online"; Bober, "Virtual Youth Research."

20. Bober, "Virtual Youth Research," 308.

21. See, for example, McKee and Porter, "The Ethics of Digital Writing Research."

22. YouTube, "A Word on Safety": http://www.youtube.com/t/safety (accessed July 1, 2008).

23. For a discussion of hyperlinks as "user-generated distribution," see Wesch, "An Anthropological Introduction to YouTube."

24. Turkle, *Life on the Screen*, 261.

25. Nakamura, *Digitizing Race*, 35.

26. Ibid., 34, 35.

27. Kang, "Cyber-Race," 1181.

28. See, for example, Jennifer González's fascinating essay on constructing avatars: González, J., "The Appended Subject."

29. See, for example, Rutten, "The Good Generation Gap."

30. Tynes, et al., "Adolescence, Race, and Ethnicity on the Internet," 669.

31. Ibid., 667, 672.

32. Ibid., 675.

33. YouTube: video posted in 2006.

34. YouTube: comment posted in 2008.

35. Ibid.

36. Ibid.

37. Ibid.

38. At the time this chapter is being written (August 2008), Christian Lander's blog is one of the most popular in the nation: it has logged over 38 million hits to date. See http://stuffwhitepeoplelike.com (accessed July 28, 2008).

39. Lander, "Stuff White People Like: Coldplay."

40. For a fascinating article on the racial differences between the Romans and Goths see Royster, "'White-Limed Walls.'"

41. *Othello*, dir. Oliver Parker. For Fishburne's views on his relationship with Shakespeare see Lennix and Fishburne, "Two Actors on Shakespeare, Race, and Performance."

42. *Titus*, dir. Julie Taymor. For an interesting take on Lennix's "gestural" performance of race in *Titus* see Hendricks, "Gestures of Performance."

43. For a discussion of the "linguistic miscegenation" that Aaron threatens in *Titus Andronicus* see Thompson, *Performing Race and Torture on the Early Modern Stage* (especially chapter 3).

44. Geto Boys, "Damn it Feels Good to be a Gangsta."
45. Butler, *Bodies that Matter*; Gubar, *Racechanges*; Johnson, *Appropriating Blackness*; and Lott, *Love and Theft*.
46. *Reservoir Dogs*, dir. Quentin Tarantino.
47. *Office Space*, dir. Mike Judge.
48. Geto Boys, "Damn it Feels Good to be a Gangsta."
49. *Jackie Brown*, dir. Quentin Tarantino; Bosso and Renzulli, "A Hit is a Hit"; "De Niro and 50 Now That's Gangster The Hollywood Issue."
50. YouTube: video posted in 2007.
51. YouTube: comment posted in 2008.
52. Although it is clear that the performance is unified (i.e., it is all performed and shot in one day), it was actually posted as two separate postings on YouTube with the labels "Part 1/2" and "Part 2/2." Because of the unity of the performance, I treat it as one.
53. Rose, *Black Noise*, 5.
54. Phillips, "Physical Graffiti West," 62.
55. YouTube: comment posted in 2007.
56. Ibid.
57. Ibid.
58. YouTube: comments posted in 2007, 2007, 2007, 2008, 2008, 2007, 2007, and 2008, respectively.
59. Wesch, "An Anthropological Introduction to YouTube."
60. YouTube: comment posted in 2008.
61. YouTube: video posted in 2007. Although it is clear that the performance is unified (i.e., it is all performed and shot in one day), it was actually posted as two separate postings on YouTube with the labels "1/2" and "2/2." Because of the unity of the performance, I treat it as one.
62. *Reservoir Dogs*, dir. Quentin Tarantino; *Pulp Fiction*, dir. Quentin Tarantino.
63. Eminem, "You Don't Know."
64. The beginning of the video includes a long written prologue about *Othello* and their "modern day" approach.
65. East Clubbers, "It's a Dream."
66. *Once Upon a Time in China* (Wong Fei Hung), dir. Hark Tsui.

CHAPTER 8

1. Als, "The Black Man Cometh."
2. Teague, *Shakespeare and the American Popular Stage*, 96.
3. Okri, "Leaping Out of Shakespeare's Terror," 86.
4. This phrase, of course, is taken from the title to Okri's essay.
5. Lennix and Fishburne, "Two Actors on Shakespeare, Race, and Performance," 404.
6. For a fascinating essay about these "unconventional Othellos" see, Pao, "Ocular Revisions."
7. Okri, "Leaping Out of Shakespeare's Terror," 86.
8. Sellars, "On Othello."
9. Ibid.

10. Edelstein, "Making a New Othello."

11. Ibid.

12. Ibid.

13. Ibid.

14. For a book that theorizes the notion that performance is adaptation see Worthen, *Shakespeare and the Force of Modern Performance.*

15. For more on this topic see Thompson, "To Notice or Not to Notice."

16. For more on this topic see Thompson, "Practicing a Theory/Theorizing a Practice."

17. Bernardo, "Othello."

18. Simon, "Megalomaniacal Director Sellars Dumbs Down *Othello*."

19. Ibid.

20. Kuchwara, "Lengthy, High-Concept *Othello* Falters Off-B'way."

21. Brown, "It's Lost Its Moorings."

22. Vincentelli, "New Shakespeare Tragedy."

23. Saltzman, "Othello."

24. Als, "The Black Man Cometh."

25. Ibid.

26. Coleridge, "Comments on *Othello*," 231.

27. Als, "The Black Man Cometh."

28. Ibid.

29. Teague, *Shakespeare and the American Popular Stage*, 96.

30. Ibid.

31. Okri, "Leaping Out of Shakespeare's Terror," 86.

WORKS CITED

Adelman, Janet. *Blood Relations: Christian and Jew in The Merchant of Venice*. Chicago: The University of Chicago Press, 2008.

Adelman, Ken. Phone interview. Published with permission. November 23, 2009.

Ahad, Nick. "Shakespeare Role is Murder for Lenny." *ExpressandStar.com*, February 9, 2009. http://www.expressandstar.com/2009/02/09/shakespeare-role-is-murder-for-lenny/. Accessed June 8, 2009.

Aird, Catherine. *Passing Strange*. Garden City, NY: Doubleday, 1980.

Ajax. *Shakespeare or Bacon?* Boston: B. Wilkins, 1888.

Akala. "Shakespeare." *It's Not a Rumour*. MSI Music Distribution, 2006.

Akhimie, Patricia. "Strange Episodes: Race in Stage History." *Shakespeare Bulletin* 27, no. 3 (2009): 363–376.

Als, Hilton. "The Black Man Cometh." *The New Yorker*. October 5, 2009.

Als, Hilton. "The Empress Jones." *The New Yorker*. March 27, 2006.

American Council of Trustees and Alumni (ACTA). *The Shakespeare File: What English Majors Are Really Studying*. Washington, DC: The National Alumni Forum, December 1996. http://www.goacta.org/publications/downloads/ShakespeareFile.pdf. Accessed November 1, 2009.

American Council of Trustees and Alumni (ACTA). *The Vanishing Shakespeare*. Washington, DC: The National Alumni Forum, April 2007. http://www.goacta.org/publications/downloads/VanishingShakespeare.pdf. Accessed November 1, 2009.

Anderson, Lisa M. "When Race Matters: Reading Race in *Richard III* and *Macbeth*." In *Colorblind Shakespeare: New Perspectives on Race and Performance*, edited by Ayanna Thompson, 89–102. London and New York: Routledge, 2006.

Angelou, Maya. "Journey to the Heartland." Address Delivered at the 1985 National Assembly of Local Arts Agencies. Cedar Rapids, Iowa. June 12, 1985.

Aronson, Donna B. "Changing Demographics: Where is Diversity in Theatre Programs in Higher Education and National Associations?" In *The Politics of American Actor Training*, edited by Ellen Margolis and Lissa Tyler Renaud, 94–102. New York and London: Routledge, 2010.

Augustine, Norman and Kenneth Adelman. *Shakespeare in Charge: The Bard's Guide to Leading and Succeeding on the Business Stage.* New York: Hyperion, 1999.

Auld, Tim. "Revelatory Brilliance: The Bridge Project Comes Up Trumps with its First Two Classics." *The Sunday Telegraph (London).* June 21, 2009.

Bamboozled. Dir. Spike Lee. Perf. Damon Wayans, Savion Glover, and Jada Pinkett-Smith. New Line Cinema, 2000.

Bartels, Emily. *Speaking of the Moor: From Alcazar to Othello.* Philadelphia: University of Pennsylvania Press, 2008.

Barthelemy, Anthony. *Black Face, Maligned Race: The Representation of Blacks in English Drama from Shakespeare to Southerne.* Baton Rouge: Louisiana State University Press, 1987.

Basset, Elizabeth and Kathleen O'Riordan. "Ethics of Internet Research: Contesting the Human Subjects Research Model." *Ethics and Information Technology* 4 (2002): 233–247.

Bate, Jonathan. "Introduction." In *Titus Andronicus*, edited by Jonathan Bate, 1–121. London: Routledge, 1995.

Battista, Denise. "Shakespeare Journeys Inside San Quentin Prison." *PlayShakespeare.com*, March 30, 2008. http://www.playshakespeare.com/stories/250-features/3594-shakespeare-journeys-inside-san-quentin-prison. Accessed November 1, 2009.

Bennett, Susan. *Performing Nostalgia: Shifting Shakespeare and the Contemporary Past.* London and New York: Routledge, 1996.

Bennett, Susan. *Theatre Audiences: A Theory of Production and Reception*, 2nd ed. New York and London: Routledge, 1997.

Berger v. Battaglia. 779 F 2d 992. No. 84–1440. United States Court of Appeals for the Fourth Circuit. 1985. Online. LexisNexis Academic. Accessed July 1, 2008.

Bernardo, Melissa Rose. "Othello." *EW.com.* September 27, 2009. http://www.ew.com/ew/article/0,20308505,00.html. Accessed November 1, 2009.

Berry, Ralph. "Shakespeare and Integrated Casting." *Contemporary Review* 285 (July 2004): 35–39.

Berson, Misha. "A Critical Look at Oregon Shakespeare Festival's Summer-Fall Lineup." *Seattle Times.* July 20, 2008.

Bland, Sheila Rose. "How I Would Direct Othello." In *Othello: New Essays by Black Writers*, edited by Mythili Kaul, 29–41. Washington, DC: Howard University Press, 1997.

Bloom, Harold. *Shakespeare: The Invention of the Human.* New York: Riverhead Books, 1998.

Bober, Magdalena. "Virtual Youth Research: An Exploration of Methodologies and Ethical Dilemmas from a British Perspective." In *Readings in Virtual Research Ethics: Issues and Controversies*, edited by Elizabeth Buchanan, 288–315. Hershey, PA: Idea Group Inc, 2003.

Bosso, Joe and Frank Renzulli. "A Hit is a Hit." *The Sopranos.* Season 1, episode 10. HBO, 1999.

Brewster, Lawrence G. "Abstract." *An Evaluation of the Arts-in-Corrections Program of the California Department of Corrections*. April 1983.

Bringing Down the House. Dir. Adam Shankman. Perf. Steve Martin, Queen Latifah, and Eugene Levy. Touchstone Pictures, 2003.

Bristol, Michael. *Shakespeare's America, America's Shakespeare*. London and New York: Routledge, 1990.

Brontë, Charlotte. *Shirley* (1849). Oxford: Oxford University Press, 2007.

Brook, Peter. *There Are No Secrets: Thoughts on Acting and Theatre*. London: Methuen, 1993.

Brown, Scott. "It's Lost Its Moorings: The Public Theater's Painfully Adrift *Othello*." *New York Magazine*. September 27, 2009.

Bruckman, Amy. *Ethical Guidelines for Research Online*. April 4, 2002. http://www.cc.gatech.edu/~asb/ethics. Accessed July 1, 2008.

Brustein, Robert. *Letters to a Young Actor: A Universal Guide to Performance*. New York: Basic Books, 2005.

Brustein, Robert. "Reworking the Classics: Homage or Ego Trip?" *New York Times*. November 6, 1988.

Buchanan, Elizabeth, ed. *Readings in Virtual Research Ethics: Issues and Controversies*. Hershey, PA: Idea Group Inc, 2003.

Burns, Christy. "Suturing Over Racial Difference: Problems for a Colorblind Approach in a Visual Culture." *Discourse* 22 (2000): 70–91.

Burt, Richard. "Civic ShakesPR: Middlebrow Multiculturalism, White Television, and the Color Bind." In *Colorblind Shakespeare: New Perspectives on Race and Performance*, edited by Ayanna Thompson, 157–185. New York and London: Routledge, 2006.

Butler, Judith. *Bodies that Matter: On the Discursive Limits of "Sex."* New York: Routledge, 1993.

Butler, Judith. *Excitable Speech: A Politics of the Performative*. New York and London: Routledge, 1997.

Callaghan, Dympna. *Shakespeare Without Women: Representing Gender and Race on the Renaissance Stage*. London and New York: Routledge, 2000.

Carby, Hazel. *Race Men*. Cambridge, MA: Harvard University Press, 1998.

"Carol and Ken Adelman." *Training and Development (TD) Magazine*. March 2005.

Carpenter, John. "'The Forms of Things Unknown': Richard Wright and Stephen Henderson's Quiet Appropriation." In *Native Shakespeares: Indigenous Appropriations on a Global Stage*, edited by Craig Dionne and Parmita Kapadia, 57–72. Aldershot, U.K. and Burlington, U.S.A.: Ashgate, 2008.

Carpio, Glenda. *Laughing Fit to Kill: Black Humor in the Fictions of Slavery*. Oxford: Oxford University Press, 2008.

Carroll, Tim. "Prologue." In David Crystal, *Pronouncing Shakespeare: The Globe Experiment*, xv–xviii. Cambridge: Cambridge University Press, 2005.

Cartelli, Tom. *Repositioning Shakespeare: National Formations, Postcolonial Appropriations*. London and New York: Routledge, 1999.

Chedgzoy, Kate. *Shakespeare's Queer Children: Sexual Politics and Contemporary Culture*. Manchester: Manchester University Press, 1995.

Cheney, Lynne. *Humanities in America: A Report to the President, the Congress, and the American People*. Washington, DC: National Endowment for the Humanities, 1988.

Citro, Joseph. *Passing Strange: True Tales of New England Hauntings and Horrors.* Boston: Houghton Mifflin, 1996.

Clarke, Breena and Susan Tifft. "A Race Man Argues for a Broader Curriculum: Henry Louis Gates, Jr." *Time Magazine.* April 22, 1991.

Cliff, Nigel. *The Shakespeare Riots: Revenge, Drama, and Death in Nineteenth-Century America.* New York: Random House, 2007.

Coleridge, Samuel Taylor. "*Comments on Othello.*" In *Othello by William Shakespeare* (Norton Critical Edition), edited by Edward Pechter, 230–234. New York: W. W. Norton & Company, 2004.

Conrad, Joseph. *Heart of Darkness* (1899). New York: W. W. Norton & Company, 1988.

Crowl, Samuel. "'Ocular Proof': Teaching *Othello* in Performance." In *Approaches to Teaching Shakespeare's Othello,* edited by Peter Erickson and Maurice Hunt, 162–168. New York: The Modern Language Association of America, 2005.

"Cultural Connections at OSF." Oregon Shakespeare Festival 2009 Playbill.

Daileader, Celia. "The Cleopatra Complex: White Actresses on the Interracial 'Classic' Stage." In *Colorblind Shakespeare: New Perspectives in Race and Performance,* edited by Ayanna Thompson, 205–220. New York and London: Routledge, 2006.

Danius, Sara and Stefan Jonsson. "An Interview with Gayatri Chakravorty Spivak." *boundary* 2 20 (1993): 24–50.

Davis, Clinton Turner and Harry Newman, eds. *Beyond Tradition: Transcripts of the First Symposium on Non-Traditional Casting.* New York: Non-Traditional Casting Project, 1988.

Davis, Michael. *The Poetry of Philosophy: On Aristotle's Poetics.* Chicago: St. Augustine Press, 1999.

"De Niro and 50 Now That's Gangster The Hollywood Issue." *Vibe Magazine.* March 2008.

Dhondy, Farrukh. *Black Swan.* Boston: Houghton Mifflin, 1993; London: Victor Gollancz, 1992.

DiGaetani, John. "August Wilson." In *A Search for a Postmodern Theater: Interviews with Contemporary Playwrights,* 275–284. New York: Greenwood Press, 1991.

Dionne, Craig and Parmita Kapadia, eds. *Native Shakespeares: Indigenous Appropriations on a Global Stage.* Aldershot, U.K. and Burlington, U.S.A.: Ashgate, 2008.

Drake, Chris. "Review." *Sight and Sound* 5, no. 2 (February 1995): 54.

Drake, St. Clair and Horace Cayton. *Black Metropolis: A Study of Life in a Northern City.* New York: Harcourt Brace, 1945.

D'Souza, Dinesh. *The End of Racism: Principles for a Multiracial Society.* New York: The Free Press, 1995.

DuBois, W. E. B. *The Souls of Black Folk* (1903). New York: Signet Classics, 1969.

East Clubbers. "It's a Dream." 2004 Single.

Edelstein, Barry. "Making a New Othello." In *Othello Briefing: Contexts & Commentary.* New York: The Public Theater, 2009.

Edwards, Gus. *50 African American Audition Monologues.* Portsmouth, NH: Heinemann, 2002.

Edward, Gus. *Advice to a Young Black Actor (and Others): Conversations with Douglas Turner Ward.* Portsmouth, NH: Heinemann, 2004.

Edwards, Gus. *Monologues on Black Life.* Portsmouth, NH: Heinemann, 1997.

Edwards, Gus. *More Monologues on Black Life.* Portsmouth, NH: Heinemann, 2000.

Eliot, T. S. "Seneca in Elizabethan Translation" (1927). In *Elizabethan Dramatists*, 11–57. London: Faber and Faber, 1963.

Ellis, Roger, ed. *Multicultural Theatre: Scenes and Monologues from New Hispanic, Asian, and African-American Plays*. Colorado Springs: Meriwether Publishing, 1996.

Ellis, Roger, ed. *Multicultural Theatre II: Contemporary Hispanic, Asian, and African-American Plays*. Colorado Springs: Meriwether Publishing, 1998.

Eminem. "You Don't Know." *Eminem Presents the Re-Up*. Shady Records, 2006.

Ephraim, Michelle. "Jepthah's Kin: The Sacrificing Father in *The Merchant of Venice*." *Journal of Early Modern Cultural Studies* 5, no. 2 (2005): 71–93.

Erickson, Peter. *Citing Shakespeare: The Reinterpretation of Race in Contemporary Literature and Art*. New York, U.S.A. and Basingstoke, U.K.: Palgrave Macmillan, 2007.

Erickson, Peter. *Rewriting Shakespeare, Rewriting Ourselves*. Berkeley: University of California Press, 1991.

Espinosa, Micha and Antonio Ocampo-Guzman. "Identity Politics and the Training of Latino Actors." In *The Politics of American Actor Training*, edited by Ellen Margolis and Lissa Tyler Renaud, 150–161. New York and London: Routledge, 2010.

Esquith, Rafe. Phone interview. Published with permission. November 10, 2009.

Esquith, Rafe. *Teach Like Your Hair's On Fire: The Methods and Madness Inside Room 56*. New York: Viking, 2007.

Esquith, Rafe. *There Are No Shortcuts*. New York: Pantheon, 2003.

Ess, Charles and Association of Internet Researchers (AoIR). *Ethical Decision-Making and Internet Research: Recommendations form the AoIR Ethics Working Committee*. November 27, 2002. http://www.aoir.org/reports/ethics.pdf. Accessed July 1, 2008.

Farley, Christopher John. "Dave Speaks." *Time Magazine*. May 23, 2005.

Farrell, Betty. "Changing Culture and Practices Inside Organizations." In *Entering Cultural Communities: Diversity and Change in the Nonprofit Arts*, edited by Diane Grams and Betty Farrell, 38–63. New Brunswick, NJ: Rutgers University Press, 2008.

Fichandler, Zelda. "Casting for a Different Truth." *American Theatre* 5 (1988): 18–23.

France, Richard. *Orson Welles on Shakespeare*. Westport, CT: Greenwood Press, 1990.

Freud, Sigmund. *The Interpretation of Dreams* (1900), edited and translated by James Strachey. New York: Avon Books, 1965.

Garber, Marjorie. *Quotation Marks*. London and New York: Routledge, 2002.

Garber, Marjorie. "Shakespeare as Fetish." *Shakespeare Quarterly* 41 (1990): 242–250.

Garber, Marjorie. *Shakespeare's Ghost Writers: Literature as Uncanny Causality*. New York: Routledge, 1987.

Garber, Marjorie. *Shakespeare and Modern Culture*. New York: Pantheon Books, 2008.

Gates, Henry Louis, Jr. Personal correspondence. May 26, 2009. Published with permission.

Gates, Henry Louis, Jr. *The Signifying Monkey: A Theory of African-American Literary Criticism*. Oxford: Oxford University Press, 1988.

Gates, Henry Louis, Jr. and Nellie McKay, eds. *The Norton Anthology of African American Literature*. New York: W. W. Norton., 1997.

Geto Boys. "Damn it Feels Good to be a Gangsta." *Uncut Dope: Geto Boys' Best*. Virgin Records, 1992.

Gilroy, Paul. *Against Race: Imagining Political Culture Beyond the Color Line*. Cambridge, MA: The Belknap Press of Harvard University Press, 2000.

Gioia, Dana. "The Method in our Madness: The NEA's Shakespeare in American Communities." *The Dramatist* 9, no. 1 (September/October 2006): 34–35.

Gioia, Dana. Phone interview. Published with permission. November 25, 2009.

Giroux, Henry. "White Noise: Toward a Pedagogy of Whiteness." In *Race-ing Representation: Voice, History, and Sexuality*, edited by Kostas and Linda Myrsiades, 42–76. Lanham: Rowman & Littlefield, 1998.

González, Jennifer. "The Appended Subject: Race and Identity in Digital Assemblage." In *Race in Cyberspace*, edited by Beth Kolko, Lisa Nakamura, and Gilbert Rodman, 27–50. New York and London: Routledge, 2000.

Gonzalez, Susan. "Director Spike Lee Slams 'Same Old' Black Stereotypes in Today's Films." *Yale Bulletin & Calendar*. March 2, 2001.

Green, Amy S. *The Revisionist Stage: American Directors Reinvent the Classics*. Cambridge: Cambridge University Press, 1994.

Greenblatt, Stephen. *Hamlet in Purgatory*. Princeton: Princeton University Press, 2001.

Greenblatt, Stephen. *Renaissance Self-Fashioning: From More to Shakespeare*. Chicago: University of Chicago Press, 1980.

Greene, Robert. *Greenes Groats-worth of Witte* (1592). In *The Norton Shakespeare: Based on the Oxford Edition*, edited by Stephen Greenblatt et al., 3321–3322. New York: W. W. Norton, 1997.

Grundmann, Roy. "Identity Politics at Face Value: An Interview with Scott McGehee and David Siegel." *Cineaste* 20 (1994): 24–26.

Gubar, Susan. *Racechanges: White Skin, Black Face in American Culture*. New York and Oxford: Oxford University Press, 1997.

Guillory, John. *Cultural Capital: The Problem of Literary Canon Formation*. Chicago: The University of Chicago Press, 1993.

Habib, Imtiaz. *Black Lives in the English Archives, 1500–1677*. Aldershot, U.K. and Burlington, U.S.A.: Ashgate, 2007.

Hale, Natalie. "Theatre Review: Lenny Henry in *Othello* at Theatre Royal Bath." *Crackerjack*. April 6, 2009. http://www.crackerjack.co.uk/bristol/theatre-news/theatre-interview-lenny-henry-othello-theatre-royal-bath. Accessed June 8, 2009.

Hall, Kim F., ed. *Othello, The Moor of Venice: Texts and Contexts*. Boston, New York: Bedford/St. Martin's, 2007.

Hall, Kim F. *Things of Darkness: Economies of Race and Gender in Early Modern England*. Ithaca: Cornell University Press, 1995.

Hamlet 2. Dir. Andrew Fleming. Perf. Steve Coogan and Elizabeth Shue. Focus Features, 2008.

Hardy, Thomas. *Tess of the D'Urbervilles* (1891). London: Penguin Books, 1985.

Harries, Martin. "On a Far-Away Island." *Hotreviews.com*. March 2006.

Harries, Martin. *Scare Quotes from Shakespeare: Marx, Keynes, and the Language of Reenchantment*. Stanford: Stanford University Press, 2000.

Henderson, Stephen. "Introduction: The Form of Things Unknown." In *Understanding the New Black Poetry: Black Speech and Black Music and Poetic References*. New York: William Morrow, 1973.

Hendricks, Margo. "Gestures of Performance: Rethinking Race in Contemporary Shakespeare." In *Colorblind Shakespeare: New Perspectives on Race and Performance*, edited by Ayanna Thompson, 187–203. New York and London: Routledge, 2006.

Henry V. Dir. Kenneth Branagh. Perf. Kenneth Branagh. Samuel Goldwyn Company, 1989.

Herold, Niels. "Movers and Losers: Shakespeare in Charge and Shakespeare Behind Bars." In *Native Shakespeares: Indigenous Appropriations on a Global Stage*, edited by Craig Dionne and Parmita Kapadia, 153–170. Aldershot, U.K. and Burlington, U.S.A.: Ashgate, 2008.

Herold, Niels. "Shakespeare and the Performance of Rehabilitation." Shakespeare Association of America 34th Annual Meeting. Philadelphia, PA: April 15, 2006.

Hicks, Heather J. "Hoodoo Economics: White Men's Work and Black Men's Magic in Contemporary American Film." *Camera Obscura* 18 (2003): 27–55.

Hill, Errol. *Shakespeare in Sable: A History of Black Shakespearean Actors*. Amherst: University of Massachusetts Press, 1984.

Hill, Errol G. and James V. Hatch. *A History of African American Theatre*. Cambridge: Cambridge University Press, 2003.

Hitt, Jack. "Act V." *This American Life*. National Public Radio. August 8, 2002. http://www.thisamericanlife.org/Radio_Episode.aspx?episode=218. Accessed November 1, 2009.

The Hobart Shakespeareans. Dir. Mel Stuart. DOCU-RAMA & POV: 2005.

Hodge, Alison. "Introduction." In *Twentieth Century Actor Training*, edited by Alison Hodge, 1–10. London and New York: Routledge, 2000.

Hodge, Alison, ed. *Twentieth Century Actor Training*. London and New York: Routledge, 2000.

Hooks, bell. "The Oppositional Gaze." In *Black Looks: Race and Representation*, 115–132. Boston: South End, 1992.

Hornby, Richard. "Interracial Casting." *Hudson Review* 42 (1989): 459–466.

In Re: Ellender. 889 So 2d 225. No. 04-0-2123. Supreme Court of Louisiana. 2004. Online. LexisNexis Academic. Accessed July 1, 2008.

Isherwood, Charles. "An Emperor Who Tops What O'Neill Imagined." *The New York Times*. March 14, 2006.

Iyengar, Sujata. "Colorblind Casting in Single-Sex Shakespeare." In *Colorblind Shakespeare: New Perspectives on Race and Performance*, edited by Ayanna Thompson, 47–67. London and New York: Routledge, 2006.

Jackie Brown. Dir. Quentin Tarantino. Perf. Pam Grier, Samuel L. Jackson, and Robert Forster. Miramax Films, 1997.

Johnson, E. Patrick. *Appropriating Blackness: Performance and the Politics of Authenticity*. Durham: Duke University Press, 2003.

Jones, Eldred. *Othello's Countrymen: The African in English Renaissance Drama*. London: Oxford University Press, 1965.

Jonson, Ben. "To the memory of my beloved, The Author Mr. William Shakespeare: And what he hath left us." *Mr. William Shakespeares Comedies, Histories, & Tragedies* (1623). In *A Facsimile of The First Folio, 1623*. New York and London: Routledge, 1998.

Jordan, Winthrop. *White Over Black: American Attitudes toward the Negro, 1550–1812*. Chapel Hill: The University of North Carolina Press, 1968.

Kang, Jerry. "Cyber-Race." *Harvard Law Review* 113 (2000): 1130–1208.

Kaplan, Carla. "Introduction: Nella Larsen's Erotics of Race." In *Passing by Nella Larsen* (Norton Critical Edition), edited by Carla Kaplan, ix–xxvi. New York: W. W. Norton, 2007.

Kidnie, Margaret Jane. *Shakespeare and the Problem of Adaptation*. London and New York: Routledge, 2009.

Know Your History: Jesus Was Black . . . So Was Cleopatra. Dir. Bart Phillips. Perf. Paul
    Mooney. Image Entertainment, 2007.

Kolko, Beth, Lisa Nakamura, and Gilbert Rodman. "Race in Cyberspace: An Introduction."
    In *Race in Cyberspace*, edited by Beth Kolko, Lisa Nakamura, and Gilbert Rodman, 1–13.
    New York and London: Routledge, 2000.

Kuchwara, Michael. "Lengthy, High-Concept Othello Falters Off-B'Way." *Associated Press.*
    September 27, 2009.

Kurzweg, Anne Salzman. "Live Art and the Audience: Toward a Speaker-Focused Freedom
    of Expression." *Harvard Civil Rights-Civil Liberties Law Review.* Boston: President and
    Fellows of Harvard College, 1999.

LaBute, Neil. "Casting for the Stage should be Color-Blind." *Los Angeles Times.* May 6,
    2007.

Lander, Christian. "Stuff White People Like: Coldplay." *Vanity Fair/VF Daily.* June 16,
    2008. www.vanityfair.com. Accessed July 28, 2008.

Landry, Donna and Gerald MacLean. Introduction to "Subaltern Studies." In *The Spivak
    Reader: Selected Works by Gayatri Chakravorty Spivak*, edited by Donna Landry and Ger-
    ald MacLean, 203–205. New York and London: Routledge, 1996.

Lee, D. T. "The African American Shakespeare Company: From *A Midsummer Night's
    Dream* to Reality." *American Visions* 14 (June 1999): 16–20.

Lee, Spike. "The Making of *Bamboozled*." *Bamboozled.* Dir. Spike Lee. Perf. Damon Wayans,
    Savion Glover, and Jada Pinkett-Smith. New Line Cinema DVD, 2000.

Lennix, Harry J. and Laurence Fishburne. "Two Actors on Shakespeare, Race, and Perfor-
    mance: A Conversation between Harry J. Lennix and Laurence Fishburne." *Shakespeare
    Bulletin* 27, no. 3 (2009): 399–414.

Levine, Lawrence. *Highbrow/Lowbrow: The Emergence of Cultural Hierarchy in America.*
    Cambridge, MA: Harvard University Press, 1988.

Lockwood, Lucinda. "Review of *Black Swan*." *School of Library Journal* (September 1993):
    248.

Locurto v. Guiliani. 447 f 3d 159. No. 04-6480-cv (L), 04-6498-cv (Con), 04-6499-cv (Con).
    United States Court of Appeals for the Second Circuit. 2006. Online. LexisNexis Aca-
    demic. Accessed July 1, 2008.

London Shakespeare Workout (LSW). *Mission Statement.* http://www.londonshake-
    speare.org.uk/Mission/prisonmission2.htm. Accessed November 1, 2009.

Londré, Felicia Hardison and Daniel J. Watermeier. *The History of North American Theatre:
    The United States, Canada, and Mexico: From Pre-Columbian Times to the Present.* New
    York: Continuum Books, 1998.

Loomba, Ania. *Gender, Race, Renaissance Drama.* Manchester: Manchester University
    Press, 1989.

Loomba, Ania. "Teaching Shakespeare and Race in the New Empire." In *Teaching Shake-
    speare: Passing It On*, edited by G. B. Shand, 160–180. Oxford: Wiley-Blackwell, 2009.

Lott, Eric. *Love and Theft: Blackface Minstrelsy and the American Working Class.* New York
    and Oxford: Oxford University Press, 1993.

Lucia, Cynthia. "Introduction to Race, Media and Money: A Critical Symposium on Spike
    Lee's *Bamboozled*." *Cineaste* 26 (2001): 10–11.

MacDonald, Joyce Green. *Women and Race in Early Modern Texts.* Cambridge: Cambridge
    University Press, 2002.

MacLeod, Sally. *Passing Strange: A Novel*. New York: Random House, 2002.

Marks, Elise. "'Othello/Me': Racial Drag and the Pleasures of Boundary-Crossing with *Othello*." *Comparative Drama* 35 (2001): 101–123.

Martin, Theodore. *Shakespeare or Bacon?* Edinburgh and London: William Blackwood and Sons, 1888.

Massachelein, Annaleen. "Double Reading/Reading Double: Psychoanalytic Poetics at Work." *Paradoxa: Studies in World Literary Genres* 3 (1997): 395–406.

Massai, Sonia, ed. *World-Wide Shakespeares: Local Appropriations in Film and Performance*. London and New York: Routledge, 2005.

Masten, Jeffrey. *Textual Intercourse: Collaboration, Authorship, and Sexualities in Renaissance Drama*. Cambridge: Cambridge University Press, 1997.

McKee, Heidi and Dànielle Nicole DeVoss, eds. *Digital Writing Research: Technologies, Methodologies, and Ethical Issues*. Cresskill, NJ: Hampton Press, 2007.

McKee, Heidi and James E. Porter. "The Ethics of Digital Writing Research: A Rhetorical Approach." *College Composition and Communication*. 59 (2008): 711–749.

Miller, Jacques-Alain. "Suture (elements of the logic of the signifier)." *Screen* 18 (1977): 24–34.

Miller v. California. 413 U.S. 15. No. 70–73. United States Supreme Court. 1973. Online. LexisNexis Academic. Accessed July 1, 2008.

Mitchell, W. J. T. *What Do Pictures Want? The Lives and Loves of Images*. Chicago: University of Chicago Press, 2005.

Monette, Richard. *This Rough Magic: The Making of an Artistic Director*. Stratford: Stratford Shakespearean Festival of Canada, 2007.

Mooney, Paul. *Black is the New White: A Memoir*. New York: Simon Spotlight Entertainment, 2009.

Nakamura, Lisa. *Cybertypes: Race, Ethnicity, and Identity on the Internet*. New York and London: Routledge, 2002.

Nakamura, Lisa. *Digitizing Race: Visual Cultures on the Internet*. Minneapolis and London: University of Minnesota Press, 2008.

National Endowment for the Arts (NEA). *All America's a Stage: Growth and Challenges in Nonprofit Theater*. Washington, DC: National Endowment for the Arts, December 2008. http://www.arts.gov/research/TheaterBrochure12-08.pdf. Accessed November 1, 2009.

National Endowment for the Arts (NEA). "National Endowment for the Arts Announces 2008–2009 Shakespeare for a New Generation Grants." Press Release: April 23, 2008. http://www.arts.gov/news/news08/Shakespeare.html. Accessed November 1, 2009.

National Endowment for the Arts (NEA). "National Endowment for the Arts Announces 2009–2010 Shakespeare for a New Generation Grants." Press Release: April 23, 2009. http://www.nea.gov/news/news09/shakespeare-for-a-new-generation.html. Accessed November 1, 2009.

National Endowment for the Arts (NEA). *Shakespeare in American Communities*. Washington, DC: National Endowment for the Arts, August 2008. http://www.nea.gov/pub/SIAC4.pdf. Accessed November 1, 2009.

National Endowment for the Arts (NEA). "Shakespeare in American Communities: Shakespeare for a New Generation 2008–2009 Request for Proposals." Press Release: April 23,

2008. http://arts.endow.gov/national/shakespeare/ShakespeareCompanies2008–2009. html. Accessed November 1, 2009.

National Endowment for the Arts v. Finley et al. 534 U.S. 569. No. 97–371. 1998. Online LexisNexis Academic. Accessed July 1, 2008.

Neal, Mark Anthony. "Does Denzel Always Have to Represent?" *The Washington Post.* December 23, 2007.

Newman, Harry. "Holding Back: The Theatre's Resistance to Non-Traditional Casting." *TDR* 33 (1989): 22–36.

Newman, Karen. "'And was the Ethiop White': Femininity and the Monstrous in *Othello*." In *Shakespeare Reproduced: The Text in History and Ideology*, edited by Jean Howard and Marion O'Connor, 141–162. New York and London: Routledge, 1987.

Newstok, Scott and Ayanna Thompson, ed. *Weyward Macbeth: Intersections of Race and Performance*. New York, U.S.A. and Basingstoke, U.K.: Macmillan, 2010.

Ney, Charles. "Force of Will." *American Theatre* 22 (April 2005): 24–27.

Nyong'o, Tavia. "Racial Kitsch and Black Performance." *The Yale Journal of Criticism* 15 (2002): 371–391.

Office for Human Research Protections (OHRP). "Human Subjects Regulations Decision Charts." September 24, 2004. http://www.hhs.gov/ohrp/humansubjects/guidance/decisioncharts.htm. Accessed July 1, 2008.

Office of Juvenile Justice and Delinquency Prevention (OJJDP). "Juvenile Arrests Disproportionately Involved Minorities." *Juvenile Justice Bulletin* (April 2009): 9.

Office Space. Dir. Mike Judge. Perf. Ron Livingston and Jennifer Aniston. Twentieth Century Fox, 1999.

Okri, Ben. "Leaping Out of Shakespeare's Terror." In *A Way of Being*, 71–87. London: Phoenix House, 1997.

Oldham, Madeleine. "Stew Interviewed by Madeleine Oldham (Berkeley Rep)." http://www.negroproblem.com/passing/pages/stew3.html. Accessed November 1, 2009.

Omi, Michael and Howard Winant. "Once More, with Feeling: Reflections on Racial Formation." *PMLA* 123 (2008): 1565–1572.

Omi, Michael and Howard Winant. *Racial Formation in the United States: From the 1960s to the 1990s*. 2nd ed. New York and London: Routledge, 1994.

Once Upon a Time in China (Wong Fei Hung). Dir. Hark Tsui. Perf. Jet Li and Rosamund Kwan. Golden Harvest Company, 1991.

Oregon Shakespeare Festival Board Meeting Minutes. March 13, 2009. http://www.osfashland.org/about/archive/minutes.aspx. Accessed July 30, 2009.

Orkin, Martin. *Local Shakespeares: Proximations and Power*. London and New York: Routledge, 2005.

Othello. Dir. Oliver Parker. Perf. Laurence Fishburne and Irène Jacob. Castle Rock Entertainment, 1995.

Oudart, Jean-Pierre. "Cinema and Suture." *Screen* 18 (1977): 35–47.

Palfrey, Simon and Tiffany Stern. *Shakespeare in Parts*. Oxford: Oxford University Press, 2007.

Pao, Angela. "Ocular Revisions: Re-Casting Othello in Text and Performance." In *Colorblind Shakespeare: New Perspectives on Race and Performance*, edited by Ayanna Thompson, 27–45. London and New York: Routledge, 2006.

Parolin, Peter. "'What revels are in hand?': A Change in Direction at the Stratford Shakespeare Festival of Canada." *Shakespeare Quarterly* 60 (2009): 197–224.

Pearson, Noel. *Up from the Mission: Selected Writings*. Melbourne: Black Inc., 2009.

Phillips, Susan A. "Physical Graffiti West: African American Gang Walks and Semiotic Practice." In *Migrations of Gesture*, edited by Carrie Noland and Sally Ann Ness, 31–68. Minneapolis and London: University of Minnesota Press, 2008.

Pickering v. Board of Education. 391 U.S. 563. No. 510. United States Supreme Court. 1968. Online. LexisNexis Academic. Accessed July 1, 2008.

Prager, Carolyn. "'If I Be Devil': English Renaissance Responses to the Proverbial and Ecumenical Ethiopian." *Journal of Medieval and Renaissance Studies* 17 (1987): 257–279.

Prashad, Vijay. *Everybody Was Kung Fu Fighting: Afro-Asian Connections and the Myth of Cultural Purity*. Boston: Beacon Press, 2001.

Pulp Fiction. Dir. Quentin Tarantino. Perf. John Travolta, Samuel L. Jackson, and Bruce Willis. Miramax Films, 1994.

Quarshie, Hugh. *Second Thoughts about Othello*. Chipping Campden, U.K.: Clouds Hill Printers, 1999.

Rauch, Bill. "From the Artistic Director." *Oregon Shakespeare Festival Playbill* 1 (2009): 5.

Rawson, Christopher. "Stage Preview: Shakespearean Company brings an Original *Twelfth Night* to Pittsburgh." *Pittsburgh Post-Gazette*. November 2, 2003.

Red Lion Broadcasting Company v. FCC. 395 U.S. 367. No. 2. United States Supreme Court. 1969. Online. LexisNexis Academic. Accessed July 1, 2008.

Reduced Shakespeare Company. Dir. Paul Kafno. Perf. Adam Long, Reed Martin, and Austin Tichenor. Acorn Media, 2003.

Rees, David. "Skin Colour in British Children's Books." *Children's Literature in Education* 2 (1980): 91–97.

Reese, Venus Opal. "Keeping It Real Without Selling Out: Toward Confronting and Triumphing Over Racially-Specific Barriers in American Actor Training." In *The Politics of American Actor Training*, edited by Ellen Margolis and Lissa Tyler Renaud, 162–176. New York and London: Routledge, 2010.

Reservoir Dogs. Dir. Quentin Tarantino. Perf. Harvey Keitel, Michael Madsen, and Steve Buscemi. Miramax Films, 1992.

"Review of *Black Swan*." *Kirkus Review*. July 15, 1993: 932.

"Review of *Black Swan*." *Publisher's Weekly* 26 (June 28, 1993): 79.

Reynolds, Gillian. "Voices from Beyond the Radio 4 Compound." *Daily Telegraph* (London). March 28, 2006.

Richmond, Hugh Macrea. "The Audience's Role in *Othello*." In *Othello: New Critical Essays*, edited by Philip C. Kolin, 89–101. New York and London: Routledge, 2002.

Roberts, Donald, Ulla Foehr, and Victoria Rideout. *Generation M: Media in the Lives of 8–18 Year-Olds; A Kaiser Family Foundation Study*. Menlo Park, CA: Kaiser Family Foundation, 2005.

Romney, Jonathan. "How Did We Get Here?" *Sight and Sound* 5, no. 2 (February 1995): 32–34.

Rose, Tricia. *Black Noise: Rap Music and Black Culture in Contemporary America*. Hanover, CT: Wesleyan University Press, 1994.

Rothstein, Mervyn. "Theater; Shakespeare on the Potomac: A Reappearing Act." *New York Times*. September 16, 1990.

Royster, Francesca. *Becoming Cleopatra: The Shifting Image of an Icon*. New York, U.S.A. and Basingstoke, U.K.: Palgrave Macmillan, 2003.

Royster, Francesca. "Rememorializing Othello: Teaching *Othello* and the Cultural Memory of Racism." In *Approaches to Teaching Shakespeare's* Othello, edited by Peter Erickson and Maurice Hunt, 53–61. New York: The Modern Language Association of America, 2005.

Royster, Francesca. "'White-Limed Walls': Whiteness and Gothic Extremism in *Titus Andronicus.*" *Shakespeare Quarterly* 51 (2000): 432–455.

Russell, Paul. *Acting: Make it Your Business: Avoid Mistakes and Achieve Success As a Working Actor.* New York: Back Stage Books, 2008.

Rutten, Tim. "The Good Generation Gap: The Way that Young People Deal with Race is a Hopeful Sign for Our Politics." *Los Angeles Times.* February 6, 2008.

Said, Edward. *Orientalism.* New York: Pantheon Books, 1978.

Sale, Richard. *Passing Strange: A Story of Birth and Burial.* New York: Simon and Schuster, 1942.

Saltzman, Simon. "Othello: A CurtainUp Review." *CurtainUp.* September 27, 2009. http://www.curtainup.com/othellolabrynth09.html. Accessed November 1, 2009.

Sandweiss, Martha. *Passing Strange: A Gilded Age Tale of Love and Deception across the Color Line.* New York: Penguin Press, 2009.

Schechner, Richard. "Race Free, Gender Free, Body-Type Free, Age Free Casting." *TDR: The Drama Review* 33 (1989): 4–12.

Schiffman, Jean. "Minority Actors Discuss University Training Programs." *Theatre Bay Area Magazine.* December 2008.

Schlossberg, Linda. "Introduction: Rites of Passing." In *Passing: Identity and Interpretation in Sexuality, Race, and Religion*, edited by María Carla Sánchez and Linda Schlossberg, 1–12. New York: New York University Press, 2001.

Scotland, PA. Dir. Billy Morrissette. Perf. James LeGros, Maura Tierney, and Christopher Walken. Abandon Pictures, 2001.

Scott-Douglass, Amy. "Shades of Shakespeare: Colorblind Casting and Interracial Couples in Macbeth in Manhattan, Grey's Anatomy, and Prison Macbeth." In *Weyward Macbeth: Intersections of Race and Performance*, edited by Scott L. Newstok and Ayanna Thompson, 193–202. New York, U.S.A. and Basingstoke, U.K.: Palgrave Macmillan, 2010.

Scott-Douglass, Amy. *Shakespeare Inside: The Bard Behind Bars.* London and New York: Continuum Books, 2007.

Seidel, Steve, Shari Tishman, Ellen Winner, Lois Hetland, and Patricia Palmer. *The Qualities of Quality: Understanding Excellence in Arts Education.* Cambridge, MA: Project Zero, 2009.

Sellars, Peter. "On Othello." In *Othello Briefing: Contexts & Commentary.* New York: The Public Theater, 2009.

Shattuck, Kathryn. "One or Two Things He Knows about Teenagers." *New York Times.* June 28, 2009.

Silverman, Kaja. "(On Suture)." In *Film Theory and Criticism: Introductory Readings*, edited by Leo Braudy and Marshall Cohen, 137–147. New York: Oxford University Press, 1999.

Simon, John. "Megalomaniacal Director Sellars Dumbs Down Othello: Review." Bloomberg.com. September 28, 2009. http://www.bloomberg.com/apps/news?pid=20601088&sid=aIondKhbyRpE. Accessed November 1, 2009.

Simonson, Lee. *The Stage is Set* (1932). New York: Theatre Arts Books, 1963.

Singh, Jyotsna. "Afterword: The Location of Shakespeare." In *Native Shakespeares: Indigenous Appropriations on a Global Stage*, edited by Craig Dionne and Parmita Kapadia, 233–239. Aldershot, U.K. and Burlington, U.S.A.: Ashgate, 2008.

Slaight, Craig and Jack Sharrar, eds. *Multicultural Scenes for Young Actors*. Lyme, NH: A Smith and Kraus Book, 1995.

Smith, Anna Deavere. *Letters to a Young Artist*. New York: Anchor Books, 2006.

Smith, Bruce. "Lenny Henry on his Leeds *Othello* Debut." *Yorkshire Evening Post*. October 3, 2008. http://www.yorkshireeveningpost.co.uk/showbiz/Lenny-Henry-on-his-Leeds.4557444.jp. Accessed June 8, 2009.

Smith, Catherine F. "Nobody, Which Means Anybody: Audience on the World Wide Web." In *Weaving a Virtual Web: Practical Approaches to New Information Technologies*, edited by Sibylle Gruber, 239–249. Urbana, IL: National Council of Teachers of English, 2000.

Smith, Ian. "White Skin, Black Masks: Racial Cross-Dressing on the Early Modern Stage." *Renaissance Drama* 32 (2003): 33–67.

Sontag, Deborah. "A Musical Star Plucked from the Underground." *The New York Times*. May 21, 2007.

Sorensen, Rosemary. "To the Point." *Weekend Australia*. June 20, 2009.

Soyinka, Wole. "Shakespeare and the Living Poet." *Shakespeare Survey* 36 (1983): 1–10.

Spivak, Gayatri Chakravorty. "In a Word: Interview." In *Outside in the Teaching Machine*. New York and London: Routledge, 1993. 1–23.

Spivak, Gayatri Chakravorty. "Subaltern Studies: Deconstructing Historiography" (1985). In *The Spivak Reader: Selected Works by Gayatri Chakravorty Spivak*, edited by Donna Landry and Gerald MacLean, 203–235. New York and London: Routledge, 1996.

Steigerwalt, Jenna. "Performing Race on the Original-Practices Stage: A Call to Action." *Shakespeare Bulletin* 27.3 (2009): 425–435.

Stern, Susannah. "Studying Adolescents Online: A Consideration of Ethical Issues." In *Readings in Virtual Research Ethics: Issues and Controversies*, edited by Elizabeth Buchanan, 274–287. Hershey, PA: Idea Group Inc, 2003.

Stern, Tiffany. *Making Shakespeare: From Stage to Page*. London and New York: Routledge, 2004.

Stevenson, Robert Louis. *The Black Arrow: A Tale of the Two Roses* (1888). In *The Novels and Tales of Robert Louis Stevenson*. Vol. 8. New York: Charles Scribner's Sons, 1905.

Stew. *Passing Strange: The Complete Book and Lyrics of the Broadway Musical*. New York: Applause Books, 2009.

Strausbaugh, John. *Black Like You: Blackface, Whiteface, Insult and Imitation in American Popular Culture*. New York: Jeremy P. Tarcher/Penguin, 2006.

Sturgess, Kim C. *Shakespeare and the American Nation*. Cambridge: Cambridge University Press, 2004.

Suture. Dir. Scott McGehee and David Siegel. Perf. Dennis Haysbert, Mel Harris, and Sab Shimono. Samuel Goldwyn Company, 1993.

Tatum, Beverly. *"Why Are All the Black Kids Sitting Together in the Cafeteria?" And Other Conversations about Race*. New York: Basic Books, 1997.

Taylor, Philip, ed. *Researching Drama and Arts Education: Paradigms and Possibilities*. Washington, DC: Falmer Press, 1996.

Teague, Frances. *Shakespeare and the American Popular Stage*. Cambridge: Cambridge University Press, 2006.

Thernstrom Abigail and Stephen. *No Excuses: Closing the Racial Gap in Learning.* New York: Simon & Schuster, 2003.

Thompson, Ayanna. "The Blackfaced Bard: Returning to Shakespeare or Leaving Him?" *Shakespeare Bulletin* 27, no. 3 (2009): 437–456.

Thompson, Ayanna. "To Notice or Not To Notice: Shakespeare, Black Actors, and Performance Reviews." *Borrowers and Lenders: The Journal of Shakespeare and Appropriation* 4 (2008): 1–15.

Thompson, Ayanna. *Performing Race and Torture on the Early Modern Stage.* New York and London: Routledge, 2008. Routledge Studies in Renaissance Literature and Culture.

Thompson, Ayanna. "Practicing a Theory/Theorizing a Practice: An Introduction to Shakespearean Colorblind Casting." In *Colorblind Shakespeare: New Perspectives on Race and Performance,* edited by Ayanna Thompson, 1–24. New York and London: Routledge, 2006.

Thompson, Ayanna. "Rewriting the 'Real': Popular Shakespeare in the 1990s." *The Journal of Popular Culture* 40 (2007): 1052–1072.

Thompson, Ayanna. "Unmooring the Moor: Researching and Teaching on YouTube." *Shakespeare Quarterly* 61, no.3 (2010): 337–356.

Tidwell, John Edgar and Steven C. Tracy, eds. *After Winter: The Life and Art of Sterling A. Brown.* New York: Oxford University Press, 2009.

Titus. Dir. Julie Taymor. Perf. Anthony Hopkins, Jessica Lange, and Harry J. Lennix. Fox Searchlight Productions, 1999.

Tokson, Elliot. *The Popular Image of the Black Man in English Drama, 1550–1688.* Boston: GK Hall and Co, 1982.

Tuan, Yi-Fu. *Passing Strange and Wonderful: Aesthetics, Nature, and Culture.* Washington, DC: Shearwater Books, 1993.

Turkle, Sherry. *Life on the Screen: Identity in the Age of the Internet.* New York: Simon and Schuster, 1995.

Tynes, Brendesha, Lindsay Reynolds, and Patricia Greenfield. "Adolescence, Race, and Ethnicity on the Internet: A Comparison of Discourse in Monitored vs. Unmonitored Chat Rooms." *Applied Developmental Psychology* 25 (2004): 667–684.

Uno, Roberta, ed. *Monologues for Actors of Color.* New York and London: Routledge, 2000.

Vaughan, Alden and Virginia Mason Vaughan. "Before Othello: Elizabethan Representations of Sub-Saharan Africans." *The William and Mary Quarterly* 54 (1997): 19–44.

Vaughan, Virginia Mason. *Performing Blackness on English Stages, 1500–1800.* Cambridge: Cambridge University Press, 2005.

Vincentelli, Elisabeth. "New Shakespeare Tragedy." *New York Post.* September 28, 2009.

Viswanathan, Gauri. *Masks of Conquest: Literary Study and British Rule in India.* New York: Columbia University Press, 1989.

Walker-Kuhne, Donna. *Invitation to the Party: Building Bridges to the Arts, Culture and Community.* New York: Theatre Communications Group, 2005.

Wesch, Michael. "An Anthropological Introduction to YouTube." July 26, 2008. http://www.youtube.com/user/mwesch#p/u/3/TPAO-lZ4_hU. Accessed July 1, 2010.

White, Armond. "Post-Art Minstrelsy." *Cineaste* 26 (2001): 12–14.

Why Shakespeare? Dir. Lawrence Bridges. National Endowment for the Arts: 2004.

Wiles, David Eulus. "Beyond Race and Gender: Reframing Diversity in Actor-Training Programs." In *The Politics of American Actor Training*, edited by Ellen Margolis and Lissa Tyler Renaud, 123–136. New York and London: Routledge, 2010.

Williams/Coleman Amendment. 20 United States Congress § 954(d)(1). Online. Lexis-Nexis Academic. Accessed July 1, 2008.

Will Power to Youth. *Impact Report*. Los Angeles: Shakespeare Festival/LA, April 1, 2008. http://www.shakespearefestivalla.org/education/will_power_to_youth/-docs/wpy_impact_report.pdf. Accessed November 1, 2009.

Wilson, August. *The Ground on Which I Stand*. New York: Theater Communications Group, 1996.

Worthen, W.B. *Shakespeare and the Force of Modern Performance*. Cambridge: Cambridge University Press, 2003.

Young, Lola. "The Rough Side of the Mountain: Black Women and Representation in Film." In *Reconstructing Womanhood, Reconstructing Feminism: Writings on Black Women*, edited by Delia Jarrett-Macauley, 175–201. London and New York: Routledge, 1996.

INDEX

Made in the USA
Middletown, DE
03 September 2023

37923364R00144